PRAISE FOR *CHANGEOLOGY*

"Changing a habit involves two things: knowing how to change and knowing what to change. This book, by a true master scientist of change, is the best book I know about the steps YOU can take to make and to sustain the changes YOU want to make."

—Mike Roizen, MD, coauthor of the bestselling YOU series

"Become more clever, more relaxed, more satisfied—and more realistic about how long it will take to make new habits stick."

—Oprah.com

"Norcross is the Billy Beane of personal-change gurus, using reams of psychological studies the way a sabermetrician uses baseball statistics. He'll be the first to tell you that this scientific approach beats magical thinking."

—*The Atlanta Journal-Constitution*

"*Changeology* is a powerful tool for those seeking the happiness lasting change can bring. Science tells us that if you can change your behavior, you can increase your happiness. This simple, research-based plan will show you how to begin a new life free of old, bad habits and full of inner peace and well-being."

—Marci Shimoff, author of *Happy for No Reason*

"The title says it all. This clearly written, easy to follow, and scientifically grounded guide provides a step-by-step map to effective self-improvement. Already widely known and respected in professional circles, Dr. Norcross is now sharing his work for use by everyone."

—Gerald P. Koocher, PhD, ABPP, 2006 president, American Psychological Association

"When you are ready to move from just 'talking the talk' to 'walking the walk,' turn to *Changeology*. John Norcross has accomplished a rare feat—translating thirty years of sophisticated psychological research into practical, understandable, doable steps that *really* work for changing behavior. I recommend this book as a top choice to achieve important goals."

—Carol D. Goodheart, EdD, 2010 president, American Psychological Association

CHANGEOLOGY

5 Steps to Realizing Your Goals and Resolutions

JOHN C. NORCROSS, PhD

with Kristin Loberg and Jonathon Norcross

SIMON & SCHUSTER PAPERBACKS

NEW YORK   LONDON   TORONTO   SYDNEY   NEW DELHI

Simon & Schuster Paperbacks
A Division of Simon and Schuster, Inc.
1230 Avenue of the Americas
New York, NY 10020

First Simon & Schuster trade paperback edition December 2013

SIMON & SCHUSTER PAPERBACKS and colophon are registered trademarks of Simon
& Schuster, Inc.

CHANGEOLOGY is a trademark of John C. Norcross, PhD.

The individual self-changers discussed in this book (except for the author and contributors)
are de-identified composites who illustrate common struggles and situations. Any
resemblance to a single real person, living or dead, is purely coincidental.

For information about special discounts for bulk purchases, please contact
Simon & Schuster Special Sales at 1-866-506-1949 or business@simonandschuster.com.

The Simon & Schuster Speakers Bureau can bring authors to your live event.
For more information or to book an event contact the Simon & Schuster Speakers Bureau
at 1-866-248-3049 or visit our website at www.simonspeakers.com.

Designed by Ruth Lee-Mui

Manufactured in the United States of America

10 9 8 7 6 5 4 3 2 1

The Library of Congress has cataloged the hardcover edition as follows:

Norcross, John C., 1957–
    Changeology : 5 steps to realizing your goals and resolutions / John C. Norcross,
with Kristin Loberg and Jonathon Norcross.
        p.   cm.
    Includes bibliographical references and index.
    1. Change (Psychology)   2. Goal (Psychology)   I. Loberg, Kristin.   II. Norcross,
Jonathon.   III. Title.
BF637.C4N67   2012
158.1–dc23   2012033059

ISBN 978-1-4516-5761-6
ISBN 978-1-4516-5762-3 (pbk)
ISBN 978-1-4516-5763-0 (ebook)

To my brothers—George, Donald, and Philip—
who have changed me in so many ways

CONTENTS

Introduction: Changeology: What It Is and What It Can Do for You   1

PART I: THE REAL SCIENCE OF CHANGE   13

How Self-Changers Succeed: The Science   15

How You Will Succeed: The Keys   35

PART II: BECOMING A CHANGEOLOGIST IN 90 DAYS   51

Step 1   Psych: Getting Ready   53

Step 2   Prep: Planning Before Leaping   83

Step 3   Perspire: Taking Action   111

Step 4   Persevere: Managing Slips   152

Step 5   Persist: Maintaining Change   178

Epilogue   The Adaptation of Changeology   204

Acknowledgments   209

Appendix A. Recommended Self-Help Resources   211

Appendix B. Selecting the Right Psychotherapist for You   219

Notes   231

Selected Bibliography   237

Index   247

CHANGEOLOGY

CHANGEOLOGY: WHAT IT IS AND WHAT IT CAN DO FOR YOU

Let's begin with the end in mind: think of one, maybe two, things that you'd like to change in yourself, something you really want to modify about your behavior. If you're like most people, it doesn't take long to come up with something. Perhaps a laundry list of goals and ambitions rushes through your mind, some harder to achieve than others. Maybe a quick smile breaks out on your face when you proudly recall a goal you have recently realized. Perhaps, too, you feel a brief pang of guilt for not trying to change certain things or a fleeting sense of dismay because your previous attempts have proven unsuccessful. All of these complicated feelings are part of the universal constellation of emotions toward change.

Now take a deep breath and consider the following: whether you're hoping to stop smoking or gambling, commit to exercising more hours a week (maybe run a marathon), eliminate fast food and bike to work, or learn a new skill that will earn you a promotion, following the scientific program outlined in this book can dramatically increase your chance of success—without drugs or other types of formal treatment. This proven program shows you exactly how to execute the steps necessary to change on your own. And best of all: you can experience lasting results within 90 days.

Sound too good to be true? Much in the way Elisabeth Kübler-Ross distinguished stages of grief, my colleagues and I have identified five distinct stages of behavior change. This is hardly an inconsequential finding; these stages, which I've simplified to just 5 straightforward steps, reflect three decades of scientific research and millions of dollars in funding. Finally, this well-documented program for successful change is accessible to everyone in this practical book.

From chronic addictions to minor habits, the range of behaviors that we can change is vast but the process of change is the same. In other words, the steps an overweight individual has to take to lose pounds permanently will be the same as those taken by a workaholic seeking to cut back on time spent in the office so he can spend more time with his family. Granted, as each person passes through the steps, he or she will have different goals, but the overall experience will be astonishingly similar.

How do I know this for sure? That's what part of this book is going to reveal to you; I'll be detailing what I've learned as a clinical psychologist and university professor helping tens of thousands of people—in both research and clinical settings—achieve permanent changes.

A LITTLE HISTORY

I was there at the beginning. Not at the creation of the world, mind you, but at the start of defining one of the most effective and celebrated systems ever for changing human behavior: the Stages of Change. Before I detail exactly how you'll create successful change in your life, let me take a few moments to introduce myself and provide the backstory. It will help you understand just how different *Changeology* is from any other program that you might have tried in the past.

It all started in 1980. Jimmy Carter was in the White House, and *Dallas* was flickering across the nation's TV screens. I had just moved to Rhode Island to earn my doctorate and to work with Dr. James O. Prochaska on his first National Institutes of Health grant to study *self-change*—how people modify their behavior without professional treatment. He and one of his recent graduates, Dr. Carlo C. DiClemente, were studying how a thousand people stopped smoking on their own. Little did any of us imagine that those early studies would lead to revolutionary advances in understanding how people change their behavior on their own.

Five years later, I had my clinical psychology PhD in hand and an internship at Brown University Medical School under my belt. I accepted a professorship at the University of Scranton, nestled in the rolling foothills of the Pocono Mountains in northeastern Pennsylvania. I continued my research into self-change and psychotherapy, much of it in collaboration with Jim Prochaska.

In the 1990s, the research got really interesting as research assistants and I conducted three nationally publicized studies that tracked New Year's resolutions. We learned, scientifically speaking, what predicted some resolvers' success and others' failures. Our investigations also looked at change in psychotherapists—the most educated and experienced change agents. How do the experts change themselves?

After the new millennium, my comrades and I conducted another series of studies—a dozen, in fact—to identify the effectiveness of myriad self-help resources. We separated the chaff from the wheat among thousands of self-help books, autobiographies, films, and websites. We managed to determine what kind of self-help resources work and what constitutes ineffective, unscientific pabulum.

Today, there is a staggering number of published studies that have been done on the stages of change—more than two thousand and counting. Our work has added to this undeniably impressive body of research, which has enjoyed the support of $80 million in federal grant funding. Although the early studies concentrated on addictions, such as smoking, drinking, and overeating, over the years they have expanded to include three dozen challenges that millions of people face in daily living, including distressed relationships, anxiety, getting ahead at work, troubling finances, depression, and procrastination.

The program resulting from this research works across a variety of problems, across countries and cultures, and across the spectrum of healing. It's been used successfully by individuals, couples, families, organizations, and entire health systems worldwide. What's more, it's been proven to work whether you're attempting to change on your own or are armed with a self-help book, assisted by a formal support group, treated by a psychologist, bolstered by medication, or any combination thereof.

Our change system has a documented track record of success. It has guided tens of thousands of research participants and psychotherapy patients to lives filled with greater health and happiness. That same research can now guide you through the labyrinth of self-change to your goal. This revolutionary system has been translated into the step-by-step program explained in this book. In other words, you can reap the same benefits of our research that our patients have experienced—just by reading and following the advice offered in *Changeology*.

HOW CHANGEOLOGY DIFFERS FROM OTHER SELF-HELP

At this point you're probably thinking, "He's making awfully strong claims!" Or perhaps you're silently protesting, "The usual oversold promises of self-help books." Correct on both counts: These are strong claims, and most self-help books do guarantee unrealistic and unproven results. Decades of research validate the methods described in this book: that's the crucial difference between *Changeology* and the morass of other self-help books. I deplore the insulting, antiscientific fare of most self-help books. In fact, that's been a huge motivator for my career as a clinical psychologist, university professor, and researcher focused on studying behavior change. I have devoted decades of my life to determining what works and what doesn't.

After investigating people's attempts to realize their goals for 30 years, I have naturally compiled a list of pet peeves about self-help resources. They tend to fail in four ways: they are not based on research; they don't provide specific, practical strategies; they focus on only one part of the solution; and they don't tailor advice to the individual reader. Let's consider each of these in turn with an eye toward how *Changeology* corrects them.

A staggering 95 percent plus of self-help books present no scientific research that they work as self-help, and some bestsellers even contain advice that is contradicted by available research. If FDA approval were required for the usefulness and safety of self-help books, fewer than 2 percent would be published. Flip through a popular diet book and look for research studies on how much weight loss was achieved for at least one year by people on that particular diet. You'll find lots of testimonials and "amazing stories" but almost never any hard numbers based on controlled research. Authors' boasts and client anecdotes don't constitute, and should not replace, scientific research. Therein lies the first crucial difference between other self-help books and *Changeology*: the science.

But a self-help book that simply imparted the science would not prove helpful; it would be about as effective, as Sigmund Freud once observed, as offering a dinner menu to a starving person! Though I do have a tendency to use scientific terminology on occasion, and though I've written this book to appeal to the most science-averse reader, it will be useful for you to learn a few key terms as you come to appreciate the science behind the magic of self-change. But I will go further and translate that science into an abundance of specific, realistic strategies. I will lead you through the most powerful means of behavior change with armloads of examples and illustrations.

Another problem with most self-help books is their narrow focus on only one part of the change process. Imagine if someone promised to help you do your taxes but gave you advice on how to organize your receipts and nothing else. The rest of the process would remain frustrating and unfinished. Well, that aptly describes most self-help products: they feature a single part of that process: setting a goal, getting inspired, securing hugs, or learning a few behavioral strategies. But the reader winds up like the proverbial blind man with the elephant, his efforts incomplete and futile.

This book, on the other hand, encompasses the entire change process. I will patiently, supportively guide you through all 5 steps of a proven system that you can use to change on your own and customize to your own life.

In truth, this isn't the first time that our scientific research and program have been published in a book for a general audience. In 1994, Drs. Jim Prochaska, Carlo DiClemente, and I published our popular *Changing for Good*. But a lot has happened since then, both in the scientific arena and in the world at large, which now operates at warp speed and sets individuals up for new challenges and behavioral problems. Hence, *Changeology* updates our cutting-edge research and expands its applications. I'll be presenting a broader approach to achieving personal improvement and goals, as opposed to our earlier emphasis on eradicating bad habits. I'll also be focusing primarily on the crucial first 90 days of the change process, which omits those people not yet ready to consider change.

THE POWER OF CONNECTION

Changeology personalizes your journey in two important ways: first, it guides you step by step and tells you exactly what to do and when to do it; and second, you'll be able to maximize this book's instructions with the help of an interactive website (www.ChangeologyBook.com) at no cost or obligation to you.

 To receive personalized support online, visit www .ChangeologyBook.com. This will allow you to save your goals, track your progress, print out the worksheets in this book, and complete additional activities. Harness the power of the Web as you read this book and beyond. All of the exercises and activities at www.ChangeologyBook.com begin in this book.

 The icon at the beginning of this paragraph, which shows 5 steps within a delta symbol (delta stands for "change"), appears throughout this book. Wherever you see it, you'll know that an online application is available to you based on a suggested exercise. There you'll have access to 12 free online activities that will assist you in executing many of the specific strategies suggested. The work you do online in conjunction with this book will help you tailor the program to your specific goals.

USING THIS BOOK EFFECTIVELY

As I've already noted, you can change virtually any voluntary behavior using the formula in this book. I will address the most popular behavioral goals and resolutions, such as enhancing relationships, losing weight, acquiring new skills, quitting smoking, starting an exercise regimen, improving your finances, boosting your self-esteem, and reducing your alcohol consumption, but this needn't be an exclusive list. In other words, while the central points in the book address these goals, you are not limited to them. The research-proven methods of Changeology can be applied toward a vast array of personal goals. You may want to help others by delivering meals to the elderly or teaching children. You may be going through a time when accepting change is necessary to weather a major life challenge, such as the loss of a loved one, divorce, unemployment, or prolonged misfortune. As we'll see in this book, following the Changcology program can help you make all kinds of changes.

To help you know what you should be doing and when, regardless of your particular goal, the Check Yourself sections will be your guide. I'll also offer some general To Dos at the beginning of each detailed step that will give you a heads-up about what to expect. Obviously, I cannot detail the specifics to every type of possible change a person may want to make; you won't find a daily menu plan for losing 20 pounds, for instance; you're going to create that on your own using the tools I provide. The examples I showcase, however, will give you guidance on what you should be doing every step of the way.

You should prepare to follow the program for 90 days. Why? Because behavioral research indicates that it takes 90 days to prepare for change, build a new behavior, become confident in the face of high-risk triggers, and move past the likelihood of relapse. Brain research also suggests that it takes a few months of practicing a new behavior to create permanent change.

More than 75 percent of people maintain a goal for a week but then they gradually slip back into old behavior. However, research shows that almost all of the people who maintain a new behavior for three months make the change permanent; the probability of relapse after that period is modest. Our aim is to get you to your goal and keep you there; that will require a 90-day commitment on your part.

I encourage you to read Part I in its entirety before jumping into Part II. Otherwise, you may not grasp the big picture of what works when, and you may inadvertently squander the power of the research. I'm not trying to hold you back; rather, I'm helping you get psyched up and make realistic plans before you jump into action. Decades of research and experience suggest that people who prepare properly and have genuine self-confidence will be far more successful at maintaining their goals after 90 days.

It's common to have at least five or six things that you want to change about yourself. I'll show you how to deal with multiple goals at once. Bear in mind that for different goals you may be in different steps. For example, you might be in the first step for improving your finances but already in the second for losing weight. Reading the pages of this book in order will improve your chances of success for all of your goals, no matter where you're starting from today. Of course, I expect that you'll return to various sections and the interactive website at different times depending on your particular needs.

Please pay attention to the Check Yourself exercises sprinkled throughout the book and take them seriously. They are not mere summaries; they are research-based, data-driven guides that will ensure your success. The Check Yourself appraisals serve as practical checkpoints along your journey through the 5 steps. They also give you the support you need to know exactly what you should be doing and when.

A final word about using this book effectively: Work the program enthusiastically. Don't read it as an intellectual exercise or as a dreaded assignment. Bring passionate effort and confidence to the book; change is not a spectator sport. Complete the Check Yourself exercises honestly. Go online when prompted, and print materials that will enhance your success. Enlist the support of another person or two when encouraged to do so. Work the program for 90 days.

This is a personal and unique journey. You may feel daunted at first by what lies ahead or fearful that others will judge you. The work you do and the exercises you complete don't need to be read by or shared with anyone else. It's your experience that counts here. So feel free to record the truth and let your success flow from the results.

Warning: Avoid Using This Book Ineffectively

Near the top of my list of pet peeves are authors who fail—intentionally, it seems—to declare the limitations of their self-help resources. In fact, the more outrageous the claim, the greater the public interest. "Jesus Himself used this approach!" "Guaranteed results from this miracle method!" "My secret strategy will work for all problems!" Self-help materials that are not forthcoming about their limits are simply not honest.

So let me be up front about the boundaries of this book's applicability and candid about its limits. *Changeology* will not help those who are in denial or unaware of their problems. This book assumes that you are aware of your goals and voluntarily pursuing them; it will not work if its methods are being imposed upon you. Remember, *Changeology* outlines a 90-day program; if you quit after a week, it will probably prove ineffective. The program is applicable to dozens and dozens of behavioral goals, resolutions, and transformations, but not disorders that lead to reality breaks or suicidal intentions.

I should reiterate that this book doesn't need to be used in combination with any other treatment program; it's not tied to or dependent on anything but your willingness to change. *Changeology* can be used with or without professional treatment, including medications, psychotherapy, support groups, and services targeted at specific goals such as weight loss.

People ask me all the time if changing long-established behaviors— such as smoking, drinking, and overeating—requires professional help. The science speaks for itself: thousands of people have successfully overcome their problematic behaviors on their own using the system outlined in this book. In fact, a whopping 90 percent of people who stop smoking and 90 percent of people who gain control of problem drinking do so without formal treatment. That said, I realize that for some, it might prove essential to incorporate additional help, but everyone will be different. My recommendation is that you try to work through this self-change program as it's outlined and then consider professional treatment if necessary.

All of the people you'll meet in this book, however, did not recruit help outside our program and my guidance. What's more, they managed to transform their lives in serious ways, extricating themselves from problems that most of us would think demand professional treatment. Now, if you're among those who choose to use the Changeology program while under the care of a professional, please ensure that he or she is aware that you are using it and that you are in agreement on the treatment plan. And, as is true of all self-help books, *Changeology* does not constitute my rendering professional services to you.

Put simply, Changeology advocates for the integration of multiple sources of healing. There's no conflict between the program outlined here and the use of other therapies. More than anything, I want you to avoid the pernicious either-or thinking that we should have outgrown by the age of twelve. We can take advantage of any combination of these strategies to arrive at successful change. Use and blend as many of the methods as you feel necessary in your own journey through the steps.

To this end, I have provided two appendices to the book: Recommended Self-Help Resources and Selecting the Right Psychotherapist for You. Both are compilations derived from my studies on, respectively, identifying worthy self-help resources and choosing psychotherapists that fit the individual person. They are offered as appendices because not every reader wants them or will use them. But many of you will be interested in expanding your experience to incorporate additional self-help materials and professional healers.

I can't think of a more appropriate time for this book. In the last decade alone we've witnessed soaring rates of chronic disease, which now outpaces infectious disease as a leading killer worldwide. Many chronic diseases, such as obesity and some cancers, have their roots in unhealthy behaviors. We are battling the lethality of lifestyles. At the same time, there's a collective feeling that we're deeply entrenched in depression, stress, and relationship dysfunction. Millions of people are struggling to end addictions and behavioral flaws that only exacerbate their health challenges.

The good news is that Changeology has rescued thousands of psychotherapy patients and research participants from a wide variety of behavioral problems that diminish their well-being. I know that it can accelerate your self-change as well, no matter what kind of goals you hope to realize today, tomorrow, and in the future.

Contrary to the negativity of conventional wisdom, millions of people have, in fact, changed their own lives for the better. They have creatively negotiated the confusing blizzard of information and misinformation. Through my research on their successes, I can now guide you more efficiently and effectively toward your behavioral goals, New Year's (or anytime) resolutions, and life transformations.

Here's what I want to scream from the rooftops: "There's no need to rely anymore on folk myths and Grandma's advice about improving your life. We now possess compelling scientific research that can guide your behavioral metamorphosis. Let science help you; let us show you the way!"

That's precisely what I intend to do in this book. It's time for you to become your own behavioral expert, your own changeologist. Now let's get started!

PART I

THE REAL SCIENCE OF CHANGE

HOW SELF-CHANGERS SUCCEED: THE SCIENCE

We have a love-hate relationship with the idea of changing our behavior. Change is desired and dreaded, venerated and vilified. No wonder we are so confused about it. Change is cumbersome, clumsy, and even contrary. In a word: difficult. Anyone who has tried to change a behavior, from biting nails or procrastinating, to a more ambitious task, such as quitting smoking or reversing a lifelong habit of overeating, knows how elusive lasting success can be. And let's not forget that we're human; we're practically programmed to make mistakes and to be led astray.

On the one hand, we crave personal growth and hope for continual improvement—to be all we can be, to use the old 1960s slogan and the more current armed forces advertisement. Change is an affirmation of life, an exuberant "Yes!" Most of our crowning achievements involve self-change: maturing into adults, mastering skills, learning professions, enhancing health, pursuing interests, ridding ourselves of destructive behaviors, and so on. Isn't that what we are set on earth to do? Change is exciting, awe-inspiring, and distinctly part of our DNA as *Homo sapiens*.

On the other hand, we fear change. Our distress and dissatisfaction about behavioral blemishes motivate us to seek relief, to be sure. We all want relief, and to live better, more fulfilling lives—but not necessarily to change. Can't I be trimmer without exercising or improving my diet? Can't I have a successful relationship and career without working so hard? Most searches for instant, painless solutions stem from the yearning for immediate relief but not effortful change. After all, we've been led to believe that change entails an unrealistic regimen of self-sacrifice that frequently meets with failure in the long run.

Resistance to change, as any half-conscious psychotherapist will tell you, is a powerful psychological force. What sorts of resistance? Various types: resistance to recognizing painful feelings and motives connected to a problem; resistance to surrendering the comfortable rewards of our self-destructive behavior; resistance to giving up short-term gratification for long-term health; resistance to doing what needs to be done as opposed to simply knowing what to do; resistance to changing what we expect and know; resistance to work and sacrifice. Even switching to a new cereal or a new pair of shoes can prove an ordeal for many of us. As W. H. Auden once declared, "We would rather be ruined than changed."

Change is at once wished for and avoided, approached and dodged. As you seek change, you also fight against it. This is expected; embrace it. In fact, this intense ambivalence can fuel your change, as you're about to find out.

But for now, as you begin to digest (and hopefully heed) the advice of this book, recognize both your positive and negative feelings about the forthcoming change. Your positive feelings are usually more apparent initially, but doubts and fears are there as well. Uneasiness toward change is universal and, to some extent, required. In this book we will use your natural desire to change while we mobilize the energy behind your resistance.

THE STRUCTURE OF CHANGE

What sorts of changes do we crave (and simultaneously resist)? There are four clusters that characterize the vast majority of people's ambitions. The first cluster focuses on bad habits—fairly discrete, specific actions that become stitched into daily life. Examples include excessive consumption of tobacco, food, alcohol, and even money. These are behavioral excesses—too much of a good thing.

A second cluster involves new goals. You may desire to acquire or improve upon your skills, be it learning to garden, asserting yourself, running long distance, or playing the guitar. These are behavioral improvements—too little of what you seek.

A third category takes us beyond the individual to the interpersonal: relationships. You may be trying to enhance a romantic partnership, deepen your friendships, reverse troubles with your in-laws, maintain better relations with your coworkers, and so on.

A final cluster addresses the larger picture of life satisfaction. Such change is supremely important, but its success can't be easily quantified in the way that achieving a new goal or improving a relationship can. You are seeking this kind of change if you make statements such as "I want to be a better person" or "I hope to deepen my spirituality" or you set slightly more detailed goals such as wanting to be more generous, kinder, and less selfish.

Many Changes, Yet a Single Solution

In practically every workshop or talk I deliver, someone immediately raises the challenge: But isn't there a big difference between changing a bad habit, such as quitting smoking, and trying to change a relationship with a teenager, for instance? Or seeking to become a better person overall? I certainly thought so 30 years ago when we began researching change. I was convinced that modifying a long-established smoking or alcohol habit was different from treating relationship dysfunctions or promoting self-growth.

I was wrong. The process of change is amazingly similar across diverse goals and problems. People progress through the identical stages—what I will call the 5 steps—for each of the 50-plus problems now researched. And they use the same fundamental strategies to speed their progress through those stages. Of course, the particular goals are different—smokers are reducing cigarette consumption and dealing with cravings, while parent-child relationships are being improved by reducing conflict and enhancing communication. But the journey to the goal is the same.

Some People Aren't Ready for Change

In my previous book, *Changing for Good,* with Drs. Prochaska and DiClemente, we defined how change unfolds over time, starting with the *precontemplation* stage. We say that someone is in precontemplation when he has no intention to change his behavior in the foreseeable future. Most individuals in this stage are either unaware or underaware of their problems; they suffer from ignorance, minimization, or denial. As G. K. Chesterton once said, "It isn't that they can't see the solution. It is that they can't see the problem."

Families, friends, neighbors, and employees, however, are often well aware that precontemplators have problems. When precontemplators seek treatment, they typically do so because of pressure from others. Usually they feel coerced into changing by a spouse who threatens to leave, an employer who threatens to dismiss them, parents who threaten to disown them, or courts that threaten to punish them. They may even change their behavior as long as the pressure is on. Once the pressure is off, however, they often quickly return to their old ways.

This book will not address or help precontemplators. Why? Because the research shows that precontemplators aren't yet ready to make meaningful efforts to change, much less in 90 days. It's also beyond the scope of this book to train people how to encourage *others* to change, so if you're the spouse, parent, or friend of a precontemplator, please understand that although this book can equip you with insights, it won't necessarily help you shift an unmotivated individual into action.

That said, let's take a look at each of the main stages so you can understand how we'll turn these into the 5 steps.

How Scientists Describe the Stages of Change

Virtually everyone has been in the *contemplation* stage for some goal or resolution. This is the stage in which people are aware that a problem exists and are seriously thinking about overcoming it but have not yet made a commitment to take action. They are mulling it over, considering it, weighing the pros and cons. This stage is epitomized by the smoker who wonders every time he lights up when he'll finally set a quit date or muster the courage to ask his doctor for help and the overweight individual who considers joining a weight loss program and goes so far as to write down information she picks up from a commercial selling weight loss products.

The essence of the contemplation stage was beautifully illustrated by the psychotherapist Alfred Benjamin back in the mid-1980s. He was walking home one evening when a stranger approached him and inquired about the location of a certain street. Benjamin pointed it out to the stranger and provided specific instructions. After understanding and accepting the instructions, the stranger began to walk in the opposite direction. Benjamin said, "You are headed in the wrong direction." The stranger replied, "Yes, I know. I am not quite ready yet." This is contemplation: knowing where you want to go, but not being quite ready to go there yet.

People can remain stuck in the contemplation stage for long periods. In one of our studies, we followed a group of 200 contemplators for two years. Typically, our research participants remained in the contemplation stage for the entire two years without ever taking significant action. Contemplators are evaluating their options. If they are to move forward in the cycle of change, they must avoid the trap of obsessive rumination—what we call chronic contemplation—and make a firm decision to take action.

Preparation is a stage made up of good intentions and small movements. Individuals in this stage are intending to take action in the next month and are taking "baby steps" toward change. Preparation might entail smoking fewer cigarettes, cutting down on desserts, making appointments with experts, or seeking support from loved ones. Although they have reduced their problems, preparers have not yet taken decisive action, such as abstaining from smoking or alcohol abuse. They are intending, however, to take such action in the very near future.

Like anyone on the verge of momentous action, individuals in the preparation stage are setting goals and priorities. In addition, they are dedicating themselves to an action plan they choose. Preparers are getting ready for the big jump into the action stage, and they take baby steps in anticipation of that moment.

Action is the stage in which individuals modify their behavior and environment in order to overcome their problems and reach their new goals. Action requires a considerable commitment of time and energy. You're in this stage if you have successfully changed a behavior for one day up to a couple of months. The overspender who develops and lives on a budget, the bickering partner who reduces the number of arguments she starts, the wannabe gardener who toils in the dirt and plants—all of them have entered the action stage.

Changes in the action stage tend to be most visible and socially recognized. People who know you will witness your attempt to change. They will see, for instance, you declining big-ticket purchases, refraining from squabbling, and working in the garden. They will find you walking the walk, probably after months or even years of talking the talk. Your friends, coworkers, and family members will note your efforts and probably congratulate you on them.

In fact, many people, including professionals, often wrongly equate such action with the entire journey. As a consequence, they overlook the necessary preparatory work and the huge efforts required to maintain change in the long run. You will not commit that error with this book. In order to be successful with Changeology, you must recognize and progress through each stage. Which brings me to the next critical stage that must follow action.

Maintenance is the stage in which people work to prevent a relapse to their old ways and consolidate the gains attained during action. The abstinent drinker may say yes to a cocktail at a holiday party but prevents that one slip from becoming a fall. The new exerciser may work out religiously for the first month but then begin slipping in the second month. She catches herself, condemns the sin but not the sinner, and gets back on track. For some problems, particularly addictions, maintenance can last a lifetime—always recovering, never recovered.

Traditionally, maintenance has been viewed as a static stage: just do nothing and keep going. However, everything we've learned in the past 30 years indicates that maintenance is a continuation, not an absence, of change. Getting there is only half the battle; the other half is staying there. Stabilizing behavior change and avoiding relapse are the hallmarks of maintenance.

Now, given these well-defined stages, let's turn to how we'll map them out in this book.

THE 5 STEPS

In the last decade or so, I have discovered through my clinical practice and speaking engagements that most everyone who makes an effort to change doesn't really care about the names of the stages or even how many there are. They enjoy recognizing where they stand in relation to the entire journey, but their focus remains primarily on their necessary tasks.

Put another way, people dedicated to change want to know *what to do*. As one self-changer memorably exclaimed, "Don't tell me where I am; tell me how to move forward!"

Each stage reflects not only a period of time but also a set of tasks that must be completed if you are to move to the next stage, the next step. Although the time that you'll spend in each stage varies, the tasks to be accomplished in each stage are, thankfully, pretty much identical.

It may sound trite, but realizing your goal, resolution, or transformation is a journey. Change, like any meaningful endeavor, proceeds sequentially through steps. The journey begins with the contemplation stage of specifying realistic goals, getting ready, or getting *psyched*. The planning stage is all about *prepping*. How exactly will I do this thing? At some point you will jump from preparing and planning to *perspiring*, the work of implementing the new, desired behavior. Getting there is wonderful, but we need to keep you there, which entails *persevering* through slips and, finally, *persisting* over time.

To simplify the path, in the remainder of the book I will speak of the 5 steps: **P**sych (get ready/contemplation), **P**rep (plan before leaping/preparation), **P**erspire (take action/action), **P**ersevere (manage slips/maintenance), and **P**ersist (maintain change/maintenance). The maintenance stage has been split into two steps because it involves two central but different tasks: Persevere refers to overcoming slips and obstacles, while Persist refers to maintaining the change over time—forever.

As you can see, I've labeled each step with a word that starts with the letter P, which helps me to remember them. Whether or not this is helpful to you, think in terms of these 5 steps from this point forward.

I probably know what you're thinking, because at this point, when I am giving a talk or workshop, someone will politely ask, "But so what? So what that you have identified different stages or steps of change?"

Knowing what step you are in is vitally important to your success. How far you advance in the steps will foretell your success or failure. Our recent analysis of 39 published studies, involving 8,238 patients, demonstrated that the further along you are in the steps, the more likely you are to succeed. Moving a smoker, for example, from Step 1 to Step 3 *doubles* that person's chances of quitting smoking.

Case in point: In an intensive smoking cessation program among cardiac patients, nearly a quarter of patients in Step 1 managed to quit smoking, whereas a breathtaking 76 percent of patients who moved through Step 3 achieved success. About 43 percent of patients in between Step 1 and Step 3 quit the habit. So one thing is clear: the amount of progress you make, on your own or in treatment, is a function of the step you are in.

The following figure from one of my studies on New Year's resolutions perfectly illustrates the dramatic differences in success due to following (or not following) the steps. For six months, we tracked two different groups of people. Both groups had identical goals, the same desire to change, and equal confidence in their ability to change. They all began in the Psych step. On January 1, one group, the "resolvers," began to move through the steps, while the second group, the "nonresolvers," did not; they still wanted to change but didn't proceed to engage in the kinds of exercises and activities that would support that change.

Thus, we had two groups at the exact same starting point, but one group progressed to action while the other group was left behind. The action-oriented resolvers (top, solid line) were ten times more successful than the people still thinking about change and stuck in Step 1 (bottom, dashed line). Forty-four percent compared to a measly 4 percent! Moving one step—from contemplating to doing, from prep to perspire produced that huge effect.

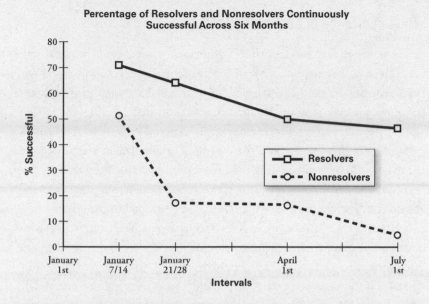

Percentage of Resolvers and Nonresolvers Continuously Successful Across Six Months

The top, solid line reflects the success of people who moved into the Perspire step at the beginning of the year. The dotted line shows those who also wanted to change mightily but failed to take the next step. Over the course of six months, those who took the next step were ten times more successful than those who were languishing in Psych.

That's the power of honoring and following the 5 steps: *each step you take nearly doubles the probability of your long-term success.*

The 5 steps predict who successfully changes and who does not—regardless of other factors involved, including a strong desire to change. The reason for this is straightforward: people can get derailed at any step. Some people never get psyched enough to move to the next step; some get psyched but don't ever prepare; others prepare but don't execute; and still others burn up before they can persevere and persist. The value of working the Changeology program one full step at a time is that it enhances the chance of lasting success. Simple as that.

The Importance of Step Matching

Have you ever watched an inspiring movie, attended a motivational talk, or walked across red-hot coals? Those experiences get you pumped and psyched, but 10 days later all your motivation has faded into oblivion. Or have you ever received personal coaching or medical counseling? They might provide you with expert direction, but you cannot seem to follow it. Perhaps you were not in a place to hear or implement the advice yet, or maybe the suggestions didn't resonate with you. In either instance you experienced *step mismatching*: the right thing at the wrong time (and let's be honest: you could also have received just plain bad information).

The research speaks for itself: respecting and deliberately following the 5 steps considerably increases the likelihood of success; moving one step at a time (i.e., now I'm preparing, next I will perspire in action) practically doubles your odds of realizing your goal or resolution. This may seem obvious, and the graph on page 23 may look like an unnecessary fact to point out because it makes sense that people who don't try to change fail. But I am compelled to show this graphically because it reflects the real research, not just anecdotal evidence.

Once you identify your step, you can complete the tasks and exercises appropriate to it. We call this *step matching*. For instance, if you're already on a diet and losing weight toward a target number, you won't need to consider the activities in the Psych and Prep steps; you'll have already done that work, but now you need to train your efforts on the Perspire step and then the subsequent Persevere and Persist steps when you get there. What works for someone getting psyched to change will not work for someone trying to maintain a change; what works for a person thinking about change certainly differs from someone trying to remain changed.

It would be unfair for my colleagues and me to claim credit for discovering the steps. In the earliest studies done decades ago, when we tried to determine what methods participants successfully used in self-change and psychotherapy, our research subjects kept saying "It depends." "On what?" we wanted to know. It depended on where they were on the change continuum. At different points they employed different strategies, some of which were useful only during certain steps along the path. That sounds obvious, but researchers and psychotherapists before us didn't know it. Now, however, we have the knowledge and the data to back up what we know is true of successful change: that it follows a well-defined, predictable pattern.

Copious research continues to confirm the importance of obeying the 5 steps. A review of 87 self-help treatments revealed that honoring the stages and each of their intrinsic strategies is *the* key to personal improvement across dozens of behavioral goals. Matching the strategies to the step generates large improvements over those achieved by usual treatments, in which everyone is treated the same and receives identical care. Put simply, personalizing treatment to you and your particular step works mightily. It's all about doing the right thing at the right time.

When Dr. Jim Prochaska and his colleagues looked at the effectiveness of stage matching in a health maintenance organization where nearly 4,000 smokers were trying to quit, he showed that step matching proved 34 percent more effective than usual care, and in a second study, it proved 31 percent more effective. ("Usual care" refers to routine treatment provided in the community by health care professionals according to their best judgment and can include any number of strategies.)

Finally, let me give you an example related to depression. Almost 500 primary care patients experiencing depression but not receiving treatment were randomly assigned to either usual care or treatment using step matching. The patients receiving specific tasks and exercises at each stage were significantly more likely than the usual care patients (35 percent versus 25 percent) to experience improvements in their depression. The patients who received treatments tailored to their step were one and a half times as likely to improve. Bottom line: the research proves that step matching is a powerful and inclusive approach to behavior change.

Although I am now a bit embarrassed by it, I specifically undertook research on depression and anxiety to demonstrate that the stages of change could not apply to such complex, clinical disorders. And I was wrong (again): anxious and depressed folks move through the same steps and employ the same strategies as people who are battling bad habits and seeking new goals and relationship improvements.

Where Are You?

I am an expert on *how* to change; you are the expert on *what* to change. So in getting started, ask yourself: What do I want to change? What would improve my health and happiness? What would make me a better person? Think in terms of the following:

♦ Bad habits
♦ New goals
♦ Relationship improvements
♦ Life fulfillment

Go ahead and list several goals, even if they fall under more than one of the above categories. Don't concern yourself with phrasing them perfectly or positively; we'll get to that later. For now, just get them out! (And for those who insist that they have nothing to improve upon, I can confidently nominate two areas for potential change: humility and accurate self-perception! Being human guarantees constant movement and evolution.)

Let's ensure that self-change is just that and does not consist of trying to control other people or situations beyond your influence. To this end, ask yourself: Is the change you want to make about you? Is it voluntary? If not, rethink your list.

I'm assuming that you picked up this book for a reason—to make one or more changes in your life. But I also realize that some of you may have been inspired to read this in the hope of changing *someone else* in your life. Although I applaud those who encourage others around them to change—that's why I'm writing this book, after all—the Changeology program is best used by the person who commits to change and embarks on a personal action plan. So if you're thinking about others at this juncture, see if you can focus squarely on yourself and identify the behaviors you want to improve in yourself. Of course, changing your own behavior can (and usually does) alter your relationships with other people, but your goals for change should still be about *you*.

Making More than One Change: Two's a Charm

Old science told us to stick to one thing at a time when it came to change. After all, the argument went, a person has only so much effort and brain agility to go around. New science, much of it coming from the University of Rhode Island, tells us that you're just as likely to be successful in undertaking two changes at once, particularly if they're related. Exercise and eating, smoking and stress management, relationships and communication are three examples of natural pairing.

When we alter something about ourselves, we increase the likelihood that we will alter other things about ourselves; we can correlate two conditions or states of being. This is especially true with regard to behavior: modifying one behavior increases the likelihood of changing another behavior. In a series of controlled studies carried out by colleagues at the University of Rhode Island, people were several times more likely to improve their exercise and eating habits if they changed the target behavior, of, say, complying with their medication use. You can leverage this power and undertake a couple of related goals at the same time. Since more than half of alcohol abusers also smoke cigarettes and because smoking frequently triggers an urge for a drink, you can immediately see how they can be targeted at the same time or in sequence for maximum effect.

Given the reality of our busy lives, two is probably the right number of goals for most humans to tackle at any one time. Go for two if they are synergistic, such as increasing exercise and eating more healthfully or enhancing relationships and communication simultaneously. Planning such pairings can produce the greatest results. You can sequence other goals you may have: as you progress through the 5 steps, you can take on additional changes, and I'll be helping you do that.

I recently consulted with a gentleman intent on renovating his house, traveling more, and starting to date all at the same time. I loved his determination and ambition but was concerned that he was spreading his commitment a bit thin. We followed the rule of two and focused on two goals, agreeing that the third (renovating his house) would wait until he was well on his way to success with the first two.

How did we decide which two goals to pursue first and which to add later? We followed several research-driven guidelines, which you can consider as well. First, as I've already mentioned, it helps to select two goals that complement and enrich each other. In my patient's case, dating and traveling were natural complements in that his dates could feature day trips and sightseeing. But he could not travel extensively while overseeing renovations to his house, so we scheduled that one for later.

Second, honor your readiness to change and pursue those goals in which you're farther along in the steps. You're far more likely to succeed with behaviors that are already in Perspire than in Psych or Prep. And we know that your confidence and dedication will zoom once you discover your change-ability. Third, prioritize any behavior problems that immediately threaten your health or your ability to change. That guideline did not apply to the gentleman in question, but it would if his goals concerned urgent health-compromising behaviors, such as depression or obesity.

And fourth, chase your energy right now: what do you want to pursue at this time? Of course, all of your goals are important—that's why they are your goals. But you're likely to feel more poised and psyched with some than others. Honor that feeling when you prioritize your goals.

PRIORITIZING CHANGE: WHICH GOALS SHOULD YOU TACKLE FIRST?

1. Select two goals that are related and work with each other. For example: reducing drinking and smoking or exercising more and eating better.
2. Focus on goals where you're farther along in the 5 steps.
3. Make any goals that seriously affect your health and wellness a priority.
4. Concentrate on those goals for which you have the most energy and desire to change today.

CHECK YOURSELF: ASSESS YOUR STEP

There are a number of ways to scientifically measure your stage of change, most of them requiring lengthy questionnaires employed in our research studies. Fortunately, my colleagues and I have determined that you can assess which step you are in by answering a few questions. This exercise, as with the other Check Yourself activities sprinkled throughout the book, requires truthful responses, not your wishes or fantasies.

Be aware that your step is specific to a particular behavior, not universal to you as a person. It's what we psychologists refer to as a *state,* not a *trait.* Your step is a state that can, and probably will, alter over time, in contrast to a stable personality trait. When you think steps, think behaviors, not people.

Each of us is in several different steps at any given time. Take me, for instance. By definition, I would be unaware or in denial of any precontemplation behaviors. I'm in the Psych step—thinking about but not quite ready to act—on my first colonoscopy. It's a goal, but I am fretting and mulling and mentally preparing for it. Granted, this is not on par with most of the larger, more ambitious goals that this book helps you reach, but for the sake of describing the steps, bear with me. And my admittedly unambitious colonoscopy usefully reminds us to define goals that are geared for our needs, not for others' approval.

I'm in the Prep stage on my New Year's resolution to work fewer than 55 hours a week. I've translated my noble intentions into baby steps; for example, I recently announced my decision to step down as editor of a journal at the end of this year, but I have not achieved 54 or fewer hours of work recently.

On the other hand, I am definitely in the Perspire step for exercising at least four times a week, even when I travel. And I can proudly say that I have maintained a host of healthy daily behaviors, such as sleeping eight hours a night, flossing my teeth, and drinking plenty of water. For those goals, I've gone through the Persist step and am currently enjoying the final, Persevere stage. (But don't pressure me to give up my caffeinated diet sodas, even though I probably just identified one of my precontemplation behaviors!)

Now it's your turn to assess the steps for your behavioral goals, resolutions, and life transformations. Let's do so for a single behavior and then for multiple goals in your life.

Consider a Single Goal

To identify your step for a single behavior, ask yourself:

> **Am I seriously intending to change the problem in the**
> **near future, typically within the next 90 days?**

If your answer is no, you're classified as a precontemplator for that behavior. If you reply that you are seriously considering changing the problem in the next three months, you're already in Psych for that goal. If you intend to take action in the next month, you're in Prep. If you are currently changing it, you're already in Perspire.

If you prefer, answer this question with a follow-up question for a particular problem:

> **Do I currently have a problem with _____?**

If yes, you're in the first, second, or third step of change. If no, you're either in the precontemplation stage or have conquered the problem and are in the final steps.

If yes, when will you change it? (Someday = Psych; in the next few weeks = Prep; right now = Perspire).

If no, what leads you to say that? (Because it's not a problem for me = Precontemplation stage; because I have already changed it = Persevere or Persist.)

Consider Multiple Goals

To identify where you currently are for multiple goals, review the statements in the box listed under the respective steps and determine the best fit for your goals or resolutions. Identify your specific goal next to

"My Goal" underneath the items that best represent your step right now. For example, my desire to work fewer than 55 hours a week fell under Prep. The items for that step—"I'm intending to change but, for now, baby steps" and "I am getting ready but not ready to fully commit yet"— accurately describe where I am in the change cycle.

Remember: you may wish to change, but that is quite different from seriously considering or intending to change. Keep the self-assessment real by sticking with your actual behavior of late.

Step 1: Psych

I've been considering changing that part of myself.

I have that problem and I really think I should work on it.

MY GOAL: _____

Step 2: Prep

I'm intending to change but, for now, baby steps.

I am getting ready but not ready to fully commit yet.

MY GOAL: _____

Step 3: Perspire

Anyone can talk about changing; I'm actually doing something about it.

I am really working hard to change.

MY GOAL: _____

Steps 4 and 5: Persist and Persevere

I may need a boost right now to help me maintain the changes I've already made.

I'm here to prevent myself from having a relapse of my problem.

MY GOAL: _____

EMMA: A TRANSFORMATION

I've given you a lot of information so far. Before moving on, let's take a look at how one individual we'll call Emma used this systematic approach to change so you'll begin to see the possibilities that exist for you, no matter the unique behaviors you'd like to change.

Emma dragged herself into my office as a gift to herself on her 40th birthday. She was overweight, a two-pack-a-day smoker, and bouncing from one bad relationship to another. She was "unhappy with life and myself," as she put it.

Bright and motivated, Emma was also demoralized by the magnitude of her challenges and her history of unsuccessful attempts to rectify them. Like many people, she had read scores of self-help books that had left her inspired for a couple of weeks but without lasting results or even specific methods to follow. I was her "last chance"; after me, there would be abject resignation and despair. Though she was not suicidal, she was depressed and feeling hopeless "about it all—me, my weight, my smoking, the whole mess." In one memorable meeting, she exclaimed in frustration, "How do all of these methods and books relate to each other? Is there no structure to how we change?"

Her medical insurance was not the best, requiring an outlandish deductible for behavioral and preventative health care and then offering practically no payment for services. Emma couldn't afford psychotherapy, but she also couldn't afford to do nothing. Hence, we opted to meet a few times with me serving as her coach. I was willing to let a few usual rules slide.

Once Emma discovered the power of following the 5 steps, success came steadily her way. She immediately grasped that people need different tasks in different steps; for a long time she'd been confused by what to do and when, which meant that she had perpetually failed to do the right thing at the right time, given where she was in the steps. What one book taught her was, in fact, effective for Psych but utter nonsense for Perspire. What another book recommended was fabulous for maintaining change but not for initiating it. A lightbulb went on in her head when she finally understood the steps as I taught them and how to fulfill them in her quest.

By working the 5 steps, Emma was able to create order from chaos, to progress systematically instead of stumbling haphazardly. In only five appointments with me as her coach, she proceeded one step at a time through her three goals of losing weight, quitting smoking, and improving her relationships. She mastered the step-matching maxim of doing the right thing at the right time.

Emma did so in three months—the crucial 90-day window—sequencing her three goals so that she was not tackling all of them at the same time. First, she modified her eating patterns and slowly initiated exercise; a few weeks later, she cut down on cigarettes until she cut them out altogether. I won't get into the play-by-play details of how she achieved so much in so little time; other examples in this book will show exactly how it's done. For now, understand that of all the things she did, the most important was conscientiously following the steps and doing the right thing at the right time. She walked the steps in sequence and executed each step's set of strategies, which I'll be detailing starting in the next chapter.

Emma noticed, as have many discouraged self-changers, that she had been seriously step *mis*matching in the past. In particular, the last time she had attempted to kick the habit, she had valiantly tried to "will" herself into new behaviors, rather than learning and practicing them. In other words, she had committed the classic mistakes of, first, approaching change as a battle of willpower ("me versus the temptations of the world") and second, ripping out an old problem without building in a new behavior. Of course, she stumbled a few times, but she discovered that a single slip didn't become a permanent fall (Step 4) and learned the tricks of the trade about long-term maintenance (Step 5).

Emma learned that she didn't require a separate or additional plan for each goal; she understood that the Changeology formula applied to all of her behaviors. She left our "coaching" relationship not only victorious in her three goals but also hopeful and confident about her ability to succeed in future endeavors: sensible, systematic, successful.

Emma reminds me of the vast potential and ceaseless wonder of self-change. If she could do it—shouldering the weight of despair at the start, overcoming a history of failure, juggling three difficult goals, and receiving minimal treatment—certainly most others can as well. And that means you. Emma also reminds me of the privilege of helping others and the value of research-informed practice. I became her coach, just as I will be yours throughout this book.

Let me, backed by decades of psychological research, teach you how to leverage the power of the 5 steps—Psych, Prep, Perspire, Persist, and Persevere—and learn to do the right thing at the right time. You may begin feeling discouraged by multiple setbacks and confused by the blizzard of advice, as did Emma. But my ardent desire and research-proven plan is that you, like Emma, become a successful changeologist.

HOW YOU WILL SUCCEED:
THE KEYS

You've just learned that my colleagues and I have been studying, for 30 years, how people successfully modify their behavior on their own—often without professional treatment. Our search for the structure of self-change determined that it unfolds over time in a predictable sequence of 5 steps: (1) Psych, (2) Prep, (3) Perspire, (4) Persevere, and (5) Persist. You also discovered that in this book you'll learn from the collective wisdom of tens of thousands of people who've mastered change on their own. This will help you to avoid traveling the painful road of trial and error to reach your goals.

I hope you are now as excited as I am about applying these lessons and about navigating the maze. I call it a maze because that's how life happens. You're not sure what to expect, and you can't know what awaits you once you turn the next corner. That's to be expected, so don't panic. Every novel behavior—just like a new pair of eyeglasses, a new pair of shoes, or a new piece of clothing—feels awkward at first, but then we adapt to it and feel comfortable.

In this chapter, I'll transition from the general to the specific, from how most people succeed to how you will celebrate your change in 90 days. First, I'll show you how this process transpires over 90 days by means of a timeline. Second, I'll describe the *change catalysts*—the strategies that provoke or accelerate significant change. Then I'll walk you through what to do (and what *not* to do) at the right time so you execute each step appropriately. Before I send you on your journey through the 5 steps in detail, I'll explode several destructive myths about behavior change that could seriously hinder your progress. You've probably been influenced by those myths in past attempts to change. Just being aware of them will give you a tremendous advantage. And then, bam! Before you know it, you'll be on your way to taking the first step in the next part of the book.

THE TIMELINE

How does all of this change fit into 90 days? Here's the general timeline across the 5 steps.

TIMELINE FOR DOING THE RIGHT THING AT THE RIGHT TIME

Step:	1. Psych	2. Prep	3. Perspire	4. Persevere	5. Persist
Stage:	Contemplation	Preparation	Action	Maintenance	Maintenance
90 days:	1 to 7–14	7–14 to 21	7–14 to 60	60 to 90	75+ onward

The first week or two is rightfully devoted to increasing your motivation, identifying resistance, and psyching yourself up for the momentous change ahead. Another week or two is spent in preparation. As a Chinese proverb reminds us, "Prepare your silken coat before it rains, and don't wait until you are thirsty to dig a well." The first two steps for a particular goal should occupy at least two weeks so you don't jump into action prematurely. However, don't let them exceed one month; otherwise, you'll spend too much time waiting for a magic moment. Not too quick and not too slow; follow the Aristotelian mean of just the right amount of time to psych and prep. Perspiring and persevering together take up the remaining 60 or so days, as the research consistently shows that meaningful transformations typically take two months to be securely established.

Of course, these are generic guides that will be tailored to your situation. Life has an uncanny knack of intruding with unforeseen complications and unexpected circumstances. Adapt the timeline, but do commit to 90 days—a month getting ready and then two months staying at it and avoiding the relapse. That's what thousands of successful changers have taught us over the years. Attempts to do so in much less time typically result in fleeting change and then despair.

THE CHANGE CATALYSTS

As in chemistry, catalysts are the agents that instigate or accelerate significant change. Think of them as the fuel of change, the "go-go juice," as one of my brothers likes to call gasoline. In instigating behavior change, the catalysts are research-supported strategies that get us to the next step. They include such activities as tracking your progress, committing to a goal, raising awareness about yourself and the problem, rewarding your improvement, securing support from other people, rearranging your physical environment, and so on. These are all vital strategies that speed up the process.

Below is a visual representation of the timeline along with the catalysts that are most useful at each step. These catalysts are involved at different steps and for different lengths of time, as indicated by the dotted lines:

90 days:	1 to 7–14	7–14 to 21	7–14 to 60	60 to 90	75+
Steps:	1. Psych	2. Prep	3. Perspire	4. Persevere	5. Persist
Tracking Progress	---				→
Committing	---				→
Raising Awareness	---------------------------------	◉			
Arousing Emotions	---------------------------------	◉			
Helping Relationships			----------------------------		→
Rewarding			----------------------------------		→
Countering			-----------------------------------		→
Controlling Environment			-------------------------		→
Managing Slips				---------------	→

Each catalyst or strategy consists of many particular techniques. Committing to your goal, for instance, encompasses an array of techniques, such as fortifying your will, taking small steps, telling others about your resolution, boosting your self-confidence, and restructuring your thoughts, among others. Rewarding yourself, for another, can take the form of self-affirmations, tangible reinforcers (e.g., a ticket to a movie for not procrastinating that day), formal contracts with other people, and joining an informal network of friends (online and off).

"Ahhhh, I see now. There are dozens of possible techniques for each catalyst, right? So I get to choose which ones to use?" That's what one woman asked during a talk I was giving on how people change. And she was right: there are lots of techniques you can try for each catalyst. For example, within the general strategy of helping relationships, there is a bunch of specific techniques you can use to cultivate and maintain social support for your change. You don't have to use all of the recommended techniques, just the ones that fit your circumstances and preferences. I'll show you myriad examples of useful techniques and help you select those that are especially tailored to your needs and are research-proven in their effectiveness. You will use each catalyst at the right time, but only the techniques that fit your needs.

For the moment, what I want to impress upon you is that the structure of change is orderly, explainable, and understandable. We know these catalysts work; you don't need to guess haphazardly, ask friends randomly, mimic celebrities mindlessly, or follow trial and error blindly. What's more, the route to success can be taught and mastered! That's my whole mission of this book—to share and teach the science of self-change. And I intend to teach as if my hair's on fire.

An Integrated Approach

Here's a second point that I wish to impress upon you: *Changeology* integrates the best of the diverse approaches to behavior change. We're avoiding the "one theory is best" tradition that has divided the mental health disciplines in favor of an all-encompassing, evidence-based approach that honors a combination of proven strategies.

Once upon a time, psychotherapists and self-help authors were trained in a single theoretical approach with little regard to scientific research. Those "dogma eat dogma" days are over. Much in the way medicine today integrates the best treatments in many areas, *Changeology* reflects the contemporary movement toward the integration of approaches and embodies the best of scientific research.

So no matter which school of thought you endorse (e.g., psychodynamic, behavioral, humanistic, cognitive, relational, neuroscience), they all have something to offer—*when* they are used at the right time and when they are sustained by research. You don't even have to know what these theories are or how they relate to the 5 steps. We're going to apply them when and where they are most effective. As it turns out, and as this book will prove, competing psychotherapies do not necessarily lead to conflicting ideas on what generates change. Different forms of psychotherapy prove complementary when worked across the 5 steps.

THE FORMULA FOR CHANGE: STEP MATCHING

As I pointed out earlier, but which bears reiterating, the most important discovery my colleagues and I have made in our 30 years of research is that the key to success resides in matching your efforts to your step. It's technically called step (or stage) matching; metaphorically speaking, it's like two dancing partners who perfectly synchronize their movements during each step of their routine.

Simply put, it involves following certain research-proven catalysts while you're in a particular step. For example, during the first step, it's important to get motivated, explicitly define your goals, and begin to track your progress. In the second step, it's critical to raise your awareness, develop a concrete action plan, and assemble your support team. Each step consists of a set of strategies to complete. Some strategies span multiple steps, while others do not. In practical terms, it's about doing the right thing (catalyst/strategy) at the right time (step).

Step matching is the basis of the self-change formula. In particular, the strategies that raise your emotions and awareness are effective in the early steps (Psych and Prep) but backfire in the latter steps (Perspire and Persevere). Likewise, the strategies that involve your environment and rewarding yourself work marvelously when perspiring and persevering but are actually detrimental in the early Psych and Prep steps. Therefore, you'll want to arouse emotions such as enthusiasm and determination as you get psyched and prepare, and you'll want to have supportive relationships on hand before change occurs and on through maintenance.

In 2000, an analysis of 47 studies proved the potent connection between the steps and their respective catalysts when it came to the success of self-change. The studies involved a wide range of problems such as smoking, substance abuse, lack of exercise, and poor diet. The fancy statistical analysis concluded that the single most powerful means of self-change was to use the right catalyst at the right step. Moreover, it didn't matter what an individual was trying to change, confirming again that this formula for change works just as well across dozens of goals and resolutions.

Once we know what step you are at in reaching a particular goal, we know what will work. Integrating the change catalysts and the steps systematically directs you to success.

STEP MISMATCHING

Step matching, as I've been emphasizing, explains much of behavioral success—and failure. Do the right thing but at the wrong time in your journey, and failure ensues, a phenomenon called mismatching. Mismatches are terribly common, and they can be lethal to your goal.

Zelma was in despair for years because her extended family was constantly asking her for financial help and monetary gifts. During and in between therapy sessions, she would act depressed, feel upset, and be consumed by thoughts about why her relatives would continue to take advantage of her. Zelma was relying primarily on the catalysts of raising awareness and arousing emotions, which didn't match what she needed to do in her journey to progress. Those particular strategies are most effective in Psych and Prep, whereas Zelma was ahead of those steps. She was ready to Perspire, to step into action, to move past the emotional side of dealing with the problem. Zelma was futilely trying to modify her behavior by becoming more aware and emotional, which kept her stuck in the early steps. We know from research that insight and emotion alone don't necessarily bring about behavior change. We can think all we want about our problem and become hypervigilant about it, but that can take us only so far. When I helped Zelma apply other catalysts that were aligned with her actual step, she set boundaries and nudged her way forward. Ever since, she has not been "guilted" into giving financially.

Let's take another example. For years, Zach had been flailing away against his dark moods and irritability by grabbing at whatever remedy he could find in town or on television. He'd participate in one-day seminars, try mood makeovers, buy motivational audiotapes, take assertion lessons, and read an avalanche of just-do-it books. He would quickly learn a few new skills and try to "make" himself change, but to no avail. He was still, in his words, a "suffering sad sack." The problem? Zach was relying primarily on countering and rewarding, but these catalysts are effective only after the requisite awareness, decision making, and readiness are provided in Psych and Prep, the first two steps. In Zach's case, he was acting too far ahead of where he was emotionally, trying to modify his behavior without being fully aware of it. This reflects yet another truth revealed by the research: action without insight and preparation is likely to produce only temporary change. For Zach to be successful in battling his moods, he needed to shift back to the work of those earlier steps and use their catalysts before moving forward.

By contrast with Zach, Zoe was experiencing unprecedented happiness and success, and for good reason: she had accomplished a major milestone in her attempts to lose weight. Zoe had a new body, a new exercise regimen, and a new sense of confidence thanks to her 30-pound weight loss. She had worked diligently for months to lose the weight with the additional help of a popular weight loss program, which offered weekly weigh-ins and occasional group support. In fact, Zoe was so confident that she abandoned both the program and the strategies that had gotten her to the goal weight. As you can imagine, the temptations started and she was no longer equipped to handle them now that the relationships she'd previously maintained to keep her on track were gone. Soon enough, she discovered she was vastly underskilled in managing slips. The temporary slips quickly deteriorated into a permanent relapse. Zoe was trying to maintain her behavior without skills in relapse prevention, which points to another fact borne out by the research: quick, dramatic change rarely lasts for long unless you have a maintenance program in place.

Zelma, Zach, and Zoe were all innocent casualties of step mismatching. All three were working hard but not smart. All three were employing effective change catalysts but at the wrong time. *Changeology* helps you work smarter, not harder, by step matching. The groundwork in this chapter ultimately prepares you to enter the first step (Psych) in the change process and begin the journey of achieving your goals, resolutions, and transformations.

EXPLODING MYTHS

I'm eager to get you into the 5 steps and the change process itself, beginning with the next chapter, but I would be guilty of mismatching myself if I did so without presenting a few more skills that will fully orient you to the book and the system's effectiveness for you.

From painful experience, I've learned that many people subscribe to a series of self-defeating myths that undermine their efforts to change. These myths have infected our society. In an effort to set our heads straight and keep our hearts open, let's demolish them:

1. People can't change on their own.
2. Most goals and resolutions are trivial.
3. Change requires only willpower.
4. It's all in my genes.
5. I can't change; I've tried before.

John Maynard Keynes, the esteemed economist, once wrote that "the difficulty lies not so much in developing new ideas as in escaping from old ones." Before jumping into the new ideas of Changeology, let's briefly escape the old ideas to which many of us still cling. Understanding why those myths flourish and how their truthful counterparts—their opposing facts—relate to successful change will further equip you with the knowledge to become your own changeologist.

Myth No. 1: People can't change on their own (and its corollary: resolutions never succeed).

The statistics, in this case anyway, don't lie. More than three-quarters of people who change their behavioral problems have done so on their own, without professional treatment. Call it Emersonian self-reliance, the do-it-yourself nation, or the Home Depot effect, but the most common way that people change is indeed *on their own*. Even for addictions such as problem drinking and smoking, a staggering 90 percent of people ditch the habits all by themselves. The history of humanity is filled with clear and compelling evidence that we can change and grow.

Understandably, most mental health professionals don't like to emphasize the fact that we can change on our own. They have occupational and economic self-interests to consider. But those who get past their therapist-centricity see the facts plainly. It's a shame that such a professional prejudice exists because it ultimately diminishes our appreciation of change and limits how much professionals encourage self-help.

Contrary to widespread public opinion, a considerable proportion of New Year's resolvers do in fact succeed. Our longitudinal research contradicts the prevailing belief that "resolutions never succeed" or, in the words of Oscar Wilde, that the origin of resolutions "is pure vanity. Their result is absolutely nil." As I've already pointed out, more than 40 percent of resolvers are successful at six months. And that's for a single attempt; count a few attempts at the same New Year's resolution, and the success rates goes even higher.

Bottom line: stop propagating, and stop believing, the nonsense. People are changing on their own all the time, without treatment. Believing otherwise imperils your own success.

Myth No. 2: Most goals and resolutions are trivial.

"Well, okay," the argument goes, "many people can change on their own, but they can overcome only the small, trivial things." In a word, baloney.

Every national study on goals and resolutions demonstrates that people fulfill impressive ambitions all the time, including losing weight, stopping smoking, improving relationships, achieving financial security, boosting self-confidence, reducing alcohol use, increasing exercise, eating healthier foods, regularizing sleep patterns, and letting go of grudges. These are not trivial; they are all life-enhancing, if not life-saving, goals. They are probably among the top 10 behaviors any of us should adopt to improve our health, life span, and peace of mind.

Myth No. 3: Change requires only willpower.

This prescientific misconception contains a grain of truth within a loaf of nonsense. The grain of truth is that your willpower or commitment contributes to your success. Believing in your ability to change and acting on that belief raises the probability that you'll succeed. And in this book I will certainly teach you research-backed methods of fortifying your will.

However, the loaf of nonsense is that willpower constitutes the only, or even the most effective, ingredient. It's only *one* ingredient in the recipe. Our research shows that resolvers who rely on willpower to the virtual exclusion of the other valuable catalysts actually fail at a higher rate than everyone else!

So despite what your mom or Aunt Lily might have told you as a child, willpower is nowhere near sufficient for lasting change—and it may not even be your most important one. People who rely solely on willpower set themselves up for failure. Stick with the science, and use your willpower as one of many tools that will help you change for good.

Myth No. 4: It's all in my genes.

This is the most recent brain-based misconception about change, and it's an unfortunate side effect of advances in neuroscience. But a few quick moments of critical thinking show that it's simply a variation on the old theme—"it's all willpower," "it's all about money," and now "it's all in my genes." This is just the either-or, black-and-white thinking of a fourth grader.

Yes, of course, biology impacts your behavior, your metabolism, your impulse control, and all of your physical features. Biology sets some practical limits on what we can accomplish in life. That fact, however, doesn't mean that we are at the mercy of our genes. Genes exert powerful influences, but they don't determine our destiny.

I meet hundreds of folks who insist that they are shackled by their genes to a lifetime of addictions, obesity, depression, and bad relationships. I immediately empathize with their family history but then respectfully challenge their thinking: Do you know anyone with a similar family history who is not suffering from your disorder? What percentage of people with parents who are addicted, obese, depressed, and/or divorced do *not* develop those problems? (It's the majority, by the way.) Do you understand the crucial difference between genetic determination and genetic predisposition? Persistent questioning often leads to a slow surrender to the truth—that genetics predispose and influence what we do, but they do not determine us. In other words, your DNA is not necessarily your fate; far from it.

Beyond the inaccuracy of the myth, the genetics hype is worrisome for another reason: people who engage in the riskiest health behaviors and who are most in need of self-change are more likely to blame their genes. They use their genes as an excuse to continue unhealthy behaviors. And the more unhealthy the behavior, the more they latch on to a genetic justification for their problems. This defensive reaction allows them to blame health problems as being "beyond their control" and then spiral down into "I can't change." Blaming DNA bodes ill for people in so many ways.

We are free to exert our will, no matter what our biological constraints may be. Remember that the brain-behavior interaction goes both ways: your behavior impacts your biology and influences the expression of those genes. So the next time you succumb to the brainwashing and begin blaming your biology for your disappointing attempts to change, get real and remind yourself that "it's just genetics, not destiny."

Myth No. 5: I can't change; I've tried before.

How many times have you heard people (perhaps yourself) say that they cannot change because they've attempted to do so oh-so-many times in the past to no avail? They won't even entertain another attempt because they are so tired of the serial failure.

This myth comes wrapped up in a lot of emotion. Anyone who has failed a number of times to modify a single behavior will express resignation, anger, apathy, fear, disgust, disillusionment, and sadness. When I work with individuals who are in this mode, I have to find a way to remind them that the consequences of not trying again are grave and that the real possibility of success using Changeology is so much higher than what they have experienced before. I wade through their feelings and with as much empathy as I can muster; I address their resignation with Socratic questions. Here's an abbreviated transcript of such an exchange that I had last year with a patient, whom I'll call "Resigned":

> *Norcross:* How would your effort to change this time, with the guidance of decades of scientific research, differ from how you have tried three times before on your own?
>
> *Resigned:* Well, I didn't know about that research the last few times. I never learned about this stuff before. Where were you three years ago when I needed you?
>
> *Norcross* (fighting off pangs of neurotic guilt): So you realize that a new attempt would be quite different and afford you a better chance of achieving your goal?
>
> *Resigned:* Yes, I suppose so. But I still don't think I can do it.
>
> *Norcross:* Naturally enough. You tried valiantly on your own and came up short each time. That was then, and now brings a new day and a better way.
>
> *Resigned:* Mmmhhh. I guess so . . .
>
> *Norcross:* But you aren't entirely convinced, huh? And perhaps I hear some fear in your voice: that if you go to all of the effort to change again, you're fearful that you might fail again. Another devastating blow . . .
>
> *Resigned:* (interrupting) Exactly! I'm afraid to fail again.

A few more minutes of this conversation confirmed my suspicion of two underlying themes that are endemic: (1) fear of failure and

(2) overgeneralizing. Resigned was understandably afraid of falling flat on her face again; empathy, support, validation, and reassurance got us through that barrier. But her cognitive error of overgeneralizing, which refers to making blanket statements ("If it was true in one case, it must be true in all future cases"), took some time to correct. I had to point out her faulty logic and teach her how the new program would indeed be different. I also drew attention to the fact that she had committed a step mismatch: she was prematurely rushing into action without sufficiently preparing for the task. That mismatch was further compromising her maintenance plan.

You've already learned the multitude of ways in which Changeology proves superior to common practice and your previous efforts, but Resigned didn't know that yet. A few more minutes of conversation enabled her to realize that her prior efforts had not been similar to what I was suggesting. She then began to convert her fear into fuel and to implement the new science of self-change.

SELF-EFFICACY AND BEYOND

It is essential to counter these corrosive fictions at the outset. When you think about it, the myth of "I can't change; I've tried before" is the complete opposite of what's called *self-efficacy*—the belief that your own efforts play a critical role in your success and in a particular task. The "I can't change myth" is anti-self-efficacy.

Let me apologize in advance for using the $12 psychological term *self-efficacy* throughout the book. I will use the word a lot because it's central to our research and there's not another term that comes close enough to it. Another way of thinking about it in practical terms is simply as your belief in your competency to complete a particular behavioral goal.

Before we leap into the 5 steps, let's discuss and cultivate your self-efficacy. You'll need to abandon the "I can't change" myth and whole-heartedly believe that you possess the power to grow in fundamental ways.

What's the difference between self-esteem and self-efficacy? Self-esteem is global, which is a way of saying that it's about you as a person.

It's about how positive you feel about yourself in general. By contrast, self-efficacy is specific; it's your ability to execute a particular task. It's about how confidently you believe you can achieve a certain goal. You may have wonderful self-esteem but still not believe that you can bake an apple pie, master chess, or paint like van Gogh. Alternatively, you may have 100 percent confidence that you won't smoke or overeat today, but at the same time you may feel lousy about yourself. Surprisingly, global self-esteem and specific self-efficacy are not that highly correlated. You can have one but not the other.

More surprisingly, self-esteem barely predicts the probability of reaching your behavioral goal, resolution, or transformation. You can have healthy self-esteem but fail to achieve any serious goal. Self-efficacy, on the other hand, has everything to do with whether or not you succeed, and that's why we will use the term.

CHECK YOURSELF: SELF-EFFICACY

Here is a brief self-assessment of your self-efficacy to change. Answer the following question "None," "A little," "Some," "Often," or "A great deal" with regard to one particular behavior:

How much realistic confidence do you have in your ability to change your behavior (your goal or resolution)?

Before January 1, resolvers who proved successful answered "Often" or "A great deal." Resolvers who were ineffective typically answered "A little" or "Some." In fact, statistically speaking, this single item was the most powerful predictor of which resolvers succeeded or failed in the new year. This simple self-assessment integrates my scientific research with your gut check. Are you realistically confident?

As psychologists like to say, the data are always friendly. Whether you are experiencing sufficient self-efficacy to change or not, use the self-assessment data to prepare yourself.

Already brimming with self-efficacy? That's a definite head start on your transformation. Coming up a little short in this department? Not to worry; I'll soon teach you ways to boost your self-efficacy. What's important now is that you recognize the important role it plays and that you guard against joining the "can't change" crew—or, for that matter, subscribing to any of the other self-defeating myths.

Before we launch into the first step, kindly check yourself on your mastery of the material you've learned thus far. As promised, I'll routinely gauge your skills and progress throughout *Changeology* by a series of checks. Please answer honestly—not to please me or to graduate to the next chapter—so that you know where you are. I'll say it again and again throughout the book: it's insufficient to say that you should think that way or you know to behave in a particular way. We are interested in actual behavior, not best intentions or empty knowledge.

CHECK YOURSELF: THE KEYS TO SELF-CHANGE

Answer the following questions using a 5-point scale: 1 = Definitely not, 2 = Probably not, 3 = Maybe, 4 = Probably yes, 5 = Definitely yes.

I now understand the general timeline for the 5 steps. _____

I accept that it takes about 90 days to create and build a new behavior. _____

I accept the idea that different strategies are most effective in different steps. _____

The secret to change (doing the right thing at the right time) makes sense to me, and I am ready to work smarter, not harder. _____

I am convinced that people do change on their own. _____

Willpower is useful, but not the only or primary way to change. _____

I acknowledge the impact of my genes but realize that they influence, not determine, my success. _____

With the assistance of the Changeology system, I believe that my next self-change effort will bring better results. _____

I am committed to strengthening my self-efficacy. _____

I promise myself to answer the Check Yourself exercises honestly and
  accurately throughout the book.   _____
I understand the principles and powers of following the 5 steps and
  am eager to proceed!   _____

You and I both know that your rating on each of these items should be 4 ("Probably yes") and 5 ("Definitely yes"). If so, well done! Turn the page and take the first step. If you're not yet giving yourself 4s and 5s, take a bit more time to refamiliarize yourself with the key points you've learned and to rework the respective skills. There's plenty of time to do so; don't rush into the book and commit a mismatch before you even get to the first step.

PART II

BECOMING A CHANGEOLOGIST IN 90 DAYS

STEP 1

PSYCH: GETTING READY

> **WEEKS 1 AND 2**
>
> Outline your goal and define the new you. Start counting and measuring the behavior you will modify. Think about the consequences of your problem and imagine a new life without it. Harness the awareness and emotions that will propel you into action.

Ask anyone on the street for the secret of change, and you will invariably receive answers such as "It only takes motivation," "You need to be really psyched," and "Lots of commitment." Those answers are partly accurate. But science tells us that self-change also requires skills. One of the colossal mistakes people make when trying to change is overestimating the value of motivation while underestimating learnable skills.

We will avoid that mistake here; you'll learn how to acquire both commitment and skills. This chapter features the specific methods, examples, and Check Yourself exercises for the four catalysts that embody your first step: Tracking Progress, Raising Awareness, Arousing Emotions, and Committing. Decades of research demonstrate that the transition from thinking about change to planning for change involves increasing your use of these particular strategies. By the end of Step 1, you'll know how to think and feel differently about your problems, how to convert fear of change into fuel for action, how to mobilize your excitement for a glorious problem-free future, and how to kindle and keep the commitment.

Let me briefly introduce you to Monique and Andrew, two individuals who successfully used this system to make big changes in their lives. We will follow them throughout the rest of the book.

Monique typifies so many people who struggle with addictions to substances and behaviors that temporarily bolster their low self-esteem. Since adolescence, Monique had been plagued by low self-confidence despite a stellar job and a loving family; she had begun to self-medicate with sweets, cigarettes, and booze. Sounds like a lot to tackle, but Monique was up to the task once she learned to proceed one step at a time and to match the right set of tasks with the right step. Monique also learned to take on only two major changes at a time and to then "sequence" the others.

Andrew, on the other hand, had troubles of another sort: people and money. He went through both within months, leaving in his wake a series of distressed girlfriends and unpaid bills. Ready for change, he wanted to create stable, solid relationships with both the women in his life and his finances. And he wanted to do it within 90 days. Possible?

Using Monique and Andrew as examples, I'll show you how they managed to move through the first step and psych themselves up for change. How did each begin the journey? What challenges did they face at the start? How did they convert their fear into motivational fuel? How did they commit themselves and maintain it? How could they realistically conquer so many changes at once? I'll answer these and other questions as we prepare you for the road ahead.

DEFINING YOUR GOALS, PART I

By this page in the book, I'm going to assume that you already have at least one, maybe two, goals in mind. You're first going to learn how to describe your goals in general terms; then you'll put them into more specific terms in the next step, which will improve the chances of your reaching them.

Defining does not imply limiting. I feel quite strongly about this point; you don't need to limit your goals simply because you define them. Make them vital, ambitious, transformative even. Keep aiming high while I simultaneously tether your feet to the ground.

An initial step in any self-management project is to select goals and define them in behavioral terms. Vague objectives, such as "to become a better person," beget vague efforts and disappointing results. Lewis Carroll summed it up nicely in one of my favorite exchanges from *Alice's Adventures in Wonderland*:

Alice: Would you tell me, please, which way I ought to go from here?
Cheshire Cat: That depends a good deal on where you want to go.

You need to choose and define your goals in a way that will enhance your probability of success. Here are five proven methods.

It's all about you. Select a behavior you genuinely want to change. I've already stated that this needs to be about you, which sounds obvious, but I spend days listening to patients and students telling me what their spouses, parents, or friends want changed. So it must be reiterated: make sure you're doing this for none other than yourself. As Mark Twain observed, "Nothing so needs reforming as other people's habits."

It should be measurable. In my world, we refer to this as *operationalizing* a goal in a way that you can measure by counting or graphing. As you'll discover in a few pages, tracking your progress increases your progress. If you cannot find a way to measure your progress toward your goal, it will be that much harder to move forward and keep an eye on your development.

It has to be real. A guaranteed recipe for failure is to select an unrealistic, unattainable goal. Losing 30 pounds in 90 days is more of a fantasy (and a dangerous one at that) than a resolution. Distinguish between realistic, short-term goals and long-term fantasies. Ensure that your general goal is real.

It has to be under your control. You don't have the power to bring about world peace and end global warming. By contrast, you can control many of your own behaviors and contribute to a cause. Select behaviors that are under your thumb.

It should be positive. Goals expressed positively, or phrased in terms of increasing a desirable behavior, typically prove more successful than goals expressed negatively or in terms of decreasing a problem behavior. Suppose your problem is that you procrastinate too much. Instead of saying "I want to decrease my procrastination," you can increase other behaviors: planning work ahead of time and then taking small steps to complete your tasks every day. As you do these, you'll automatically reduce your procrastination. Even if you want to terminate a problem, specify your goal as a healthy alternative behavior. Psychologically, it's easier to build in a new behavior than to root out a problematic one.

As you master the skills and motivations presented in this chapter, state your goals as I suggest. Monique and Andrew certainly did, and we can use them as role models.

As you may recall, Monique initially came to me with an exhaustive list of problems: low self-esteem, high weight, cigarette smoking, and unhealthy alcohol use. She followed the rule of two and took on only two major changes at a time, sequencing the others. Instead of speaking about getting rid of her problems, she learned to look forward positively. She declared goals of elevating her esteem, improving her food and beverage selection, and initiating exercise. Smoking cessation, for Monique and practically everyone, is difficult to phrase realistically in positive terms, so we have left it at reducing the number of cigarettes smoked per day (although I would immediately add with a smile, "and thereby improving your health!").

Andrew's two core conflicts—"dropping money and women like flies," as he once memorably phrased it—easily translated into positive goals. The first became saving money and buying only what was essential. The second became communicating his intent to women honestly and moving toward a meaningful, monogamous relationship. Notice that these meet our criteria: reasonably specific, measurable, personal, realistic, attainable, positive goals.

In order to reach your goal of acquiring a new behavior, you can define a series of subgoals. For example, I recently worked with a student whose goal was to improve her grade point average for the next two semesters, before she graduated. Her subgoals entailed consistently increasing her study time by a third, meeting privately with her professors at least twice a semester, and getting some tutoring for a couple of courses.

That's how a single goal quickly becomes a number of interrelated behaviors. For those targeting weight, for instance, your subgoals may be upping the number of times each week you spend exercising, decreasing the number of times per week that you consume sugary desserts, and increasing the number of times that you substitute healthy fruit for junk food. Multiple behaviors are encouraged for each of your goals. They point the way to victory!

The last two people who approached me as I was finishing this book vividly illustrate the effective use of subgoals. One wanted me to coach her about diabetes management; the other wanted guidance on conserving energy in the environment. Those are both laudable goals but involve lots of subgoals or objectives. The diabetic grappled a bit with getting specific, but within 15 minutes she identified her subgoals as engaging in regular exercise, monitoring her blood sugar daily, taking her medications, and modifying her diet. The wannabe energy conserver got the point immediately: "So my goal is the destination, and my subgoals are how I get there, right?" Exactly. From the dozens of possibilities, she decided to walk and bike more around town, to use air-conditioning less, and to insulate her windows.

Before proceeding, please double-check that you are conceptualizing your goals in these ways. Do you have one or two behaviors that are meaningful to you? Can you measure, count, or graph them? Would your friends consider them realistic and attainable? Are they largely under your control? Are you thinking of them in positive terms? When you can say yes to all of these questions, let's move forward. (And remember, we'll sharpen your goals further in the next step.)

TRACKING YOUR PROGRESS

What did Monique and Andrew do once they decided upon and prioritized their goals? They began to monitor their behavior. This is taking the very first step in the right direction. Research in many disciplines—psychology, business, health care, and more—indicates that tracking yourself increases the probability of success. As the famed business consultant Peter Drucker once said, "What's measured improves." Precisely.

Obviously, Monique and Andrew weren't tracking real progress yet (unless you view mere vigilance as progress). Before they could begin to actively change their behavior, they needed to establish their current, or baseline, behavior. They began to track the behavior that they wanted to change and that would evolve over the course of time and effort. And as you may recall from the timeline on page 36, this strategy continues throughout all five steps.

Tracking the progress of your goal works for at least three reasons. First, it keeps your attention on the goal, your eye on the ball. Recording a behavior each day makes it almost impossible to "forget." Second, it provides useful feedback, alerting you when you veer off course and telling you to adjust. There it is in black and white: you have plateaued or fallen behind your pace. Third, tracking your progress is highly rewarding. Watching the minutes of exercise skyrocket and the number of cigarettes fall led Monique to exclaim, "Better than sex!" Andrew was more reserved but was excited to track his newly made savings account twice a day. He was so excited, in fact, that he began going online to access his bank account four or five times a week instead of twice.

That's why we incorporate tracking progress into every step: it begins before you change and persists throughout the 90 days of Changeology. Of course, the purpose of tracking evolves along with your progression through the steps. But its value remains the same: you are guaranteed rewarding feedback that makes it difficult to forget or stray from your goal. You might even discover some surprising information about your behavior.

One day I was arguing with my then collegiate son about his work habits, as fathers are apt to do. During the winter break, he preferred to start work late in the morning and, in my view, worked erratically—on some days hardly at all and on other days in a burst of productivity. Jonathon took offense at my "gross mischaracterization," and we decided to collect data to settle our dispute. He agreed to record on his laptop the number of hours worked per day on this book during his college break.

Jonathon's work hours for 31 days are graphed in the following figure.

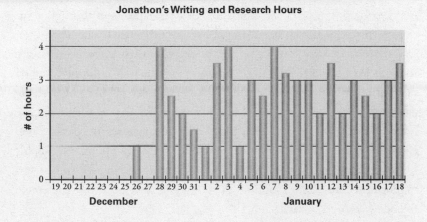

Jonathon's Writing and Research Hours

The first seven days were baseline recordings before Christmas, when he was not expected to work. On the remaining 24 workdays, he devoted at least one hour on 23 of them. His work performance was steady, averaging two to three hours of writing and research on this book per day.

In fact, Jonathon was correct; he worked 96 percent of the days. I was surprised and impressed; my elevated expectations and my own preference to begin work in the morning had led me to mistaken conclusions. He can now see my public admission in print: I was wrong!

But I am hardly alone. We are all misled by biases, selective perception, and convenient forgetting. Numbers don't lie. And they provide the truth you're seeking when you use this strategy.

Tracking your progress is especially valuable if you're unaware of how often you engage in your behavior. Counting the number of cigarettes you smoke in a day, for instance, can shed light on the extent of your problem and provide you with a tangible number that you can then begin to lower as you move through the steps. Sometimes people will censor themselves without intending to or even realizing it. They may underreport the number of calories they consume or drinks they have or cigarettes they smoke. Sometimes tracking your progress may result in surprising data. You may find yourself thinking "Wow, do I really consume that many calories every day?"

If done regularly and honestly, this catalyst ensures that you aren't underestimating a problem. You can track your progress through a variety of methods, including a graph, a diary or journal, calendar notes, or a daily record on your computer or cell phone. For many years, my wife has tracked her daily caloric consumption the old-fashioned way by maintaining a handwritten estimate in our kitchen. It keeps her aware and on track. A neighbor wears a pedometer every day to ensure that he is a member of the 10,000-steps-a-day club. His simple, inexpensive step counter records all of his steps—at home, working, shopping, walking his two dogs. He clips the pedometer to his belt upon getting out of bed and monitors his progress throughout the day. Hard data are always preferable to guesswork and speculation.

Still other changeologists journal or blog their progress. Journaling will help you stay focused and more aware of your behavior. Blogging lets you share your behavioral struggles and successes with friends and brings the bonus of cultivating helping relationships (which we will address in the next step).

Smart phones and the Internet can be excellent tools for monitoring yourself. Websites can provide you with easy graphs, charts, and reminders. There are health text message services that will remind (or perhaps nag) you about keeping track of your habits and thoughts. Google Calendar is one of my favorites since it can be used as a comprehensive self-management application, including tracking your progress. Such devices can keep the information and reminders coming. It is sometimes hard to remember to track your progress, especially if you are swamped with work and other responsibilities.

If tracking your progress involves counting or estimating stats such as calories, cell phone applications (apps) can do this work for you. For example, you can download, either for free or at minimal cost, apps that will tell you how far you've walked and give you an estimate of how many calories you've burned. Other apps can tell you roughly how many calories are in certain kinds of foods.

Sites such as SparkPeople (www.sparkpeople.com), DailyBurn (www.dailyburn.com), and Sharecare (www.sharecare.com) are great time-savers. Their food databases allow you to enter what you've consumed and then keep track of your calories, protein, carbs, and fats for the day. We don't always know offhand how many calories are in a sandwich and a glass of lemonade, for instance. Though the apps usually can't provide precise information, they can certainly give you close estimates in a short amount of time. There are countless apps and Internet resources at your disposal. Be sure to use them if they work for you, as they can make your life much easier.

Go online to access monitoring tools to customize your own journey. While there, visit www.ChangeologyBook.com for other vital tips on tracking your success.

At least once a week, a dieter asks me about the pros and cons of using photographs of themselves naked as a means of tracking progress. He will have heard from friends or read somewhere that one should take a seminaked picture of oneself before commencing a diet. I understand the potential upside: looking at that picture every week and taking more recent pictures could help you notice physical improvements over time. But the downside can be significant: the photo can create self-loathing and despair. Although it's stored on your cell phone camera and intended to be private, other people might somehow access your photos. And if you don't believe the weight is falling quickly enough, you can slide into self-rebuke and hopelessness. In fact, that's what Monique had experienced when she tried the method in an earlier, failed bid to shed pounds.

So here's my ambivalent position on using photos to track progress: carefully consider the advantages and disadvantages, avoid them if you are sensitive to your body image, and hide them safely should you choose to use them. A better, probably more effective idea is to weigh yourself two or three times a week and track your exercise minutes or distance.

As you continue to track your progress, be prepared for spontaneous improvement in your behavior, even though you have not yet moved into the later steps. This phenomenon is known as *reactivity*: measuring something usually improves it. Increasing your awareness of the goal frequently leads to gains in the monitored behavior. Sweet! That's another or fourth way that tracking progress increases your chances of success.

Bottom line: track your baseline during the first (Psych) step, which will last for a week or two. You'll then continue to track your progress for the entire 90 days and reap the rewards of doing so. We'll revisit this invaluable strategy during each subsequent step and examine how it can speed you along the road to success.

RAISING YOUR AWARENESS

This change catalyst entails becoming more conscious of the causes of, consequences of, and cures for your problems. Beginning with Freud's objective, "to make the unconscious conscious," all so-called insight methods begin by working to raise the individual's level of awareness. Knowledge is power to change.

My longtime collaborator Dr. Jim Prochaska likes to think of consciousness as a beam of light. Unavailable or unknown information is like the darkness. In the darkness, we are blind; we don't possess sufficient sight or light to guide us effectively in pursuing personal change. In the light, however, we are sighted and lucid; we hold the light and the power of personal change.

Jim's metaphor hails back to Plato's allegory of the cave as told to his students in *The Republic*: All mortals come into this world barren of knowledge and innocent of all truth. Of reality we know nothing. Like prisoners in a dark and cavernous chamber, arms shackled and weights about our necks, we are chained in the dungeon of ignorance. Only knowledge, hard-earned awareness, frees us from our ignorance and superstitions. That's how awareness leads to behavior change.

Albert Einstein once said, "No problem can be solved from the same level of consciousness that created it." We need to elevate the dialogue, the awareness, the consciousness, before modifying our behavior. Everyone agrees on the value of awareness, but what everyone doesn't agree on is how to cultivate it. Are education and information effective? How about interpersonal feedback? Or perhaps observations from professionals? Lessons gleaned from books, movies, poetry? Online education? The disagreement lies in which methods are most effective in raising awareness.

We don't need to enter these unproductive debates because you can choose the method that fits your unique goal, situation, and preferences. It might help to keep in mind my "AEIOU and always Y" guide: Available; Effective; Innovative; Open to modification; User-friendly; and always right for You (the vowels in the English alphabet). It's imperative that you select techniques that are:

♦ **A**vailable: the techniques within your reach and grasp; it makes no sense to try to use those that are unavailable to you.
♦ **E**ffective: techniques that you have determined to work for you.
♦ **I**nnovative: techniques that bring novelty and creativity to your change rather than the old standbys with which you are most familiar.
♦ **O**pen to modification: techniques that can be adapted or individualized to your personality, preferences, and problems.
♦ **U**ser-friendly: simple and teachable skills, as opposed to abstruse theories or vacuous psychobabble.
♦ **Y**ou: this is about you, so you must feel a connection with the techniques; what works in general is meaningless unless it works specifically for you.

Use these guidelines for every catalyst we will consider. I will present only techniques that have received at least a modicum of research support, and I will help you select those that are especially adapted to your needs.

What sort of self-awareness will inform and propel you through the 5 steps? Answer: knowing the causes, consequences, and cures of your problems. It helps to ask yourself three questions: (1) What led to my particular problem, and what maintains it now? (2) What are the consequences, both desirable and undesirable, of my current behavior? (3) What are the cures, the paths to my goal?

As you begin to think about the answers to those questions, consider the following proven methods of enhancing your awareness and insight.

Face the facts. Seek out information on the causes and consequences of your problem from unbiased sources. This might be uncomfortable, because we're genetically engineered to avoid unpleasantries and pain. What are the probable long-term consequences of obesity, a sedentary lifestyle, smoking, alcohol abuse, or loneliness? Learn the objective facts and apply them to yourself instead of casually dismissing them, which is easy to do. Monique, for one, was surprised when she realized the health ramifications of lugging an extra 50 pounds around for the rest of her natural-born days. She committed to, in her words, "truth telling" and began calling herself obese instead of minimizing her condition by referring to herself as "big-boned." Self-help books, health care websites, and government guidelines offer the sobering facts when you are ready to look.

Ask for trouble. Now we're getting personal. Request feedback from loved ones about the costs and consequences of your problem. Tread carefully here, but do ask for a heart-to-heart from people you have not heard from on the subject. Andrew was "floored," as he put it, when he asked a coworker about his partying and overspending. She asked for a day to think about it and then sincerely informed Andrew that he was compromising his reputation and career by acting like a "bratty, superficial frat boy." He discovered that his self-image as a suave bon vivant was probably an elaborate defense; others saw him as quite the opposite.

Ask Doc Brown. If loved ones are too biased or critical to provide objective information, or if you seek more in-depth information, get a professional opinion from a psychologist, physician, nutritionist, or clergyperson. Request a straight answer from someone whose business it is to know. Many years ago, my internist looked me straight in the eyes and said, "If you don't lose some weight, I'm putting you on a statin" (to lower my blood cholesterol). That was enough to raise my awareness quickly!

See you at the movies. I confess that I find most information sources somewhat stale and uninteresting; I prefer my awareness with some drama mixed in. If you share my preference, watching a movie, attending a play, or reading a moving autobiography might be more up your awareness alley. Appendix A presents the most highly recommended self-help books and autobiographies for dozens of goals. Andrew was visibly shaken after devouring Pete Hamill's autobiography, *A Drinking Life;* Monique could not finish reading Caroline Knapp's *Drinking: A Love Story* because she was crying intensely. She realized what her own drinking was doing to her two darling children. Increasing the drama also increases the impact, so prepare for a powerful experience.

A week or two of concerted effort at raising your awareness typically suffices. How much information is sufficient? The following Check Yourself provides an answer to the question. Remember that the benchmark scores in these self-evaluations are derived from our research with thousands of people on the road to change. But they are rules of thumb; the general pattern is more important than the particular numbers. What you need to ask yourself is: are you hitting the mark of effective changeologists?

CHECK YOURSELF: RAISING AWARENESS

What are you doing to elevate your knowledge about your problem, yourself, and your forthcoming change? Answer the following questions about your behavior in the past week using a 5-point scale: 1 = Never, 2 = Seldom, 3 = Occasionally, 4 = Often, 5 = Repeatedly.

I sought out information about the problem behavior. _____
I reflected on things I read in articles and books about how to
  overcome my problem. _____
I recalled information people have given me about the benefits of
  altering my behavior. _____

People who successfully move forward and eventually conquer their problem report at least a 3 on each of the above items. On the other hand, those who get stuck in the early steps and fail to launch their change report lower scores.

The results of this and the other Check Yourself exercises have repercussions. If you score less than 3 on each question, the research strongly advises additional work on raising your awareness. If you score 3 or higher, congratulations. Your efforts here presage movement through the five steps and ultimately to the new you.

That's Enough!

Receiving information from factual sources, loved ones, health care professionals, and the dramatic arts has led you to greater awareness of yourself and the nature of your problems. Now use this awareness to reevaluate yourself: which values will you act on, and which will you let die? You must think hard about the effects of your behavior on yourself and the people you care about most.

In the past, colleagues and I have wondered if such self-reevaluation was its own independent catalyst, but over the years I've come to think of it as a natural outcome of raising awareness. If raising awareness doesn't result in deep reflection and, later, determined action, it's nothing but empty contemplation.

So much of our behavior is on automatic pilot. We develop habits that make our lives efficient. We don't need to think about how to walk, sit, take a shower, drive a car, brush our teeth, or type on a keyboard. Habits are marvelous time-savers in so many ways, except when they become problems. The easy, the familiar, the habitual win every time—until we declare "That's enough!"

The point at which you declare "That's enough!" marks a decisive shift. It's the moment we realize that who we are is not who we want to become. We begin to align our deeds with our best selves. This step requires forceful self-reevaluation if we are to break the habit and change.

Monique cried out "Enough!" She would no longer allow smoking, overeating, and drinking to damage her health or her children. She vocalized her decision to enact it. Andrew proved less dramatic in his declaration but came to recognize that a superficial party boy was not who he wanted to be. I'll say more about arousing emotions and enhancing commitment in a few pages, but the work of raising awareness and reevaluating your life should lead to a gnawing sense that something should be done, something *will be* done.

A few weeks ago I was consulted by a baby boomer who had fallen into the habit of watching mindless television every night for three or four hours. It had begun when she occasionally indulged in the guilty pleasure of watching a soapy drama after work to decompress; however, she soon found herself watching several reality television shows a night. She was in TV hell! What catapulted her out of the habit was her anguished answer to the question "Is this what my life has come to?"

Let's ensure that your awareness raising is producing the desired results. Please complete another Check Yourself to ensure that you're on track.

CHECK YOURSELF: REEVALUATING YOURSELF

Answer the following questions about your behavior in the past week honestly using a 5-point scale: 1 = Never, 2 = Seldom, 3 = Occasionally, 4 = Often, 5 = Repeatedly.

I thought about my problem hurting me.   _____
I acknowledged the fact that being content with myself includes
   changing my problem.   _____
I thought about my problem hurting other people.   _____

A 3, 4, or 5 on each item is the goal here during the Psych step. That's the benchmark for progress. A 1 or 2 indicates the need for additional deep reflection on how your problem is impacting yourself and loved ones.

AROUSING EMOTIONS

Awareness without emotion is like a flame without fuel. Awareness without emotion is like a well-intentioned teacher who tells you what you *should* be doing but doesn't provide you with the practical skills or the motivation to do it. In fact, that phenomenon has earned the name "the teacher's fallacy": information and scolding alone have practically no effect on behavior. It's like telling someone that he should not smoke.

Here we employ the strategy of arousing emotions. Information and noble intentions cannot bring about permanent change; we need to mobilize our emotions! People rarely change because of logic or facts; if so, hardly anyone would be drinking in excess, smoking, overeating, or procrastinating. People change when their emotions compel them to confront facts.

Our goal is to harness your emotions and redirect them in support of your change. The time to do so is now, not once you enter Perspire. I'll teach you how to delicately balance feeling shameful about your negative past behavior while being drawn toward your positive future behavior—just like Dr. Doolittle's two-headed, push-pull llama. You'll identify and rally your motivations to change while simultaneously dealing with your fear of change. Instead of denying or dismissing the universal fear of new behavior, I'll demonstrate how to harness the fear and put it to work.

Arousing emotions has one of the longest traditions as a catalyst for change. The ancient Greeks believed that expressing emotions was a superb mechanism for providing personal relief and spurring behavioral improvement. Humans have used the power of cathartic release for centuries. An emotional experience often facilitates a psychological correction and movement into the future. But just releasing your emotions indiscriminately, as in the now-discredited primal scream therapy, has all the long-term success of a three-year-old's tantrum. The key is to stir up emotions in ways that propel you forward, rather than leaving you feeling emotionally agitated.

Let's return momentarily to the paradox I mentioned at the start of this book: we want to change, but at the same time we resist doing so. Why? Mostly because of fear. Your old problem behavior, for all its faults, is familiar, comfortable, and easy. It's probably established as a habit. But change, the new behavior, is unfamiliar, initially uncomfortable, and difficult at first. Naturally this breeds fear—fear that you may not like the change, fear that you will not accomplish it, fear that you'll be embarrassed in front of others, fear that the new behaviors will cost you too much, fear that you'll feel guilty. Fear, fear, and more fear keeps the problem entrenched.

Being hard-wired as *Homo sapiens,* we avoid fear and pain. Psychologically, that means we deny the fear or otherwise dismiss it. We try to convince ourselves that we don't need to change, that we can change in another year, that the consequences aren't real, that everyone "needs" a vice or two. These are all familiar and perfectly human means of avoiding the fear of change.

Yet the painful consequences of not changing do come. We suffer the health consequences of overeating, the relationship fallout of not committing, the planetary costs of not conserving. Back in the day, Freud coined the term "neurotic paradox" for this ubiquitous cycle: humans behave to avoid anxiety and to experience short-term pleasure, while ignoring the long-term inevitable consequences. Overconsuming alcohol, tobacco, and fossil fuels brings short-term pleasure but long-term misery.

Internal battles between our intellects and our emotions result in inconsistent, sometimes bewildering behavior. Freud had that right, as my conflict with undergoing a routine colonoscopy attests. Intellectually, I know the procedure is relatively safe, a healthy preventive measure, a half day of minor inconveniences. It's a good and important thing to do, rationally speaking. Emotionally, however, a colonoscopy represents mortality, growing older, the onset of frailty. It's a dreaded and avoided task, fearfully speaking. And fear is not a wise counsel.

So that you firmly grasp what it means to arouse emotions and avoid the neurotic paradox, let's proceed step by step through a collection of research-proven methods of doing so.

Let the Pain Linger

Feel the fear in manageable amounts, instead of reflexively dismissing it. Monique had pushed away her fear of dying early to protect her unhealthy behaviors. Once she let the fear seep in a bit, it began to motivate her. It didn't overwhelm her; it inspired her to change. Psychotherapists like to call this "dosing the anxiety."

The fear can also be rooted in prior life events, such as the disease of a family member or death of a friend. We tend to push such memories away, especially if they are related to our problem. A few moments lingering on those awful events will bring back the associated memories. They are never gone; they are merely shoved away and stored. In my case, I can readily call forth the memory of my father's premature death, largely caused by his lack of control over his weight and blood pressure. That's a painful memory, to be sure, but also a useful warning to me.

What's the deepest level of feeling that you can summon? Think about a threat, a fear, or an insult to yourself that is related to what you want to change. Let that fear linger, and let the pain fuel you. Turn the frightening into the exhilarating, the infuriating into the motivating.

Watch Others in Pain

For some of you, the fear of change might prove too overwhelming, so I recommend that you expose yourself to other people who are experiencing similar fear-based struggles. That can be done in the theater, on television, in books, or online. The belief that we can have cathartic reactions just by watching others dates back at least to Aristotle's writings on theater and music.

One of my patients, for example, downplayed her prescription drug abuse until she heard about Amy Winehouse's drug overdose and subsequent death in 2011. Suddenly my patient could strongly relate to Amy and see herself in the singer whose life had been cut short. She wept for Amy and for herself, which motivated her to pull back from the ledge of her own drug abuse and commit to abstinence.

Dozens of my clients have rented Ingmar Bergman's *Scenes from a Marriage* and found that they had traded a gratifying marriage for security. The movie yanked them out of their despair and prompted them to either work on or leave their relationships. (Appendix A presents top-rated self-help books and autobiographies that may help you identify the fear of change in other people. In addition, www.ChangeologyBook.com provides a list of the 50 most highly recommended movies for the same purpose.)

Go Long

When I played football with my friends, our favorite pass route was to "go long"—run far out for the long pass. That's essentially what we need to do to quash the neurotic paradox: focus on the painful long-term consequences instead of the short-term comfy rewards of the behavior. Your hard wiring will ensure that you seek immediate pleasures; instead, think of their delayed dangers. When Andrew enjoyed being the man around town on weekends, drinking and spending "like a drunken sailor," he trained himself to think about his dreadful Sunday hangover, missed commitments, and empty bank account. That sobered him up quickly!

You can train yourself into feeling the long-term pain as happening immediately. Some folks imagine a doughnut as gumming up their arteries or padding their thighs as soon as they ingest it. Other people visualize their relationship arguments as leading to marital separation and estrangement from their kids. Is the long-term pain worth the short-term gain? These handy tricks arouse the emotions and direct you to healthier decisions.

The following three methods are designed to let you safely feel the fear of change, to reverse engineer the human tendency to push away painful emotions. They will enable you to convert your fear into self-change fuel. What you previously dreaded and avoided will now actually propel you forward.

Envision a Better Tomorrow

Addressing the fear of the change is only half of arousing your emotions; we also want to embrace your positive future. This method entails conjuring up emotionally laden images, thoughts, and mottos about the benefits of changing. Monique, for example, thought about living longer, thinking more clearly, and relating more meaningfully to her children, her spouse, and her faith. Andrew thought about making the vision of his better self a reality.

Imagery or visualization works best for most of us in arousing emotions. Think about how you'll look after you change, how you'll feel, how you'll approach other people. Envision the weather (almost always sunny and temperate), the surroundings (usually in Arizona earth tones or Florida tropical colors), and the good vibes surrounding you.

Likewise, you can conjure up a memory of a time when you achieved success in the past. How did it feel? How did your body react? How did it change you? Vividly recall the amazing feelings of your previous achievements and then visualize your new goal. Imagine that you've already achieved your new goal and you get to experience that same sense of accomplishment again. Try to harness the power and confidence that came with past achievements and apply them to this new endeavor.

Tell a New Story

Psychologists have long known that the stories we tell ourselves impact our intentions and moods. Depressing tales leave us feeling discouraged and weak, whereas inspiring stories prompt us to be active and successful. We can alter our self-image by rewriting our own stories or narratives with better endings. Instead of listening to those who don't believe that we can change, we can weave a compelling tale of self-improvement and transformation. It's just like imagery but with words.

Write and edit your own narrative about the goal you seek. Describe the challenges, add a plot twist, but end up victorious. Some people prefer expressive writing in which they write journal entries or a formal story. Other people opt for a verbal bedtime tale. In both cases it winds up motivating and shaping your behavior in directions you feel are valuable. That's always an award-winning story.

Two Heads Are Better than One

The preceding methods will teach you how to balance your fear of change and your desire for change, how to be simultaneously repulsed by your negative past and drawn toward your positive future. As you might have guessed, my favorite analogy or image of this process is Dr. Doolittle's two-headed, push-pull llama.

On the one "head," you are pushed away from the problem because you can't stand it any longer. On the other "head," you are pulled toward change and a new behavior. Two energy sources—pushed and pulled— will prove superior to only one. Double your emotional commitment by being repelled by the negative past while being drawn to the positive future.

Achieving this balance is no easy trick. Some of you, particularly those raised in households relying on punishment and fire-and-brimstone tactics, will spend too much time feeling the fear and ruminating on your behavioral sins. Guilt can initiate behavior change but can rarely sustain it over the long haul. Others of you, particularly those raised in more permissive households with humanistic or New Age leanings, will rely excessively on the imagery of your flowery, sunny future. Please engage in a healthy mix of both.

When you encounter your emotional sweet spot, you may well tap into the purity of human feelings. You might access raw, undiluted emotions of fear and love—fear that you cannot or will not change; love for the change and its impact on people around you. Andrew was initially struck by his fear, wondering if he'd get trapped in a self-destructive cycle for years. Monique experienced primal love when she thought about what her transformation could do for her young children and, later, her husband and eventually herself. These are abiding motivations that can see you through for 90 days and more—when you learn to harness and use them.

Practicing as a Two-Headed Llama

When I coach people or present workshops on the push-pull balance, almost everyone immediately grasps its value. Then comes the question "How can we achieve that balance?"

Here are four practice exercises for finding the middle way between too much of the dark past and too much of the bright future. First, analyze the amount of mental time you devote to ruminating about the current problem versus the amount of time you devote to fantasizing about the glorious future free of that problem. Literally count the minutes or hours; assign a number to each activity. That will help you to maintain a 50-50 division.

Second, every time you reflect on your problem, develop a habit of considering both the nasty present and the wonderful future after you change. Train yourself to reflect on both, especially if you've been concentrating on a single side. Keep in mind that your goal may not necessarily be a "problem" per se, but you can still do this exercise by considering how your life will be different—for the better—once you achieve that goal. So if you're aiming to acquire new skills to get a new job, for instance, you can think about the obstacles you currently face in scoring a better job and how much more marketable you will be once you have those valuable abilities.

Third, write a good-bye letter to your problem or old way of being.

Put your heart into the letter or, as one recent patient did, a video. Explain the harm the problem has caused you and others and then how leaving it will improve your life. Ensure that both the push away from the past and the pull toward the future are equally represented in your letter or video.

Four, spend some time in front of the mirror. Talk to yourself and emotionally release your disgust or hatred of how the problem has controlled you. Then spend an equal amount of time and emotion letting yourself know how excited and eager you are to move toward that bright future. Mirror work may feel a bit odd or foolish, but it works convincingly for many self-changers.

These are all good ways to access emotions to complement your raised awareness and propel your change. Here's a Check Yourself to ensure that you've completed enough of the emotional work to move onto the next step.

CHECK YOURSELF: AROUSING EMOTIONS

How are you coming along? Answer the following questions about your behavior in the past week using a 5-point scale: 1 = Never, 2 = Seldom, 3 = Occasionally, 4 = Often, 5 = Repeatedly.

I talked about my problem and expressed my feelings about it.   _____
I was emotionally affected by dramatic reminders of my problem.   _____
I had a strong reaction when realizing the consequences of my problem. _____
I emotionally connected with the better future ahead of me without that
    problem.   _____

Here, during the first step, a moderate amount of emotional arousal predicts success and readies you for the next step. You should score a 3 or higher on each item—corresponding to "Occasionally" or greater. If your scores are lower, I recommend spending additional time on arousing your emotions before moving on. You are seeking both awareness and emotions that will inform your planning and will fuel you throughout the 90 days.

THE PROS AND CONS

All of your efforts to raise your awareness, evaluate your values, and arouse your emotions can coalesce into the following exercise, which documents your attraction to and fear of change. It's a way of weighing the pros and cons of change, another powerful means of leveraging your awareness. And, as you'll see, it predicts who will succeed at self-change and who will not.

On one side of a piece of paper, write the pros—the reasons for your change of a particular problem. On the other side of a paper write the cons—the arguments for not changing and continuing your comfy and familiar behavior. On both the pros and cons sides include reasons to change/not change from your own perspective (Self) as well as from other people's (Others). The result will be four quadrants.

The following table shows what Monique wrote in this exercise about quitting smoking and drinking when we first got started. As you can see, it's relatively sparse, with few entries. She used little detail, little effort, and little emotion, which accurately reflected how she was feeling

MONIQUE'S INITIAL ATTEMPT AT PROS AND CONS

Pros of Changing	Cons of Changing
Self	**Self**
More energy to do things I enjoy	Some free time will be lost
Save money and buy things for myself	Miss out on social opportunities
Live longer, maybe	Tired, exhausted
Others	**Others**
Better relationship with my kids	Friends could think less of me
More energy and enthusiasm	Kids upset that I'm so busy
More money to spend on others	Friends could see me as less fun and social

at the time. What's more, the pros-cons balance was about even: she was as comfortable remaining stuck in her smoking and drinking as she was excited about changing. This list represents a failure in the first step: paltry effort, little self-awareness, lack of emotions, and the cons equaling the pros. That's where Monique was at and why she had failed repeatedly before she began working the Changeology program.

By contrast, when Monique completed a couple of weeks of work in the Psych step, her pros and cons grew to three times as long. Her second attempt reflected her efforts in recording her baseline behavior, raising her awareness, reevaluating herself, and arousing her emotions. That time, her pros easily outweighed the cons of changing.

The moral of Monique's story is twofold: work the change catalysts of Psych before completing the pros and cons, and do not move forward until the pros outweigh the cons. Hundreds of research studies now attest that the number of pros should be higher than that of the cons before you attempt to change a behavior. It makes perfect sense: how likely are you to succeed when you adore your comfy problem and cannot see the advantages of changing it?

Of course, your instinctive fear of change may lead you, like Monique, to initially attach greater weight to prospective losses than to gains. That's human enough. That's why you fully work Step 1 before jumping into the next step.

We don't expect the cons to disappear completely. In fact, when people try to convince themselves that there is no downside—no loss to giving up their problems—I don't believe it, and I ask them to dig deeper. Problems always satisfy some needs and offer some (short-term) benefits. You will change because, intellectually and emotionally, the pros outweigh the cons. But the costs and cons of change are inevitable; as Samuel Johnson remarked, "Nothing will ever be attempted if all possible objections must first be overcome."

The pros of changing will eventually outweigh the cons, but in this Psych step you may be surprised to find that the pros equal the cons. That's the definition of ambivalence. Not to worry; the work you do in the first two steps (Psych and Prep) almost always raises the pros. Cleverly balancing the painful past of your problem with the happy future of your goal is accomplishing that already.

On www.ChangeologyBook.com you will find blank pros and cons sheets. You can complete them for diverse goals, and, like Monique, you can complete them at different points in time.

COMMITTING, PART I

I often return to the words of Ralph Waldo Emerson, the apostle of self-reliance and advocate for change. He once wrote that "Nothing great was ever achieved without enthusiasm." That certainly applies to the pros you just completed and to the final change catalyst for completing the Psych step: commitment.

Committing entails more than the mysterious, ineffable "willpower." Contrary to popular thought, committing actually encompasses a set of identifiable skills that you can develop and practice. Committing begins in this first step and carries through the next two steps.

What do I mean by *committing*? It's becoming aware of new alternatives, including the deliberate creation of new alternatives for living, and then avidly pursuing that choice. As we've seen, your pursuit will involve experiencing some anxiety, which is inherent in taking responsibility for your change and moving past your fears. By commitment, I mean the power of your choice and the power of your will to see that choice through. (That's the origin of the now-abused term "willpower.")

Today people wrongly assume that willpower is about forcing yourself to do something you don't want to do. But we want to respect willpower for what it really is: the strength to make a choice and take decisive action. Here are several ways to fortify your will (and the next chapter will offer yet more).

Say It Out Loud

In this Psych step, declare your goal or resolution by saying it to yourself and perhaps one other person: I am getting ready for change. Monique roared in private, "I am about to stop drinking and smoking!" What a liberating feeling. It's not time yet for a massive public declaration; that will occur in the next step. For now, say it and own it within yourself. "I choose to _____!" And say it like you mean it!

Push-Pull Redux

The two-headed llama metaphorically illustrates the negative consequences of the problem and the positive features of change. That's the mental picture that keeps commitment ticking. Keep the push-pull llama in your mind by posting your pros and cons for change and reminding yourself of your dual motivations in the morning or at bedtime. Harness both energy sources; there is no damnation without salvation.

Literally keep the abiding motivations in front of you. One creative resolver in our research studies drew a two-part picture—a dark side of her current problem and a sunny side/the force of her change—and posted it on the ceiling above her bed. That may be taking a good idea too far, but it was front and center for her every morning and evening.

Repeat Your Slogan

Many people create one or two short, emotive reminders that encapsulate their commitment. Monique's were a calm, reassuring "I can do this" and "For the kids and me." Andrew's motto became "Think of the future." My anxious patients remind themselves, "It's only anxiety" and "All growth requires a challenge." A popular saying a few years back was "What doesn't kill me strengthens me." Develop a few phrases that capture your change's emotional meaning for you.

Internalize Your Model or Mentor

Courageous models and successful mentors can spark your commitment. Seek a virtual mentor that you can tuck inside your mind as a reference point for inspiration. For example, having recently read a set of excellent autobiographies about Theodore Roosevelt, I began channeling him in an informal "What would TR do?" To wit: Here's what Roosevelt wrote about commitment and action:

> It is not the critic who counts; not the man who points out how the strong man stumbles or where the doer of deeds could have done them better. The credit belongs to the man who is actually in the arena, whose face is marred by dust and sweat and blood, who strives valiantly; who errs, and comes short again and again, because there is no effort without error and shortcoming; but who does actually strive to do the deeds; who knows the great enthusiasms, the great devotions; who spends himself in a worthy cause; who at the best knows in the end the triumph of high achievement, and who at the worst, if he fails, at least he fails while daring greatly, so that his place shall never be with those cold and timid souls who know neither victory nor defeat.

That became my informal slogan—the man in the arena—and my internalized representation of taking action. This might not work for you, but it does for me. Find a person or two, dead or alive, who manifests what you seek in commitment and to whom you can turn for inspiration.

Mix in Some Realistic Doubt

A dollop of doubt about the prospect of change keeps the challenge alive. This might strike you as counterintuitive, but respecting your enemy keeps you sensibly wary, makes you prepare even harder, and guards against overconfidence. "The relationship between commitment and doubt is by no means an antagonistic one," wrote the psychologist Rollo May. "Commitment is healthiest when it is not without doubt but in spite of doubt."

Group Action

We'll be recruiting your change team in the next step, but we can reiterate the point here that commitment occurs within you as well as within a group. You can accomplish many of the commitment-enhancing strategies outlined above by joining a group of like-minded individuals who are also attempting to change. They will fortify your will and see you through the steps.

Here's another self-assessment on your commitment skills to date.

CHECK YOURSELF: COMMITTING I

Are you still with me? Yes, there's a lot of work to be accomplished in this first step, but here's the final Check Yourself for this chapter. Check off the following activities that you have completed—not what you hope to accomplish soon, but what you have actually done already.

I have made a private declaration of my intentions. _____

I remind myself of the negative consequences of my problem. _____

I understand that my fear of change is natural and that it can be
converted into productive fuel for changing. _____

I visualize my positive future after I have changed. _____

The pros of my anticipated change are equal to or higher than
the cons. _____

I tell myself I can choose to change or not. _____

I have a personal slogan and/or internal model of my self-change. _____

Overconfidence is not a concern; my commitment includes a dollop
of realistic doubt. _____

In order to proceed to the next step, all these items should be checked off. If not, do not pass "Go" yet. Take a deep breath, and do some additional Psych work before proceeding further. If you have honestly checked them all off, feel free to pass "Go" and collect health and happiness.

Clearly, this first step involves considerable effort and capitalizes on the benefits of several change catalysts: sketching your goal(s), tracking your behavior, raising your awareness, reevaluating your priorities, arousing your emotions, and committing. You might understandably be tempted to rush through this step and minimize its psychological work. But that would be a serious error that would materially reduce the probability of your eventual success.

It is *never*—repeat, *never*—a good idea to rush through Psych in order to get to the later steps. The old adage of Benjamin Franklin rings true: by failing to prepare, you are preparing to fail. Whether it takes a couple of days or a couple of weeks, the work of Step 1 will inform and fuel your action. Rash action without genuine preparation and commitment is doomed to flair out.

Thus, before venturing forward in your self-change and in *Changeology* to the Prep step, make sure that you've completed the Check Yourself exercises honestly. When your activity meets the benchmarks of successful changeologists, then you can dash forward brimming with realistic confidence. I'll meet you there soon and prepare you for the next great leap into action.

STEP 2

PREP: PLANNING BEFORE LEAPING

WEEKS 2 AND 3
Build your commitment and then make your goal public. Pick your start day and identify people who will support you. Take a few small initial steps—and prepare for liftoff!

By now you're sufficiently aware of the causes and consequences of your problem, you're tracking or recording its frequency, you're emotionally activated to do something about it, and you're committed to doing so within the next week or two. Congratulations! That's impressive in a world where most people live complacently in a state of quiet desperation ruled by fear of change.

This step describes what you need to do before jumping completely into action. Why? Because it turns out that most people get so antsy and eager that they jump before they are prepared. They sew the parachute *after* they leap from the airplane. They sabotage themselves by a lack of preparation and planning.

So that you understand fully what the planning process entails, in this chapter I'll be taking you on a guided tour of acquiring and mastering the essential skills you'll need before leaping. I'll help you define your goals more specifically, learn more about tracking your progress, assemble your change team, solidify your commitment, and finalize your action plan. Supported by examples, exercises, and Check Yourself benchmarks, you will be prepared for an outstanding liftoff into action!

ON PLANNING

Whenever I start describing the planning process, about a third of my audience will audibly sigh or roll their eyes. I'll ask, "What's up with that?" I'll get three groups of responses: planning is boring (it's the kind of stuff overeager parents do); you cannot plan for the uncontrollable mysteries of life; and it never works. Well, I cannot speak to earlier annoying experiences with obsessive, superplanning parents, but I can address the other two concerns.

I often hear something along the following lines: "Ahh, why bother planning, when you know you cannot predict life?" Alcoholics Anonymous has a maxim: "If you want to make God laugh, tell him your plans." It's true that we can neither perfectly control nor predict the future. But it's just plain wrong not to plan. I'm all for spontaneity and adaptability, but attempts to change often fail because people fail to plan. So, sure, your plans will be tentative and you'll frequently need to revise them. Plan your self-change, and plan to be flexible as you proceed.

Some people think that planning doesn't work for them. That's also true, but I would ask a bigger question: why has planning not proven effective for you, when we know from decades of research that preparation favors your chances greatly? If I press the doubter with a few more questions, I usually uncover the underlying problem: the person knows the goal but not the road. Hope is not a change method! That is, planning fails when you know the destination but not how to get there. Monique's prior efforts to change failed because she was certain of her goals but had virtually no idea how to achieve them other than gritting her teeth. When planning focuses on only the goal or destination, it makes perfect sense that your planning will not work because it does not identify the road or the methods to get there.

And let's face it: hardly anyone has been taught the science of behavior change. When it comes to self-change, we are blamed by society when we fail but never formally trained to succeed. Not to worry; in this step we'll be identifying both your goal and the action plan to get you there. Planning for change works!

There's a tiny exception to the rule: planning can be unsuccessful when conducted with dysfunctional perfectionism. A fascinating line of recent research suggests that extensive planning can backfire for some perfectionists. For them, the road to Hell is paved with good intentions. Planning that triggers constant critical self-examination can obstruct progress. The solution? Tame your self-criticism, understand that no plan is perfect, and keep moving forward. If you keep criticizing yourself, add not doing so to your list of resolutions.

DEFINING YOUR GOALS, PART II

Begin with your goal in mind. As discussed in the last step, it's difficult to reach the destination when you don't even know where it is. Remember, vague goals beget vague efforts.

Being specific doesn't mean, however, that you need to restrict yourself to minor or inconsequential goals. Dream big and bold. We can break down any ambitious goal into subgoals. As President Harry Truman put it, "You can always amend a big plan, but you can never expand a little one. I don't believe in little plans. I believe in plans big enough to meet a situation which we can't possibly foresee now."

Decades of research demonstrate that *how* we express and measure a goal dramatically increases our success rate. Based on the new science and proven methods of setting goals, we'll get **SMART**: express goals in **S**pecific, **M**easurable, **A**ttainable, **R**elevant, and **T**ime-specific terms. We briefly covered several of these elements in the Psych step, but let's rework them so that you can specify your goal SMARTly here in Step 2.

> **Specific:** Tell me exactly where you will be in 90 days using positive terms. "A better person," "a kinder spouse," "save more money" fail the test. Give me observable characteristics of behavior (not inner states or global traits) that are phrased in positive language. For example, "I will be exercising at least five days a week for at least 30 minutes each time" or "I will be enjoying conversation with my

children at dinner every night." Avoid phrasing your goals in negative language, even if they are specific, such as "I will not have confrontations with my kids after school."

Measurable: In the previous step, we talked about the importance of defining your goal in ways that can be measured; you'll need to log, record, or track the frequency and triggers of the behavior (which we'll cover at greater length in the next section). Give an unambiguous definition that can be read, repeated, and measured by others.

Attainable: Otherwise, it's not a goal but an impossible dream. Better to try to "lose and keep off 15 pounds in 90 days" than a health-compromising and nearly impossible 50 pounds. Monique, for instance, converted her vague dream of losing weight into measurable, attainable objectives of consuming 1,200 calories a day and exercising at least 30 minutes four times a week.

Relevant: To you, of course, but also in terms of your life priorities. Does your immediate goal serve the pursuit of becoming the person you want to become? Or are you settling for less because a less ambitious goal might be easier to achieve and get other people off your back?

Time-specific: Specify the time frame, which in this book is typically the next 90 days. That's long enough to reach and maintain important goals, while short enough to keep it practical and doable.

Using the SMART format, practice defining your goal or goals below in concise and positive language. Try writing it or them a couple of different ways to determine what works best for you:

My goal is: _____
My goal is: _____
My goal is: _____

Now let's distinguish intermediate, or short-term, goals from long-term goals. This is an important distinction to make, because it's easy to be too ambitious with short-term goals and destroy your chances of success in the long run. Andrew, for example, sabotaged himself by seeking to eradicate—overnight—years of disastrous relationships with money and women. He was too eager for quick, unrealistic change. With me, however, he learned to avoid pursuing the fantasy of instantaneous change and instead took one methodical step at a time—from Psych to Prep—understanding that giving himself 90 days would improve his chances of success dramatically. No longer climbing a psychological Mount Everest, he felt prepared and empowered to pursue his goals with enthusiasm and confidence, while still following an orderly process that would take a certain amount of time.

Let's say your 90-day, or long-term, goal is to lose 15 pounds. Your intermediate goals could be to exercise regularly, skip most desserts, keep to a 1,200-calorie diet, and so forth. Or perhaps your 90-day goal is to become a better parent by teaching your child responsibility. Your intermediate goals might be to declare your expectations only once with a single reminder, follow through on threatened consequences, and spend five more minutes reading to your child at bedtime. In both cases, you would have one superordinate goal with a series of subgoals.

Small steps together equal a giant leap. Start small, and then incrementally increase your subgoal activity. If you're trying to lose weight, increase your exercise or activity level by a maximum of 10 percent per week, particularly if you are a baby boomer. Even if you increase it by a few minutes each day, that translates into several extra minutes of exercise a week. If you are teaching your child responsibility, read books that give you insights into communicating better with your child, and schedule more time with your child every day.

Please specify your goal again, using the language you preferred from above. Then, define the subgoals to reach it.

My goal is: _____

The subgoals are to: _____

_____

Let's conclude with a Check Yourself to ensure that your goal meets all of the SMART criteria and the other guidelines provided in the previous step.

CHECK YOURSELF: SETTING GOALS, PART II

Check off the activities on the following list that you have accomplished in defining your goal(s). Please check off only those you have actually done, not those you intend to do in the future.

I have written my goal; it sounds and feels right.   _____

That goal is reasonably specific and can be measured or tracked.   _____

My goal is realistic and attainable.   _____

My goal is for and by me, not other people.   _____

I have delineated a time frame for accomplishing it.   _____

Subgoals to achieve the larger goal have been specified.   _____

My goal is defined in a positive, healthy direction.   _____

You should be checking off all items here if you are taking full advantage of the science of change. If check marks fill the page, off you go to the next section on tracking your progress. But if you are missing a few check marks, take a few moments to complete this vital planning and preparation.

TRACKING YOUR PROGRESS

As you know, nurturing self-awareness is a well-documented and time-honored catalyst for change. Raising your self-awareness entails enhancing your insight into yourself, your problems, and your goals. In the first step of Psych, you began to track your problem behavior in order to raise your awareness of it. Now that you've gained some experience in charting or recording the problem and established a fair sense of its frequency, we'll build on that. You'll learn to become a "behavioral detective" and identify what triggers the problem and what maintains it. This process requires a bit of detective work on your part, but it will certainly pay off in informing your action plan later on.

Triggers occur before and may precipitate the problem in question. What are the environmental, interpersonal, and mood triggers for your smoking, poor parenting, low esteem, drinking, or arguments? Your answers will expose key clues to your behavior pattern. Monique began recording her smoking frequency and discovered that she smoked twice as much when stressed, tired, or celebrating with friends. Both bad times and good times triggered more tobacco use. Her action plan would need to address both sets of triggers.

Consequences occur after the problem and are usually contingent on it. As you know, the short-term consequences of our behaviors can often be very rewarding—yummy, soothing, releasing, sedating, and so on. But the long-term consequences can be painful and destructive; sadly, we tend far more to the immediate than the delayed consequences. In the moments of stress and celebration, Monique was focusing on what would happen to her mind and body in the next 20 minutes, not 20 years. She realized that she had trapped herself in a cycle of reward, precisely the reverse of her goal.

Here's how to sleuth out your triggers and consequences. On a daily basis, track four features of the behavior that you'd like to change:

1. Time of day
2. Triggers: both the situation (where you were, what you were doing, who you were with) and your feelings (sad, happy, stressed, relaxed, bored, lonely, etc.)
3. Behavior: the magnitude or amount of the problem behavior (the number of drinks, the amount of money, the number of arguments)
4. Consequences: the short-term results of the problem behavior as well as the longer-term impact on your feelings and others' reactions

Track these four elements of your behavior in a journal, create a document or spreadsheet to use on a continual basis, or go online and use the Determine My Behavioral Chain found on www .ChangeologyBook.com. Remember that for consequences, you want to record both immediate and delayed results of your problem behavior.

By tracking yourself for several days (I recommend at least five days), you'll learn a lot about the pattern of your problem and, more important, how to correct the pattern. First, you'll probably discover that you can increasingly view your problem as a predictable behavior that can be increased, decreased, or even eliminated. Monitoring your progress can help you see it as a voluntary, controllable behavior rather than an insurmountable problem. Second, you may well find yourself experiencing the gift of reactivity: monitoring and measuring your behavior improves it, even though that was not your immediate intention. As discussed in the previous step, what's measured improves.

Your behavioral detective work will reveal the culprits: time of day, triggers, and consequences. You need not be Sherlock Holmes to see the obvious: that certain times of day, certain situations, certain feelings, and certain rewards predictably lead to the same behavior.

Let's record the results of your investigation and see what kind of patterns you can identify. These results will be used later in this step and subsequent steps to fine-tune your action plan.

Times of day that are problematic:

Situations that trigger the problem:

My feelings that trigger the problem:

Immediate rewards that maintain the problem:

Delayed consequences of the problem that I typically forget:

The benefits of this exercise should be evident. "On those nights when I come home stressed from work, the chart says that I argued or yelled almost every day." "Morning and coffee always lead to a cigarette!" "Hanging out with people at work increases my overspending, but time spent with Mary rarely does." "Wow! When I am bored and watching TV, I eat twice as much as when I am reading or out at night." "I get it now: I immediately reinforce my empty threats to the children because I don't have to do anything to correct their behavior. My frustration and anger are the long-term consequences." Scientists like to say that data are always friendly; even when we don't like what we discover, data are useful nonetheless.

We'll return to your behavioral detective work throughout Change-ology, as it provides a road map to instigating change and maintaining it across the 90 days. Before we move to the next change catalyst, please complete another Check Yourself to determine if you're tracking your goal clearly and frequently enough to ensure success.

CHECK YOURSELF: TRACKING PROGRESS

You're getting the hang of these assessments now: Check off the following items that you have actually accomplished. Let honesty rule; you'll only be hurting your-self if you fudge the results.

I have recorded, logged, or charted my problem behavior for at least
    five days.   _____
I have clearly identified times of day and situations that trigger my
    problem.   _____
I know which emotions are more likely to lead to the troubled behavior.   _____
It's clear to me how I unintentionally reinforce and maintain the problem.   _____
The results of my behavioral detective work are written so that I can
    refer to them in the future.   _____

How many check marks appear on your self-test here? You already know how many *should* appear. The difference between all of them being marked and how many you marked indicates what work you still need to do. If the difference is zero, you are ready for the Detective Hall of Fame.

ASSEMBLING YOUR CHANGE TEAM

Anyone who has succeeded at change and every behavioral researcher will give you the same advice: buddy up. Helping relationships, or social support, are a vigorous predictor of behavioral success. We work better by working together. Sure, it takes some effort, but cultivating supportive relationships can make the difference between reaching your resolution and not doing so. Now I'll help you assemble your change team as part of your preparation and planning.

At this point in the Prep step, you need only to recruit your team, not ask them for much intense work. Here are some tips for doing so.

Who's Got Your Back?

Identify people around you—family, friends, coworkers, schoolmates, and neighbors—who will support your self-change. One or two solid people will do, but three or four might be ideal. The perfect support team consists of people from at least two different locations, be they from home, work, or school, friends, or online contacts.

Make a list of potential candidates, and consider their availability, their shared interests, and their ability to support (as opposed to criticize). Also factor in the type of support you seek: a good listener, a fellow gym rat, a lunchtime companion, someone who's had success at personal change, or a strict coach? You want the support of those most able to help, not simply those who are most convenient or close to you.

Cyberfriends

You might want members of your team to be relatively new to your life, independent of your ordinary routine, or you might want fellow travelers who are working to improve the same problem you are. In both cases, consider joining an online support group. Search the Web for an inexpensive (or free) group devoted to your goal. We'll return to cyberfriends in the next step, but now is the time to expand your view on who makes up your social support network through a little online research.

No, but Thank You

Not all of your friends or family members will match your needs. There's no need to apologize or explain to them. Monique, for example, realized that her best friend "would do anything" for her, but the friend could not stop herself from giving unwanted advice. She would definitely clash with Monique's efforts to bolster her self-esteem! We're seeking positive helpers here. If someone inappropriate offers to be your number one source of support, say "No, but thank you." Let the person know in a kind fashion that you appreciate his or her offer but you've already enlisted help from someone else and that your relationship will be the better for your decision.

Beware of Toxic Helpers

Enshrined in the Helper Hall of Shame are the naysayers and the my-wayers. Please avoid adding to your team the Eeyores, named after the gloomy gray donkey from *Winnie-the-Pooh*. Their pessimistic "It'll never work" can be contagious. Let them hang with the my-wayers, the narcissistically inclined folks who insist that what worked for them will automatically work for you (and everyone else on the planet). Their advice might be well intended, but chances are that it will not fit your agenda and will conflict with the science of behavior change. Instead, seek out supporters who encourage your dreams, celebrate your successes, and nourish your commitment.

A Formal Invitation

It might sound a bit hokey, but I recommend that you ask your team members for support by a formal invitation in person or by telephone (no tweets or emails here, friends). Make a sincere request for assistance. I've known a few creative individuals who have crafted formal written invitations, like those used for weddings or anniversary parties, and mailed them to their intended supporters before calling them personally. If you make a personal, formal request, you have a much better chance of receiving a favorable response; most people feel honored to be asked.

For some people, asking for help can feel weak; others don't want to risk embarrassment. Getting your head straight, focusing on your desire for self-improvement, inviting one person at a time, and adhering to the steps outlined here should help you overcome the natural instinct to avoid this baby step. And remember, we like to be asked to help others; we derive immense satisfaction from assisting others. Don't think so? After you successfully change, won't you welcome the opportunity to assist others and pay it forward?

Articulating What You Need

Be prepared for immediate queries from those you ask to help: What can I do to help? What are you expecting from me? Here you can be concise and state just four things:

- For starters, you've already done the first thing, which is to support my efforts and be part of the team.
- Second, for now, listen to me as I express both my fear and excitement (you can even explain to them about the two-headed, push-pull llama).
- Third, help me track my problem—what triggers it and what maintains or reinforces it.
- Fourth and final, as I proceed along, I'll probably ask you for help in keeping me on track, reminding me to keep going, and being around should I slip.

That's it: a two-minute conversation that leaves them feeling honored and you feeling empowered.

Put Them to Work if Need Be

Several members of your support network will probably desire to get busy immediately and start helping you right away. For them, just agreeing to help isn't enough. They want to do more. But it's not time yet. Ask them to be an extra pair of eyes monitoring your behavior. They can be your assistant detectives, watching for your triggers and helping you keep track of your progress. They will naturally watch what you say and do, looking for potential pitfalls.

But please don't ask them for advice or coaching yet. That will come later. Now is the time to assemble the troops, build trust, and develop a shared vision.

What Am I, Chopped Liver?

It appears that you forgot to put one name on your team roster: me! It's true that I'm not available to return your check-in phone calls and emails, but I want you to know that I'm here for you through this book and its supporting website at www.ChangeologyBook.com. I'm not going anywhere. I'm in it for the long haul and will be providing lots of support and skills throughout. Keep in mind that you're also being guided by thousands of veteran self-changers who've gone before you.

The Two-Way Street

You cannot realistically expect that any friendship will meet only your needs; aim to develop reciprocity. Spend time nurturing your helping relationships, and prioritize your supporters' important events, birthdays, and so on. Ensure that some of your time and conversations together pertain to them; this is not psychotherapy, where 99 percent of the time is spent on you alone! As they listen to you, you can listen to them with deep interest, genuine empathy, and an optimistic outlook.

Minimize Collateral Damage

Some people in your life will not be suitable as members of your change team; still others will probably be opposed, directly or indirectly, to your efforts. Andrew, for instance, was dreading his partying buddies' ridicule for leaving clubs early, attending church on Sunday morning, and not fooling around with multiple women.

Based on research and experience, we know that it helps to address potential saboteurs from the get-go. That's address, not confront. A polite but direct conversation along the lines of "[Name], I will be working hard soon to become [fill in your goal]. It's important to me. I realize that you may disagree with it or it may inconvenience you. I'm telling you early and up front so that my change does not compromise our relationship. It would be great if you can support me, but I understand if you don't."

If you view change as a battle, you can recruit your allies while simultaneously minimizing collateral damage. You may be pleasantly surprised when a person supports you, or you may find that you were correct when you anticipated opposition. Either way, congratulations on approaching the uncomfortable topic. It takes a hunk of courage to do so.

Getting your change team in place early enhances your prospect of success. It also creates a small victory and improves your level of competence in this endeavor—your self-efficacy—before your start day. We'll discuss in subsequent steps what you'll request from your team when the time comes.

In the meantime, please complete another Check Yourself to determine whether you have enlisted sufficient social support. Will your team live up to the challenge? Do they understand their duty? Here's a precombat checklist:

CHECK YOURSELF: ASSEMBLING THE CHANGE TEAM

Check the following activities that you have completed, soldier.

I identified and then invited potential members of my change team.   _____

At least two people from two different settings have agreed to serve.   _____

I explicitly informed them of my change needs.   _____

Several friends and family were not asked because they did not
match my needs or interests.   _____

Difficult as it was, I did address potential saboteurs about my
forthcoming self-change.   _____

I feel comfortable and confident in my change team.   _____

   Get your team on board now, and improve your probability of success considerably. Not doing so weakens your will and your plan.

COMMITTING, PART II

We know from a multitude of studies that people's mere desire to change does not predict success, but their level of commitment does. We also know that commitment alone, even when it's intense at first, can result in failure. How can we make sense of these paradoxes?

The answer lies in harnessing both motivation and skills in the change process. A desire to modify a problem is necessary, of course, but "I'll make it because I want it desperately" rarely works. Monique learned that lesson the hard way after multiple failures at what she called the "true grit" approach. Desire alone doesn't get the job done, as you can quickly see if you apply it to any of life's challenges. We also need competence and experience.

Commitment to the task at hand does predict success. But there's a profound difference between commitment and desire: commitment implies work; desire implies wish. If you commit to washing the car, making dinner, or paying some bills today, there is a plan and a particular method to accomplish the goal. If you simply desire those things, however, you're far less likely to achieve them. In the words of Peter Drucker, unless commitment is made, there are only promises and hopes, but no plans.

As to the other paradox, I suspect you have already figured that one out on your own. Overreliance on commitment at the expense of skills often leads to an intense burst of motivation for a week or so, but then nothing is left to sustain you thereafter. You're at a loss as to how to proceed. That's why you need to rely on particular change catalysts to get you through all the steps. Put simply, commitment is necessary but not sufficient.

In the first step of Psych, we began to address your commitment and motivation. Now we'll boost your level of commitment before you leap into action and then continue to build it in the subsequent steps. There's no doubt that commitment is required in each step of the journey, but it will differ depending upon where you are in the change process.

Here is how we'll use commitment as we Prep in this second step.

Make Narrow Choices

Groundbreaking research on willpower by psychologist Roy Baumeister, author of the aptly titled book *Willpower*, shows that we are easily depleted by endless choices. We have a finite store of mental energy for exerting self-control. As you plan for the great leap forward, now is the time to focus on your high priorities rather than ruminating about all of the possibilities. That's why, if you have not yet noticed, I typically limit the menu of methods for each catalyst to half a dozen. Simplify your path, prioritize your goals, and decide which methods you will use to achieve them. In self-change, less can be more.

Rest

Your store of willpower is depleted when you direct your thoughts, control your feelings, and modify your behaviors. Accordingly, prepare for the major operation, whether you think of it as a surgical or a war operation, by resting. Let other, nonessential tasks slide for a while so your willpower is conserved for the work you need to do to change. Your support team can help keep your energy aligned with your goal. Like a runner before a big race, don't run the day before; save your willpower muscles for the event itself.

Say It Loud and Proud

In the Psych step, you made a private declaration of your behavioral intentions. In this Prep step, we're looking for a public commitment to your goal. It's time to share your resolution with others. That means informing people in your life—your friends, family members, and close work colleagues—and putting your written goal(s) on display.

A wonderful example of how a public commitment can lead to prolonged effort is found in a famous social psychological experiment conducted in the mid-1950s. Drs. Morton Deutsch and Harold Gerard asked college students to estimate privately the length of lines shown to them. Then some of the students were asked to share their estimation publicly, some were instructed to write their judgments down knowing their estimations would be erased before anyone else saw them, and a third group was asked to keep their estimations to themselves. All of the students were then shown that their initial estimates of the line length were wrong. What happened? The students who had committed publicly refused to admit they were wrong; going public had made them far more resolute and persistent.

But what if you fail? I can hear you protesting already. "What? If I tell everyone and fail, I'll be embarrassed and ashamed!" The research tells us that going public is a double-edged sword: it increases your commitment but also increases the risk. That's why public commitments are so much more effective than private declarations. (You may have astutely observed that you already made your goal somewhat public when assembling your change team.) Don't go public if you are not prepared; better yet, don't go into action if you are not prepared.

Remember Your Goal

If you wanted to remember an important date, how would you do so? You'd probably put it on your calendar, post reminders around your home or workplace, or record it on your smart phone. These are all ways in which you can prioritize and remind yourself about your commitment. Post not only the goals but also the baby steps toward that goal. Some people prefer an inspirational quote, some opt for a direct reminder, and still others go for a picture. Find which works best for you and use it.

Propel the Virtuous Cycle

You may think that you must feel motivated and inspired before acting. It's a cherished myth. But research and experience prove otherwise: start changing your behavior, and as a result your motivation will improve. Success fuels motivation; motivation fuels success. If you wait for inspiration, you're ignoring half of the virtuous cycle. The sixteenth president of the United States (Abraham Lincoln) liked to remind citizens that "Things may come to those who wait, but only the things left by those who hustle."

Writers and procrastinators, in particular, are notorious for waiting for the magic moment or their muses to arrive. They stop writing when they feel blocked or uninspired and then cave in to temptations to do other things first. The research, by contrast, shows that writing regularly, in small amounts, and even though you feel momentarily blocked causes motivation to improve and inspiration to return.

Nothing sparks motivation like early success, as Andrew's story shows. He was reluctant to track his spending habits, calling it "beneath" himself, until he discovered where and why he wasted his hard-earned cash. Assessing his spending through his behavioral detective work and creating a realistic budget turned the tide; suddenly, he could literally see his progress and the light at the end of the tunnel. "I can do this!" The motivation-action link goes both ways.

Take Baby Steps

Prime the pump prior to leaping into action by taking small steps. You have already taken several baby steps by defining your goals, tracking your problem behavior, assembling the change team, going public, and so on. Notice how sequential small steps add up quickly and how, although you are not yet in full action, you are progressing steadily.

Practice Before You Need It

Your behavioral detective analysis has shown you where, why, and when your problem occurs with irritating regularity. One baby step entails practicing the healthy opposite of your problem. You cannot simply rip out and discard the problem behavior like a weed; rather, you'll replace it with a healthy alternative.

Now that I reflect on my analogy, it goes further: you will rip out the weed and then replace it with a flower. Assertion instead of passivity; relaxation in place of anxiety; on schedule as opposed to procrastination; acceptance as an alternative to trying to control the uncontrollable.

We'll devote more time to this strategy, known as "countering," in the next step of Perspire; for now, simply identify the healthy alternative behavior and begin practicing it. Acquire some comfort and confidence in performing it before you leap into the fire. What, specifically, are you going to do differently to counter the problem? How will you act, think, feel, and relate to others as a new person?

How did Monique and Andrew get started on their baby steps? Monique took a few small steps by cutting her smoking and drinking by a third for a full week. She also purchased a relaxation tape. For her, developing skills in self-soothing and relaxation proved to be the healthy alternative to consuming alcohol and nicotine. For his part, Andrew spoke with his parents and brother about his impulsive behavior, dating from childhood. He opened a savings account at his bank, since all he had was

CHECK YOURSELF: COMMITTING, PART II

Check off the following activities that you have actually completed.

I'm focused and prioritized on what I intend to change; other things
    may have to wait temporarily.   _____
I have made public declarations of my goal.   _____
Reminders and notes of encouragement are posted in places where
    I cannot forget or miss them.   _____
I have learned that my early behavior change raises my motivation,
    and I am working both sides of the change-motivation cycle.   _____
I have taken baby steps toward action.   _____
I have begun to practice the healthy opposite of my problem in
    anticipation of the great leap forward.   _____
I have made an active, personal choice to change; it's my
    inner choice.   _____

Most, if not all, of these items should be checked in order to complete the planning process. If they are, on you go. If three-quarters of them are not checked, spend some more time here before proceeding. Remember: these self-test results go onto your permanent record!

a checking account. To counter the money only going out, he planned to save some of the money coming in.

There is plenty of scientific evidence demonstrating that commitment is most effective in improving your self-image and realizing future goals when it is active, public, and effortful. What's more, the science of change has shown that we accept personal responsibility when we've chosen it ourselves, in the absence of, or in spite of, external pressures. It must be a profound inner choice.

Let's keep that commitment and motivation alive and, in fact, peaking. Here's another self-assessment to make certain that you're on the right path.

FINALIZING THE ACTION PLAN

We are now close to your leap into action. You are on the verge. You are about to transition from Prep to Perspire, from planning to action, from being an armchair hopeful to a change agent.

Building on all this planning, you will finalize your action plans in the last part of this step. I'll share Monique's and Andrew's action plans as examples and remind you to go online at www.ChangeologyBook.com for additional support in mapping out your plan for each goal or resolution. Here we go.

You Gotta Start Someday

Select a start or "go" date. Research highlights the value of beginning within a week of completing your plan. Pick a start day with fewer than usual pressures so that it is less stressful. That will enable you to commit your willpower muscles to your change and not squander your efforts on lower priorities.

Make the First Day a Special One

Although little research has been conducted on this next method, it's been repeatedly endorsed by the triumphant. Plan to start on a day that signifies a new beginning (the first day of a week, month, or year), a meaningful personal date (a birthday or anniversary), or a day when fellow resolvers are ready to start, too. The following table offers a sampling of 50 possibilities.

Fifty New Beginnings

American Diabetes Alert Day
   (4th Tuesday of every March)
Birth of a relative
Boxing Day (December 26)
Chinese New Year
Christmas
Cinco de Mayo
Class reunion
Beginning or end of Daylight Saving
   Time
Anniversary of the death of a
   loved one
Earth Day (April 22)
Family Health & Fitness Day
   (last Saturday in September)
Father's Day
First day of school or work
First day of summer (usually June 21)
Graduation
Great American Smokeout (third
   Thursday in November)
Anniversary of a health scare
Independence Day
Islamic New Year
Krishna's birthday
First day of Kwanzaa
Labor Day
First day of Lent
Nava Varsha (Indian New Year)

New Year's Day
Mother's Day
National Depression Screening Day
   (Thursday during National Mental
   Health Awareness week in October)
Lung Health Day (Wednesday of last
   week of October)
Memorial Day
Monday
National Alcohol Screening Day
   (designated day in early April,
   during Alcohol Awareness Month)
National Women's Health & Fitness
   Day (last Wednesday in May)
Nirvana Day (February 8 or 15)
First Thursday of Passover
Patriot Day (September 11)
First day of Ramadan
Rosh Hashanah
Thanksgiving
Valentine's Day
World Diabetes Day (November 14)
World Health Day (April 7)
World No Tobacco Day (May 31)
Yom Kippur
Your birthday
Your child's birthday
Your wedding anniversary
Any day you are prepared

No Waiting for Godot

I once remained in Prep for several years with regard to my weight. As my work schedule became more hectic and I enjoyed the fruits (and calories) of my labors, the poundage rose to the occasion. Of course, as a psychologist, I knew only too well the perils of obesity. But emotionally and behaviorally I was not ready to change.

I fell into the pit of *chronic contemplation:* creating rationalizations, waiting for the magic moment, and blaming external situations. But chronic contemplators never find the right time to act; like the characters in Samuel Beckett's play *Waiting for Godot,* they are perpetually waiting for someone else or something else to activate them. Our research has established that about 40 percent of people who are troubled with any particular problem are chronic contemplators waiting for Godot. That can't be you; finish the Prep and graduate to Perspire within a week.

Share the News

After enlisting your change team and publicly announcing your intentions, please don't forget to tell your team when you intend to start. Politely remind them of what you want from them as well as what you do *not* want.

Start Off with a Bang

William James, the philosopher and psychologist, was among the earliest to write about developing healthy habits. He insisted that "securing success at the outset is imperative"; in fact, he said, "failure at first is apt to damp the energy of all future attempts, whereas past experiences of success nerve one to future vigor." Although James wrote those sentences in 1890, subsequent research has supported his contentions.

The upshot for you: Start strong and fast. Begin when you, your change team, and your skills are at full force so that you secure success at the outset. As James put it, "our self-feeling is in our power."

Learn from Your Mistakes

My grandmother, bless her heart, used to tell us that our mistakes were merely lessons to be learned. Before you leap, make sure that your action plan attends to the reasons you failed in your previous attempts to change. Those are lessons to be learned, mistakes to be harvested. As mentioned previously, Monique learned that sheer willpower was insufficient and therefore built in skills before she began her last, successful change. Andrew learned the hard way that change cost more than he had budgeted for and thus took along a support team and additional commitment the next time.

Mantra for a Week

Dozens of people I've worked with in the process of change have begged me to supply a few gems of inspiration to keep them going in the early days of Perspire. In the past, I suggested a few standbys, but those individuals were dissatisfied because my recommendations didn't quite capture their experiences and hopes.

Now I refrain from offering any prepackaged mantras and instead help them develop their own. What's the mantra, slogan, or image that will inspire you? Now's the time to generate it—or him/her. Sometimes the mantra or slogan proves to be an inspirational person. As the poet Virgil wisely advised, "Follow an expert."

For the sake of illustration, here's one of my favorites from, of course, Ralph Waldo Emerson: "We are all inventors, each sailing out on a voyage of discovery, guided each by a private chart, of which there is no duplicate. The world is all gates, all opportunities." That's my mantra in the early throes of action: *The world is all gates, all opportunities.* Please find your own spiritual vibration or sacred chant; you can easily find online sites that list oodles of examples.

My inspirational experts or models tend to hail from the human rights movements—those fighting against oppression and for their inalienable rights, be they the founding fathers, labor leaders, civil rights pioneers, and so on. Select words, images, and experts that stir you.

Write It

You have learned in previous sections to define and write down your goals, to identify and write down the pros and cons of change, the triggers and reinforcers of your problem behavior. Guess what? You can now write an action plan that incorporates those and adds more elements.

Additional blank forms for writing your action plan are available on www.ChangeologyBook.com.

Put your plan on paper, using the following template, to summarize the key points.

My goal: _____

Key pros of changing: _____

Key cons of changing to be vigilant: _____

My triggers: _____

Reinforcers of my problem: _____

Negative consequences of the problem that I tend to forget: _____

_____

Members of my change team: _____

Healthy alternative/opposite of the problem: _____

_____

Lessons to learn from previous failures: _____

_____

My inspiring words, images, or experts for the first week: _____

_____

My start/go day: _____

Once your action plan is completed, hang it in a prominent place. Share it with a few members of your change team; perhaps post it on your

Facebook page. If you like, you can also post it on the Forum section of www.ChangeologyBook.com for others to model and emulate. Review others' action plans there, and print out blank forms for creating a revised action plan or one of another goal.

Now let's determine whether you have in fact put the action into your plan. Another self-assessment is coming your way.

CHECK YOURSELF: FINALIZING YOUR PLAN

Check off the following activities that you have completed to date.

I have selected my start/go day. _____

My change team and others know when that day is. _____

That day occurs within a week of completing this chapter; no waiting
around for Godot for me. _____

My action plan addresses or incorporates the reasons I failed in
the past. _____

I will build in success from day one by starting strong and fast. _____

I have found inspiring words, images, and experts for the early weeks
of the Perspire step. _____

The action plan is written and prominently displayed, at least for me. _____

You know the drill: practically all of these research-supported methods should be checked before you proceed.

READY FOR LIFTOFF?

"Just how long do I need to plan?" is a recurrent question. "As long as it takes to prepare and plan for the leap into action" is my equally recurrent answer. That might be a couple of days or a couple of weeks. It is not determined by a set number of days but by your level of preparation.

Think back to our analogy of not jumping out of an airplane until your parachute is sewn. You could fuss around for weeks, months, even years without finishing the parachute—in which case you are strongly advised not to leap into midair! But you could finish the parachute in a couple of days and be ready to leap into the bright blue yonder by the weekend.

If I sound overly insistent about the need for active preparation and meeting the Check Yourself benchmarks, it's because I respect the three decades of watching thousands of our research participants and my psychotherapy patients suffer, sometimes with dire consequences. They suffer when they wait interminably to take decisive action, on the one hand, or jump recklessly into action, on the other. Either can be disastrous, but the good news is that you can learn to avoid both extremes when you follow the Changeology program.

During a recent conference, Dr. Judith Beck and I were discussing what she had learned from years of working with dieters and writing her excellent book *The Beck Diet Solution: Train Your Brain to Think Like a Thin Person.* Judy's most important lesson involved the imperative of preparation: dieters need to learn the skills *before* they begin an active dieting phase. It's too darn hard for a dieter to start changing her eating plan while simultaneously learning the skills that will enable her to stick to it.

Early on, most dieters find the process relatively easy because they are losing (water) weight and feeling highly motivated. But once into the process for a few weeks, most dieters hit a wall and find themselves at a loss. They lack the skills to keep going. And trying to teach them skills when they are frustrated and disgusted amounts to a step mismatch. The time to repair the roof is when the sun is shining.

I have prepared you thoroughly and armed you with the skills you need before you leap. If you haven't completed the entire process, you'll be back on that vicious cycle of two weeks of behavior change followed by years of regret and discouragement. I realize this step has asked a lot from you—cognitively, emotionally, interpersonally, and behaviorally. But, my friends, that's exactly our objective.

Here's the first of two self-assessments to end this step. This is *the* bottom-line question.

Are you psyched and prepped, ready to go?! I certainly hope so but respectfully remind you that the desire to change does *not* reliably predict success. Sure, desire is necessary, but it does not separate the successful from the unsuccessful.

But preparation does reliably predict success. So before you jump into Perspire (and into the next chapter), take a moment to complete this Check Yourself. Answer the following question not at all, a little, somewhat, often, or a great deal.

Overall, how prepared or ready are you to change this behavior?

We hope you answered "often" or "a great deal," because that's what more than 80 percent of successful resolvers said before taking action. If not, please rework several of the sections in the Psych and Prep steps before proceeding.

In space-travel terms, all systems need to be "go" before liftoff, before leaping into action. Not some or most systems, but all of them. Like NASA engineers' final systems checks before blasting a rocket into space, here's the second and final Check Yourself before you embark on the next step.

Look back over the Check Yourself assessments in Psych (Step 1) and Prep (Step 2) and then determine if you have reached the right benchmarks. Circle GO if your score on those self-assessments equaled or surpassed the required level of preparation; circle CAUTION if any of your scores on those self-assessments fell short.

Raising awareness	CAUTION	GO
Reevaluating yourself	CAUTION	GO
Arousing emotions	CAUTION	GO
Committing I	CAUTION	GO
Setting goals	CAUTION	GO
Tracking progress	CAUTION	GO
Assembling your change team	CAUTION	GO
Committing II	CAUTION	GO

In a perfect world, we would require all GOs. But in the self-change world, we do not expect perfection; we accept good enough. So if you fall short on one of these eight Check Yourselves, please don't fret or berate yourself. Having seven of eight GOs clearly demonstrates your preparation. Let's leap, confident that you have now secured both the skills and the motivation to do so effectively.

STEP 3

PERSPIRE: TAKING ACTION

WEEKS 2 TO 8

Walk the talk—take action! Develop healthy alternatives to the problem, and build new behaviors. Reward yourself for a job well done. Cultivate your environment and support team to keep moving forward.

A group of graduate students at the University of Miami once summarized the steps of change in a series of sounds. Precontemplation is a disinterested *naaah*. The early steps sound like a take-it-or-leave-it *eehhhh*. And my favorite is Perspire: *rooaarrrr!*

That sound perfectly captures the high-energy excitement of this step. I prefer the term "Perspire" over "action" since all of the steps require action of one sort or another. What's more, I adore the overused (and admittedly trite) statement by Thomas Edison: Genius is 1 percent inspiration, 99 percent perspiration. Achieving your goals will require work and commitment, but following the steps of *Changeology* will markedly decrease the amount you sweat and enable you to work smarter rather than harder.

I'll never forget the day Andrew walked into my office and declared, "I'm in the grip." The first time he said "the grip," I thought he was referring to a fever or flu, as though he were physically perspiring. But Andrew meant that he was possessed of a psychological fever, a powerful "I can do this, I will do this!" That's precisely what your earlier work in Psych and Prep has led to.

Step 3 is all about the fury of action, and it takes place at least two weeks—and perhaps up to 30 days—into the 90 days of change. To help bring this step to life, I'll return to the experiences of Monique and Andrew. We'll revisit their stories and hear about their diligent work to achieve their goals. After taking a few baby steps to decrease her smoking and drinking, Monique now stops completely. After the excitement of discovering his triggers to and patterns of overspending, Andrew, in his words, "puts the pedal to the metal" on achieving satisfying relationships with money and women.

Successful action requires four catalyzing strategies:

- ◆ Rewarding
- ◆ Countering
- ◆ Controlling your environment
- ◆ Helping relationships

But—and here's the catch that so many people ignore—you have to abandon the earlier strategies of raising your self-awareness and arousing your emotions. In fact, research shows that using these two strategies, which are critical to Psych and Prep, typically spells failure in Perspire; it constitutes a step mismatch, like dance partners tripping over each other. I'll explain why and how they can now ruin the entire enterprise. Let's start with what *not* to do and then jump right into the four catalysts that will propel you along.

GOING FORWARD, NOT BACKWARD

In the Psych and Plan steps, raising self-awareness and arousing emotions about yourself, your problems, and your goals were indispensable allies. But doing so now, in the Perspire step, can be destructive. That's the profound difference, the continental divide, between getting ready and taking action.

Let's say that you're tackling a weekly chore such as baking a pie, paying the bills, mowing the lawn, or taking a stroll. You have performed the chore before with success and satisfaction. You certainly understand why you are doing it, you are committed to seeing it through, and you possess a sensible plan of action. But now imagine that halfway into the chore—the pie is about to be popped into the oven, the bills are half paid—you begin asking yourself emotional, self-critical questions: Why do I need to do this? How come someone else is not doing it instead of me? Why do I waste my time on this nonsense? Maybe I should just stop! I don't even want to do this damn thing! And I'm probably not even doing it the right way! As your questioning and resentment escalate, the likelihood of your completing the task plummets.

That's what happens when you continue to raise your self-awareness and arouse your emotions as you take serious action. Scores of research studies indicate that such rumination produces foul moods, compounds negative thinking, impairs problem solving, derails goals, and erodes helping relationships. Put simply, it sends you reeling backward at exactly the moment you are roaring forward.

It's what happened when the Toad in *Alice's Adventures in Wonderland* inquires of the Centipede how he manages to walk so gracefully with all those legs. The Centipede, who has been happily and successfully ambulating for years, gets so discombobulated that he cannot walk anymore and gives up the now-impossible task!

When I introduce this story and the research findings, a few people immediately challenge me: "How can you advise against self-awareness and authentic emotions? Don't you prize the Socratic dictum of 'Know thyself'?" Of course I do, and anyone who has read up to this page knows that that is the case. I value the centrality of raising awareness and arousing emotions, but at the right time. Step 3 is not the right time.

This lesson is precisely the reason I am frequently paid to consult with health care marketers. They are brilliant advertisers and easily create awareness among consumers. But they are failures in establishing behavior change among those consumers. Their marketing skill set takes them only so far; something altogether different is required to modify behavior.

The very purpose, the raison d'être, of Perspire is transforming preparation into action. In C. S. Lewis's *The Screwtape Letters,* a demon imparts the following advice to his apprentice for capturing souls for Hell:

> The great thing is to prevent his doing anything. As long as he does not convert it into action, it does not matter how much he thinks about this new repentance. . . . Let him do anything but act. . . . The more often he feels without acting, the less he will be able ever to act, and, in the long run, the less he will be able to feel.

In this step and this chapter of *Changeology,* we're aiming to act, to stay forward, to lean into the winds of change. Second-guessing your feelings now will often backfire and entangle you in thoughts that make you feel worse and create doubt about your capacity to change. In the words of Ralph Waldo Emerson again, "An ounce of action is worth a ton of theory." Avoid the step mismatch and rely now on the following four research-proven catalysts.

REWARDING

Since time immemorial, rewards have been used to modify and strengthen certain behaviors. The ancient Greeks, Romans, and Chinese all used reinforcement and punishment. Principles of reward are deeply woven into the fabric of social institutions and human relationships: child rearing, education, government, and business. And virtually every adult has practiced rewarding pets, children, spouses, roommates, students, parents, and others.

However, the moment I begin speaking about using rewards to change behavior, most people give me a quizzical look. "Well, sure, I use them on others, but not on myself," they say. The time has come to learn how to reward *yourself.* We will use rewarding to strengthen your goal behavior in a systematic, intentional way.

A reward—or reinforcement, as we psychologists call it—consists of any consequence that increases the frequency or strength of a target behavior. Note that it must be contingent on the behavior; if it's not, it rapidly devolves into a superstition. The classic superstitions about walking on cracks, opening an umbrella indoors, and seeing a black cat cross your path all probably originated when someone mistakenly noticed an accidental association between one of those behaviors and an unfortunate result, including breaking a mother's back.

In rewarding the baby steps you take toward your goal, you can employ all types of healthy incentives, including:

Consumables: coffee, diet sodas, sweets (if you're not dieting), cookies, and so on. Of course, these are stronger incentives when you are feeling more deprived.

Activities: watching television, attending a play, telephoning friends, getting a massage, riding a bicycle.

Interpersonal strokes: verbal praise, attention, affectionate touches from others.

Positive self-talk: internal congratulations, personal affirmations, soothing praise.

Tokens: secondary reinforcers to be exchanged for rewards at a later time, such as chips, stars, and happy faces.

The list is endless, which is fortunate, because you can continue to bathe yourself in different types of rewards and avoid getting tired of the same ones over 90 days.

It should come as no surprise that what rewards one person, say, chocolate or a movie, will be a punishment for another person. Personal preferences must come into play here. The secret is to identify what rewards can modify your behavior and to create a reinforcement plan that you'll stick with for a couple of months. A large number of reward techniques are effective; for example, you can:

Reinforce yourself for reaching target behaviors. Examples abound: dinner at your favorite restaurant, a ticket to a play, a nap, a manicure, and so on. Select from the above list of consumables, activities, people, self-talk, and tokens.

Keep the rewards contingent on meeting a prespecified step. "Cheating" by giving yourself a reward even though you didn't meet the stated goal only weakens your resolve. Set up a cause-effect relationship, and stick to it!

Reward each baby step taken toward the bigger destination. As discussed, you will not reach your final goal overnight, so plan to reinforce each and every baby step toward it with a reward. (You may recall from Intro to Psychology that this is known as "shaping.") Most complex human behavior develops this way, be it speech, exam taking, or sports. So reward yourself for the successive small steps and then up the ante slightly: give yourself a reward, say, for walking a half mile; then give yourself another reward for going three-quarters of a mile and so on.

Deliver the reward immediately and every time. Decades of research have revealed that, to achieve the best performance, you should give yourself the reinforcer immediately after the desired response. If it is delayed, other behaviors will occur—some desirable, some not—that will then be reinforced instead. Early on in Perspire, give the reward on each occasion. You can gradually fade the rewards out once you hit the next step.

Follow Grandma's rule. First you work or study, then you play. Allowing yourself to engage in desirable and more frequent behaviors will reinforce the goal. Just avoid the child's mistake of recklessly rushing through the goal behavior to get to the pleasurable activity. If you commit to 30 minutes of practicing the piano daily, rewarding yourself afterward with 10 minutes of playing a computer game, don't knock five minutes off your piano practice so you can get to that reward sooner.

As another example, a client of mine was struggling to exercise consistently; some weeks she was on track, other weeks she wasn't. I asked her to think of what she truly enjoyed doing most evenings after work. She immediately answered, "Sitting and watching television for an hour or two while petting my dog after a long day of work." Perfect. We agreed that she would not turn on her television or do more with her dog than pat its head until she exercised for at least 20 minutes. This quid pro quo worked like a charm. She rarely missed exercise because she didn't want to miss her shows and snuggling with her lapdog. Her "not motivated" exercising soon became a daily habit. In fact, within a month, it was no longer an onerous chore but simply part of her daily life.

Use many rewards of many types for maximum effectiveness. If you maintain your exercise regimen or healthy eating, for example, choose a reward from a rotating menu of possibilities. It can include any number of options, from a self-congratulatory "Excellent!" to time spent hanging out with a friend.

Reverse the usual sequence. Most consumptive and addictive behaviors are reinforcing in the short run—the delight, the *ahhh* of smoking, drinking, overeating, and so forth. But in the long run these problems are quite punishing and harmful. As I stated earlier, this is what's called the "neurotic paradox": unhealthy behaviors are, perversely, rewarded immediately and punished only in the dim, unforeseeable future. As humans, we tend to respond to those immediate effects. Reverse this sequence by reinforcing yourself immediately and potently for healthy behaviors and by avoiding any reinforcement for unhealthy behaviors.

Create a contingency contract with a loved one. Contingency contracts are mutual, transparent agreements between you and a member of your change team that specifies what rewards will occur when you meet your goal behaviors. "If I avoid fast food for a month, you'll reward me by accompanying me to the spa on a Saturday afternoon." Such contracts are particularly useful for those of you who have trouble rewarding yourself.

Contracts work best when they specify rules for the change team: "No nagging"; "Help me when I look overwhelmed"; "I pick the movie when I'm on track for a week"; and "Tell me you're proud when I reach an accomplishment toward my goal." Though establishing rules and putting them on paper may sound corny, this method has proven to work time and time again. Considerable research indicates that such contracts are quite beneficial when they are carefully created in good faith. And you can create several of these with different people or for different goals. Here's how:

Define the goal (target behavior) in SMART terms as you did in Prep. Provide specific, measurable behaviors that everyone can agree on.

Construct a contingency contract and determine what exactly will happen when you achieve your goal or target behavior.

Review your contract in terms of the following checklist and then revise it accordingly.

Checklist

My contingency contract:	Yes	No	NA
Is constructed by both parties	___	___	___
Identifies, concretely and tangibly, the goal behavior(s)	___	___	___
Allows for some exceptions under unforeseen circumstances	___	___	___
Defines parameters (what is late, what is minimum standard, etc.)	___	___	___
Includes rewards contingent on the goal	___	___	___
Specifies rewards that are health-enhancing or positive	___	___	___
States that the rewards will *not* appear if the goal is not met	___	___	___
Allows for the goal to be gradually increased over time (start with smaller steps and then graduate to bigger goals)	___	___	___
Is written and/or signed by both parties	___	___	___
Is publicly available to all affected parties	___	___	___

(go to www.ChangeologyBook.com to see a completed example and to print out formal contracts for yourself)

Sign the contract and give a copy to everyone involved or post it where both parties can see it.

Incentivize your health. The new U.S. health care law permits employers to offer a financial reward of 30 percent of the total cost of health insurance to their employees. This can take the form of lower insurance premiums, insurance rebates, and/or outright payments to you for adopting healthier habits. Take advantage of these as a means of reinforcing your progress. And kick up the incentives by using this technique in your self-reward program or your contingency contract with a friend. By contributing to a savings account, Andrew literally "paid" himself half of what he would have spent by drinking late into the wee hours of the weekend—an instant cash rebate!

Give yourself reassuring compliments. Remind yourself that you're becoming successful at changing, which will counter the years—maybe decades—of defeatist messages. The intent is to internalize and own a positive self-image, not only to reinforce the new behavior.

Remove a dreaded chore, such as cleaning the bathroom or decluttering a closet, when you're successful in the small steps you're taking toward permanent change. Sometimes we only think of giving ourselves a pleasurable consequence, but remember that removing an aversive chore by getting someone else to do it constitutes a powerful reward indeed. One of the most effective rewards in my life has been to hire a housecleaner; I'll engage in all sorts of target behaviors to have someone else do that.

Should You Punish Yourself?

A question frequently arises: "If rewards are so powerful for moving me toward my goal, I should punish myself when I don't perform, right?" Well, actually, no. Psychologists prefer not to use punishment too often because of nasty and unintended side effects that can derail you. More specifically, punishment can leave you feeling discouraged, make you feel like a failure, cause you to avoid productive behaviors, and increase your aggression toward other people. Punishment tends to foster certain behaviors that do nothing to reward the positive behavior and can actually trigger a whole other set of problems. Punishment does not direct us to the better alternative; it only suppresses behavior temporarily.

For these reasons, minimize punishing yourself, both in your daily behavior and in your thoughts. Rewards are more effective in the long run. In other words, use more carrot and less stick.

To be sure, thoughtful individuals can avoid most of these pitfalls of punishment. However, most of us are not calm or scientific when it comes to dispensing self-punishment. So if you decide to use self-punishers—and I know that some of you will (perhaps it's just human nature)—here are some pointers:

Punish like a tree. Properly applied, punishment should be immediate, contingent, and calm. When you run into a tree, you experience the same response. Emulate a tree should you decide to punish yourself in addition to giving yourself rewards, and avoid having an emotional "gotcha" response.

Punish each and every time. Be consistent with your punishment even though daily life might get in the way. We are caught only on rare occasions for speeding in cars or cheating on examinations. That's a weak way of shaping behavior; instead, apply a mild punishment every time you slip.

Catch a problem early in the behavior chain. Punishing yourself is more effective when it's done early, before the unwanted behavior culminates in a more serious outcome. Reaching for the forbidden cookie jar while dieting, for instance, can be punished mildly. Don't wait until after you've already eaten four cookies.

Remember that variety is the spice of punishment, too. By definition, punishment is any contingent consequence following an undesirable behavior that weakens or discourages that particular behavior. It's not necessarily a penalty; it's anything that decreases the behavior. Thus, use a wide range of mild forms of punishment so that they do not lose their impact.

Double the consequences. As you punish yourself for what *not to* do, simultaneously reinforce what *to* do. This has the effect of encouraging the positive behavior. In our cookie example, you could mildly punish yourself for reaching for the cookies and then immediately reward yourself for eating a more healthy substitute. Always combine punishment with a reward for doing the healthier alternative!

Put yourself in time-out. Much as you might ground adolescents or put youngsters in a "time-out" for their misbehavior, you can punish yourself by removing a pleasurable event or activity. You can cancel a planned night out if you procrastinated too much that day. You can skip your favorite television show or lose some other "behavioral freedom" if you didn't get eight hours of sleep the night before as planned.

Ignore, don't punish. In punishment, strictly speaking, a consequence follows a behavior. But you can also choose to ignore the unwanted behavior, in which case no consequence follows—nothing is added, nothing is removed. What's important is to withdraw any previous reinforcement. Do nothing; don't punish and certainly don't reward yourself. This eventually helps erode the undesirable behavior. In fact, ignoring can prove more irritating than punishment, since there is no response at all. Much as with disciplining kids, we do not want to punish each and every small misstep. Instead, alternate between ignoring some undesirable behaviors and punishing others.

Given my general mistrust of punishment, I encourage self-changers to reward the small steps toward the goal and to ignore the old problem behavior. But Monique was having no part of it. Raised in a conservative religious household, Monique was uncomfortable with the idea of rewarding herself a lot. In her religious worldview, quick punishments were given for transgressions. In fact, she occasionally called her drinking, overeating, and smoking "sins" for which she should be punished. Alas, this worldview had backfired in all of her previous attempts to change. She would "damn" herself for the original problem and rarely reward herself for her impressive changes since "I shouldn't have to." This was a self-defeating cycle from which she could not extricate herself.

I began reversing Monique's downhill slide by asking her to accept another proven method of change and to emphasize worldly rewards, not spiritual damnation. She immediately acknowledged that her old view of rewards was neither successful nor sensible. It took only a few questions to get her to switch thinking modes. I asked her, "Are punishment and damnation how you are raising your children to think of themselves?" She snapped, "Of course not!" I smiled, we shared a laugh, and she got it.

Monique then created a reward program, devoid of punishments, and mapped out a contingency contract with her husband for avoiding junk foods and desserts. One of the provisions in her contract with her husband was that if she ate only healthy foods for three days (no junk food and no sweets), she'd receive a 20-minute foot massage in bed that, she bashfully told me, "led to other things in the bedroom." Now, that's a reward system!

Andrew, too, initially avoided the use of any rewards. He thought rewarding was "bribery" and didn't represent genuine change. He is hardly alone in this line of thought. But immoral bribery is different from justly earned reinforcement. Bribery is using gifts or favors to distort someone's judgment or to corrupt someone's conduct. By contrast, the rewards we are encouraging are open, contractual, and used to improve your judgment and behavior. It took some time, but Andrew eventually came along, realizing that tangible rewards are an ordinary part of life and work.

If you, like Andrew, oppose self-rewards because you think they are bribery and don't lead to real change, or if, like Monique, you rely on punishment and condemnation to modify your behavior, please reconsider your beliefs in light of the science. You don't need to be a radical behaviorist to see that rewards work well—both for others and for yourself. Here's a prime opportunity to harness Changeology and add a powerful catalyst to your plan.

Before we jump into the next catalyzing strategy for this step, let's do a Check Yourself on rewards. This is a perfect time to remind you that it's not enough simply to know that you should be using rewards; you must actually implement them! Otherwise you'll fall prey to the *insight fallacy*: understanding something isn't the same as changing it. One of our most enduring societal myths is that once we understand a problem, the understanding will automatically solve it. My overriding commitment in this book is to ensure that you apply these strategies and put them into action. The following self-assessment is designed to do just that.

CHECK YOURSELF: REWARDING

Answer the following questions using a 5 point scale: 1 = Never, 2 = Seldom, 3 = Occasionally, 4 = Often, 5 = Repeatedly. Fill in the number that most closely reflects how frequently you used rewards in the past week to sustain your behavior change. Of course, be honest and realistic.

I rewarded myself for changing. _____

I did something nice for myself in return for not giving in to my problem. _____

I rewarded myself for taking small baby steps toward the larger goal. _____

Successful self-changers average 3 and higher on these self-assessment items. By contrast, the unsuccessful give themselves 2 and below. If you are not rating yourself as at least a 3, reengineer your reward system. The research suggests that you need to reward yourself more using the methods described earlier.

COUNTERING

Countering, a shorthand expression for the technical term "counter-conditioning," is simple in principle: do the healthy opposite of the problem behavior. There is a healthy alternative for every problem: relaxing instead of fueling stressful emotions, asserting yourself instead of passively avoiding conflict, exercising instead of sitting on the couch, thinking realistically instead of neurotically, and so on. Two opposite behaviors cannot exist at the same time; it's impossible to be simultaneously relaxed and anxious, to maintain a budget while overspending. That's the power of countering. "A new love drives out the old," as a French proverb says.

Note the emphasis on *doing* the healthy opposite. Decades of research have confirmed the obvious: you must engage in the healthy opposite, not simply know that you should do it. Put another way, Perspire requires that you learn how to talk to yourself in instructional ways rather than talking to yourself to get motivated as you did during the Psych and Plan steps.

We talk to ourselves all the time; sometimes our self-talk is motivational, and sometimes it's instructional. Motivational self-talk entails psyching yourself up (Let's go!), maximizing effort (Give it your all!), building self-efficacy (I can do this!), and creating a positive mood (I feel good about myself). You have learned these and many other methods in the earlier steps. Instructional self-talk, on the other hand, is about focusing your attention (Keep my eye on the goal), providing instruction (Reward myself now, or do the healthy opposite), and walking yourself through the particular steps. In other words, it's the how-tos of action. And that's what you are learning in this chapter—how to guide and instruct yourself to enhance your performance.

All sorts of studies have shown that once you're in the action of Perspire, instructional self-talk is more effective than motivational self-talk. As I was putting the finishing touches on this chapter, a journal arrived on my desk that contained an analysis of 32 research studies on the effectiveness of various types of self-talk for performing in sports. Sure enough, self-talk for athletes worked, and training them in self-talk worked even better. And sure enough, instructional self-talk was more effective than motivational self-talk in facilitating learning and reaching goals. Put another way, less "rah, rah, rah" and more "do this, do this, do this."

In this section, I'll show you how countering works in the real world with instructional self-talk. We'll cover the eight most common countering methods:

1. Diversion
2. Exercise
3. Relaxation
4. Assertion
5. Healthy thoughts
6. Exposure
7. Imagery
8. Acceptance

Of course, I cannot teach every possible countering method, but the beauty of Changeology is that once you become familiar with the concept, you can apply it to other problems. Just ask yourself: what is the healthy opposite or alternative to my problem? That's countering.

As an example, let's take excessive worry. For this example, I'll use myself as a parent who worries about my two grown children and their happiness, health, employment, insurance, safety, romantic interests, environment, future, ad nauseam. I also worry that they will not experience the security of job opportunities and material wealth that many of my generation were afforded.

What, in heaven's name, is the healthy opposite of this behavior? For starters, there is *diversion* from worry—keeping busy, enjoying life, engaging in fun activities, cultivating friends and hobbies. There's *exercise,* a well-known and potent antianxiety remedy. As one of my university friends claims, "I'd go crazy if I couldn't exercise. My head would probably explode!" *Relaxation* is an effective counter to physical anxiety but is slightly less effective for mental worry. Meditation, progressive muscle relaxation, deep breathing, prayer, and massage are other forms of relaxation. I can picture myself in a circumstance that would typically trigger excessive worry (*exposure*), but then imagine myself peaceful and confident (*imagery*). *Healthy thoughts* also counter worry. When my head is screwed on correctly, I realize that I am blessed with two healthy, educated, loving children who don't have any serious illnesses. My worry stems more from perfectionism and parental love than from any rational basis. And don't forget about the countering power of *acceptance:* all parents need to learn to accept that they cannot control or foretell their children's futures, no matter how hard we try. All we can do is provide them with secure roots and then wings to fly away.

As you can see, the more the merrier when it comes to countering methods. It's better to possess a number of countering tools than to depend on a single one, particularly when countering chronic worry. As you can also see from my struggles with parental worry, you'll tailor the countering to your needs and preferences. With time, experimentation, and practice, you'll discover which countering tools work best for you.

Monique impressively acquired and employed many of these countering methods: she diverted herself when tempted to smoke and drink, she exercised four times a week, she restructured her thoughts into positive messages about herself and her probability of success, and she asserted herself in saying no to unwelcome offers of alcohol and yes to her healthy needs. And she accepted that she might never weigh 110 pounds again. But she would become a healthier and happier 130-pound woman!

Virtually everyone knows the first four countering methods: diversion, exercise, relaxation, and assertion. If you have lived in the Western Hemisphere in the past few decades, you know that these have been frequently explained and commonly practiced. But the four other strategies may be unfamiliar to you and thus deserve a few moments of training in instructional self-talk. Let's review them.

Healthy Thoughts

The rising popularity of cognitive therapy has introduced many people to the general idea of healthy thinking but perhaps not how to do it. The premise of all cognitive therapies is that one's *interpretations* of an event may be more important than the event itself. Our beliefs largely establish our feelings, not the activating event. My perfectionism (not my kids' life events), for example, leads to my unrealistic worry. I am (mis)interpreting my kids' situation from a biased perspective rather than looking at their circumstances from an impartial, reasonable standpoint. And in my case, illogical, neurotic thoughts produce unnecessary feelings of anxiety and guilt. To change my feelings, I have to change my thoughts.

Though there are thousands of potential unhealthy thoughts, most of them thankfully boil down to a few recurrent patterns. The cognitive therapy pioneers Drs. Albert Ellis and Aaron Beck first identified many of these patterns back in the 1970s. As you may have guessed by now, my faulty thinking about my kids follows a pattern of perfectionism: that we as parents must do things perfectly and that our children should meet all of our elevated expectations; anything else is a failure. When I detect these cognitive errors, I forcefully dispute them and then try to think more realistically about my parenting performance and my children's lives (which, I should add, are quite wonderful for the most part but not perfect). And don't be surprised when early childhood injunctions—"get it perfect," "do it again until it's 100 percent correct"—come springing forth as you do so. I certainly hear my father's voice behind my own perfectionism.

Here's a distillation of other common mistakes we make in our thinking, along with guidance on how to replace them with their healthy opposites.

Unhealthy thinking: *If it's true in one case, it applies to any case that's even slightly similar.* This is a classic case of "overgeneralizing." A good example would be a woman who experiences a string of bad dates. Every guy she's ever dated has turned out to be a jerk, so she decides that all men must be jerks. Or picture a man who falters during a presentation at work and tells himself, "I'm always going to fail" or "I'll never do things right." Suddenly, that single experience is generalized to all others.

Countering: Tell yourself that your logic is faulty and that one negative experience doesn't mean it will happen again, especially in situations that aren't even similar. You can recognize that the past does not create the future. When you examine the overgeneralization more closely, you'll realize that it's based on a simplification, whereas reality is far too complex for overgeneralizations. Some words to be cautious of in this type of inner chatter are "always," "every," and "never."

Unhealthy thinking: *The world must treat us all fairly.* This misconception is similar to the child's complaint "It's not fair!" It's what psychologists term "a belief in cosmic justice." We tend to feel resentful because we think we know what's fair, but then the world does not behave accordingly. Discouragement and rage set in.

Countering: In case your parents did not tell you, cognitive therapy will: "Life is *not* fair." We may promote fairness, but we cannot routinely expect it. Don't assume that people will agree with what you think is "fair," and never assume that the world operates that way. Tell yourself that the world is rarely fair and that your need might really be a wish.

Unhealthy thinking: *The only events that matter are failures.* You make a judgment based on partial information but disregard other information. You take the negative details and magnify them while filtering out all positive aspects. For instance, a person may pick out a single, unpleasant day and dwell on it exclusively so that his or her reality becomes darkened or distorted. Let's say you attend a party and afterward focus on the one awkward look directed your way, ignoring the hours of smiles from others. This is known as "selective abstraction."

Countering: Identify the many successes that are present (the smiles!). Challenge the thought "I am defined by my errors." Log your daily successes to determine if you are accurately judging your experience.

Unhealthy thinking: *I am responsible for all the bad things that happen.* People who engage in this kind of "hyperresponsibility" thinking see themselves as the cause of external events that they are, in fact, not responsible for. For example, "I was late to the dinner party and caused the hostess to overcook the meal. If I had only pushed myself to leave on time, it wouldn't have happened. It's all my fault."

Countering: Determine what is and what is not reasonably your fault. The healthy opposite of hyperresponsibility is to attribute events that are out of your control to the environment, fate, or luck. "Stuff happens."

Unhealthy thinking: *The worst. Disaster will certainly strike.* This kind of catastrophic thinking magnifies the ordinary into the extraordinary, using "what if?" questions (e.g., "What if tragedy strikes?" "What if my boss discovers my mistake?"). For example, you might exaggerate the significance of one of your tiny errors or inappropriately shrink the magnitude of your accomplishments.

Countering: Evaluate and calculate real probabilities. Collect evidence to prove that an imperfection is not the end of the world and that tragedy is unlikely to happen to you. Distinguish between molehills and mountains.

Unhealthy thinking: *I must be loved by practically everyone for everything I do.* The thought pattern frequently continues with "I cannot be happy unless others are happy."

Countering: Really? Where is that written? Accept the fact that not everyone will love you and what you do. Be realistic. Also, accept the fact that your happiness and ability to change are *not* dependent on other people's approval.

Common to all these thinking distortions is their irrational, demanding, and absolutist nature. "Shoulds" and "musts" can easily tyrannize us. The countering methods outlined above can help us become more logical and realistic in approaching the frustrations of the world. Every time you entertain a negative thought, pause for a few seconds and then replace it with something positive or an "I can" statement. We want healthy adult reasoning, not antiquated childish beliefs, to rule our lives and therefore our emotions. (If you would like detailed instructions on healthier thinking or other countering methods, please consult Appendix A for the most highly recommended self-help books on the topics of assertion, depression, relaxation, and anxiety.)

The whole point of these examples of how we sabotage ourselves with unhealthy thoughts is to get you to begin seeing where your thought processes go wrong. It's also to equip you with the mental strategies for transforming those self-defeating thoughts into positive ones that will drive you through Perspire. Indeed, this is the essence of Perspiring.

Exposure

It's human nature to avoid fear and anxiety. In fact, that may be our most human of responses. Our brains are hardwired to maximize pleasure and to minimize pain. But if allowed to go unchecked, our avoidance builds and becomes a problem itself. By evading the feared situation over time, you wind up rewarding yourself—"Whew, no anxiety, and I avoided that one again." Constant avoidance is the hallmark of self-defeating behavior.

Take the common fear that children develop toward large or un-known dogs. A child will become fearful—trembling, crying, sweating, protesting—and then immediately try to escape the encounter. If the avoidance happens a couple of times, no problem. But if the avoidance persists, that fear can easily spread or generalize to other dogs, pets, and unfamiliar situations. Then there is a problem.

The healthy opposite—the effective countering of avoidance—is called "exposure." It means directly confronting dreaded situations. Some people say "Just do it" or "Throw them into the deep end of the pool," but that kind of drama is unsophisticated and largely ineffective. Instead, we teach people a series of skills: (1) relaxation, (2) gradual exposure to the fear, and (3) not to prematurely escape from the fearful situation. And, as you have undoubtedly sensed, the once-gigantic fear becomes quite manageable within minutes or a few hours.

Let's continue with the example of fear of dogs, which unfortunately occurred to my son when he was young following a single unpleasant en-counter with a stray dog. In a few minutes, my wife and I taught Jonathon to relax by breathing deeply and imagining a pleasant scene. We asked him to imagine dogs approaching him in our suburban backyard. Once he was able to do so, we walked around the neighborhood to meet some local friendly dogs. He naturally protested for a minute, but then, with encour-agement and my modeling, began to pet them and step away. I wouldn't let him back away too quickly, because I knew that that could compound his fear and reinforce his avoidance. I encouraged him to stay until half or more of his fear diminished. Within an hour or two, his fear was virtually gone, and to this day he only has the foggiest of memories about the incident.

To bring in an example relevant to adults, let's say that you want to become more assertive. In the past, you've pandered to your colleagues at work rather than speaking up and confronting them on ideas that you don't agree with. Not only has your submissive behavior in meetings left you feeling frustrated, it's also had the unfortunate effect of stifling your chances of a promotion.

To get over your fear, you intentionally introduce yourself to situations that are "safer" than the work setting. You make a conscious effort to spark conversations and respectfully offer a different perspective with people in a social setting. This affords you a more relaxed environment, one in which you can take a few deep breaths beforehand and plot out your moments of exposure. Perhaps you imagine speaking to someone in your life who has irked you or who has disappointed you for whatever reason. In the past, you would have let it go, but now you're slowly easing your way into being more assertive. At some point you feel ready to assert yourself with that person in real life. And when you feel that you're ready to take your new behavior to work, you make it a goal to be the first person to speak your mind at your next meeting. By then all the exposure outside of work comes to good use. Over time your fear diminishes and you find that asserting yourself is much easier.

Decades of research can guide us in using exposure most effectively. First, relax before confronting a fearful situation. Second, if your anxiety is intense, expose yourself initially only in your imagination until you become less fearful, and then approach the actual situation. Third, don't escape from the situation too quickly; remain until you achieve a 50 percent reduction in your anxiety. Fourth, the first few exposures typically proceed better if you have a member of your change team accompany you. And fifth, bring out the big guns of reward: you deserve huge, plentiful reinforcement for facing the fear and practicing exposure anyway.

In fact, exposure combines several countering methods: relaxation, assertion, and healthy thinking. When the exposure is complete and successful, add a healthy dose of cognitive therapy: acknowledge that your runaway or catastrophic thinking intensified the fear. Confronting the fear didn't cause you to lose control, the fear doesn't continue forever, and recalling the fear is not the same as experiencing it again. These are all healthy countering thoughts.

Exposure is a nifty strategy that's useful for all sorts of avoidance and anxiety-related problems. Let's circle back so I can remind you of the science of behavior change here: implementing the opposite behavior of your problem becomes the permanent solution. You're not simply rooting out the old behavior; you're actually building in the desired goal. (More on that subject when we hit Step 5, Persist.)

Imagery

What's the healthy opposite of imaging yourself failing or being embarrassed? Visualizing yourself succeeding and thriving. Now you're getting the gist of this countering strategy: learning and building the opposite behavior. Successful resolvers visualize the rewards of success, while unsuccessful resolvers visualize the penalties of failure.

Let's embolden the new you with some instructional training in imagery.

Make your own movie. Create a new movie in your mind about an upcoming stressor. Let's say that you're facing a competitive job interview or confronting a delicious buffet when dieting. Replace the images of yourself as vulnerable and shaky with images of yourself acing the interview and confidently declining offers of desserts and sugar-laden dishes. Then see how much better you are at handling those high-risk triggers in the future.

See yourself in a new light. Imagery can be used for specific situations, as above, or more generally. Spend five minutes visualizing yourself showing your strengths and capabilities. Imagine, for instance, that a light is shining on you, as on a film or television set. You're confidently speaking in front of a large group or patiently teaching a child to read. That positive image will spill into your daily life and efforts to change— as long as you don't get grandiose about your abilities (a drawback of many self-help tactics).

Create new scenes. Many people find it useful to collect ideas, phrases, and pictures in imagery notebooks or on goal boards. They jot down an inspiring quote or collect pictures that symbolize what they're trying to achieve. In this way, you can create new or optimal scenes in your developing film about yourself.

Read a new script. In keeping with our movie analogy, let someone else give you a few ideas and a positive narrative. You can find plenty of guided imagery exercises online by googling "guided imagery audio." Typically combined with relaxation techniques, such exercises introduce you to novel ways of seeing the world and yourself in it. For many, myself included, it's easier and more relaxing to let others' words guide you as you float along in your imagination.

Start by practicing imagery for 10 minutes daily. Some people prefer to practice twice a day, once upon getting up and once at bedtime. The amount of time spent on the task is more important than the time of day, so decide what works for you. Find a comfortable, quiet place. Decide whether you are visualizing a particular goal or a general feeling, but be as concrete and specific as possible until you acquire more experience. Close your eyes and breathe deeply. If you are visualizing a goal, vividly imagine yourself accomplishing that specific behavior: eating well, exercising joyfully, building a better relationship, depositing money into the bank, having a productive workday, or sending a basketball swishing through the net. See it as already complete, already happening. Then intensify the clarity and depth of the picture with vivid details. Capture the colors, the textures, in your mind's eye. Listen to accompanying sounds that make the moment realistic. Toward the end, take a few relaxing breaths and add a few empowering affirmations to top off the 10 minutes of imagery.

Andrew was a gifted visualizer; when he told me about his imagined scene, I could practically see, hear, and taste the bar scenes with him. He would imagine himself on a weekend frequenting nightclubs with his friends—taking in the party atmosphere, enjoying a drink or two, and living "the good life" he worked hard to attain. But in place of parting with hundreds of dollars and staying into the next morning, he now imagined himself enjoying his time, pocketing the extra money, and leaving by 1:00 A.M. In his mind's eye he created a new movie in which he enjoyed life without defeating himself. That movie soon became his reality as life began imitating art.

Acceptance

Most of us cling to the notion that we can control practically everything, that we can adapt and overcome virtually anything. But some life situations must be accepted as they are. This realization adds an Eastern or Buddhist twist to the Western faith in change.

The preceding countering methods are intended to reduce problem behaviors; by contrast, this method aims to train you to accept some problems. The first noble truth of Buddhism reminds us that life is suffering; it inevitably entails frustration, pain, loneliness, disease, and ultimately death. This irrefutable fact becomes useful because Buddhism explains how some suffering can be avoided: accept it.

Avoiding pain is, paradoxically, one of the biggest sources of suffering. Instead of relentlessly trying to change what we don't like, there are times when we can learn to accept. As Buddhists advise, invite your troubles to sit beside you.

The challenge, of course, is deciding what can be changed and what should be accepted. Uncontrollable problems, such as inclement weather and fateful accidents, are things we should accept, whereas controllable behaviors, such as overeating and gambling, are those we can change. But exactly which can we control and thus change? As the celebrated positive psychologist Martin Seligman likes to point out, life experience and scientific research point the general way, but much depends on you.

As you have seen throughout this book, we now have the tools to alleviate stress, phobias, anger, addiction, and depression while enhancing relaxation, assertion, and relationships. My own bias, as a Western clinical psychologist and university professor, is that we can change more than most of us believe—that our powers are within our own hands, to paraphrase Goethe. Even when behavior change is unfeasible or impossible, we can modify how we think about it and relate to it. For example, we largely control our physical fitness, even though many diseases have genetic origins.

Overestimating our ability to change leads to grandiose plans and behavioral wipeouts, as I call them, like surfers coming off a huge wave. On the other hand, underestimating our ability to change results in apathy, resignation, and millions of people unnecessarily leading lives of compromised health and quiet desperation. Our hope, expressed in the Serenity Prayer by Reinhold Niebuhr and adopted by 12-step programs, is:

> *God, grant me the serenity to accept the things I cannot change,*
> *Courage to change the things I can,*
> *And wisdom to know the difference.*

When you know that difference, you can counter the tenacious desire to change by learning acceptance. This skill requires considerable practice, as it runs contrary to our human need to control the world.

We can begin, like Buddhists, with meditation and mindfulness; I won't teach these two techniques here, but you'll find plenty of resources online and in other books. Breathing has always served as a cornerstone of the Eastern traditions. Mindful breathing embodies "being" instead of "doing" or "fixing," and it creates distance from the immediacy of distressing thoughts and feelings. As your breathing deepens, you calm yourself and remember that you do not need to like or endorse a problem; rather, you learn to accept that it is what it is. The problem, in reality, is not bad or good; it "just is." In this way, you eventually learn to become less blaming, less judgmental, and less distressed.

Monique, as an example, knew that genetics were against her. Going back at least two generations, the women in her family had been heavy and large. Monique didn't subscribe to genetic determinism, but she knew that weight was heavily influenced by genes. She accepted that she would never be 110 pounds again, as she had been as a teenager. Several decades, a couple of biological children, and genetics probably sealed that deal. Monique accepted that as part of her fate; as a result, she didn't feel the need to be self-damning, and she became more "settled" in her mind.

But at the same time, she acknowledged that there was no reason to be a sedentary couch potato and 50 pounds overweight. Acknowledging her DNA, she set a realistic goal to become a healthier, active 130-pound woman who controlled her emotions and fitness.

At one point, Monique muttered something about "Render unto Caesar . . . " I initially missed her reference, but then she explained how the biblical passage (Render unto Caesar the things that are Caesar's and unto God the things that are God's) related to her weight: "I give up control for things due to others but keep what I can." That's the middle path of acceptance.

To be honest, mastering the art of meditation and mindfulness will take months of daily practice, usually with a trained expert. My intent here is to instruct you in the basics of acceptance and to argue for its important role as a countering method. The healthy opposite of senselessly trying to change the unchangeable is to accept it. Acceptance is a learnable skill, not simply a slogan. When you are faced with fateful situations, as you certainly will be in life, you can develop a middle path. This will allow you to be prepared for more balanced, and effective, responses to the vicissitudes of life. Change the things you can, and accept the things you cannot.

The countering methods I've described can be used singly or in combination, and they promote the very goal behaviors that push out the old problem. Countering is a two-for-one deal: shoving aside the problem while moving toward your goal.

There are two complaints I often hear from people when it comes to these countering methods, and they will probably cross your mind at some point. Number one is that the new behavior doesn't feel "natural, like me. I feel anxious, uncomfortable." Of course! The old problem has grown comfortable over the years, and a healthy alternative will feel awkward for a while, as do most new habits. Remind yourself that the early awkwardness is a sign of growth, not a harbinger of failure. Then continue to act "as if" or fake it till you make it. Like a new pair of shoes, new habits eventually get worn in, and soon you cannot imagine how you can do without them.

The second concern is that you know the healthy countering behavior but you might not want to implement it. That's a reasonable concern, but it's precisely why I first taught you how to reward yourself. Should you experience fits and starts in countering, please use rewards. If you're procrastinating or avoiding instead of exposing yourself to a dreaded situation, start cleaning toilets or performing another chore until you confront the fear. If you're inconsistent in your use of diversion, relaxation, exercise, or assertion, arrange to reward yourself well once you do use them and remove rewards when you don't. You may even want to consider a contingency contract with a member of your change team to fortify your use of countering. Put the science of change to work!

In addition to using rewards, let's set your thinking straight: far too many people wait for energy or motivation to arrive before implementing a healthy substitute. You will recall, by contrast, that I advocate priming the pump: first implement the countering behavior and then watch your energy swell and your motivation intensify. Don't wait to strike until the iron is hot; *make* it hot by striking.

The following self-assessment aims to keep you on track and ensures that you are countering enough to be successful.

CHECK YOURSELF: COUNTERING

Answer the following questions about your behavior in the past week using a 5-point scale: 1 = Never, 2 = Seldom, 3 = Occasionally, 4 = Often, 5 = Repeatedly.

I employed behaviors that are incompatible with or replace my problem. _____
I engaged in some physical activity or relaxation when tempted to give
   in to my problem.   _____
I enjoyed doing my healthy alternative and find it to be a good substitute. _____

   Success in Perspire is predicted and facilitated by regular use of countering, a minimum of 3 on the above items. If your score is lower than that, more countering is needed. If your score is there or higher, you are on track for moving on to the next step.

Congratulations! We're halfway through the change catalysts of Perspire. See how quickly it goes when you're having fun, learning new skills, and transforming your life? Now let's move on to controlling your environment and enlisting more help from others on your journey. These two strategies are similar in that both require you to take charge of the people and things around you to foster change and avoid reverting to your old ways.

CONTROLLING YOUR ENVIRONMENT

We routinely underestimate the power of our environment to shape our behavior. That's been *the* key lesson of social psychology in the past 50 years.

Based on now-famous experiments, we know that if we were to take healthy college students and tell some that they are to play the role of prisoners and others to play the guards in a mock prison setting, we'd witness an incredible, primal transformation. Within days, the prison environment and culture would lead students into their respective roles—either submissive or authoritarian—to the point that the experiment would have to be halted because of the level of brutality displayed by the "guards" toward the "prisoners." If we were to ask a few research confederates to state that two plainly unequal lines look the same length, they would be able to get other people to agree with them. If we were to hold a fund-raiser for a good cause and introduce reluctant donors to avid volunteers, we'd watch peer pressure generate huge contributions. These three scenarios are not hypothetical; they were actual experiments that prove the power of our environment over us.

"Man is a child of his environment," Shinichi Suzuki, the inventor of a method to teach violin to young pupils, wrote. But it turns out that that's only half the truth: we shape the environment that shapes us.

In this section, I'll help you select and create a climate in which positive change can flourish. You'll learn, in other words, to harness the power of the environment; the child will become the parent.

Controlling one's environment is, sadly, the least frequently used change catalyst in dozens of our studies, yet it can be tremendously beneficial. People can be so preoccupied with examining their inner thoughts and feelings that they neglect to keep their surroundings in sync with their goals. But you will not ignore the environmental strategy, at least not if you're following the steps of *Changeology*.

We all know that a poorly managed environment can easily trigger a lapse in judgment and a quick return of the problem behavior. Consider an overeater who enters a buffet restaurant, an overspender who accepts another credit card, or a chronic procrastinator who lets bills and paperwork pile up on the desk. Borrowing a phrase from AA, I'll show you how to modify "people, places, and things" that will help, not hinder, your goals. We'll harness the power of the environment with several methods of controlling it.

Think people, places, and things. Your environment is not defined simply by where you are; it's also characterized by the people who surround you and the situation you're in. Know that you have the ability to modify your contact with people, places, and things.

Sniff out the detractors and the facilitators. The behavioral detective work that you did in the Psych and Prep steps pays off again here. You've already identified several situations that lead to more goal-oriented behavior and several that trigger more problematic behavior. If I want to stick to my exercise regimen, for example, keeping a regular work schedule increases my time at the gym, while travel and late nights lead to fewer workouts. Certain people have similar effects; when my colleagues Tom H., Mary E., and Tom S. are around and willing, I am more likely to be active. Put your sleuthing to work here by reminding yourself what detracts from and what facilitates your change.

Select, but also create. When I discuss environmental control during workshops, most self-changers talk about choosing an environment, as if they had a finite list of situations or people. But you can actually create an environment that doesn't exist yet. In the words of Orison Swett Marden, a prolific writer at the turn of the 20th century, "A strong, successful man is not the victim of his environment. He creates favorable conditions." If you don't see the appropriate environmental options around you, create the environment you need.

Bring things in. Add things to your home and work environment that remind you to keep on track: pictures on the fridge, stick-it posts on the bathroom mirror, to-do lists on your desk, reminders on your smart phone, daily messages on your computer, regular calls from special people. Recent studies show that text messages help smokers quit and reminder calls help drinkers remain on track.

Years ago I consulted with a major pharmaceutical company on a project that aimed to increase patient adherence to a complicated regimen of medicine. The problem was that the drugs were very effective but had to be taken three times a day for two weeks—"nearly impossible," as the drug company's vice president characterized it. Not so when several of us began brainstorming practical reminders. We sent the patients special plastic pill boxes for their kitchens, inexpensive watches programmed to go off three times a day, stickers for their calendars, robo-calls on the telephone if they requested them, incentives for their children to bug them, and other freebies to cue them to reliably take the medications. A little ingenuity and a lot of reminders produced 90 percent compliance (and a sweet consultation fee for me).

Populate your life with reminders and people that make it better; maximize the circumstances that promote health. The list of possible reminders is endless, particularly if you enjoy technology.

Go to www.ChangeologyBook.com to request that weekly reminders be sent to your email or smart phone.

Take temptations out. Avoid high-risk situations and people that rekindle the problem. Remove temptations from your home. Build literal barriers between temptations and yourself.

Monique found that controlling her environment was a terrific way to make steady progress toward her goal of healthier living. She actually suggested using this strategy before I did, joking that her snack drawer at work was possessed by unholy spirits. "Dr. Norcross, I swear, it opens itself and pops snacks into my mouth!" It certainly felt that way to her and to tens of millions of us in other ways.

Monique rid herself of those devilish temptations. She discarded all of the unhealthy snacks at work, politely declined trips to the doughnut shop, and didn't purchase any replacements for the things she had thrown out. She did the same at home, but encountered howls of protests from her kids until she agreed to keep small bags of multigrain chips for them in the pantry. Portion control combines "things out" (huge portions) with "things in" (reasonable amounts of foods). Her things-in list included vegetables, nuts, fruits, and other healthy snacks that were easy and convenient.

There are many creative means to alter the external cues that impact our eating behavior. We know that using smaller plates leads us to eat less. Making healthier snacks more convenient induces us to eat more of them. Repackaging foods into smaller bowls or bags decreases our consumption. Eating more consciously and deliberately, as opposed to mindlessly chomping while watching television, slows us down. But these types of proactive environmental modifications don't just pertain to weight loss. They can also be used to help us conquer practically any goal.

Andrew's attempts to stop overspending and overpartying provide good examples. He had inadvertently selected and created an environment that made it easy for him to party every weekend and waste money. His default behavior was to go out late Friday and Saturday nights with friends, drinking and spending, and it would require a huge effort from him not to be with them. As a result, he took his environment into his own hands. He made the default behavior a quiet night at the movies with nondrinking friends; he had his employer put his paycheck into direct deposit so that he was not flooded with cash on Friday; and he scheduled chores, church, and breakfasts for Sunday morning instead of sleeping into the afternoon. He constructed an environment, in other words, that supported and sustained his goal. You can do the same with a little thought and creativity.

We now know that behavior we once thought was the individual's responsibility can often be caused by the environment. Continuing with our obesity example: we used to assume that if people had more information about dieting and more willpower about nutrition, they would make better choices. But we have recently learned that our culture conspires to make it difficult for people to change, since economic and environmental factors shape what and how much we eat. Food marketing, in particular, exerts a powerful and pernicious influence on our eating patterns, as well as those of our children. At the end of the day, we adults are responsible for our behavior, but the environment influences those choices. When society regulates food marketing and increases the availability of fresh foods, we quickly find that diets improve and diabetes declines.

All of this sounds simple and commonsensical, right? Well, it is. But the vast majority of people on the road to change fail to control their environment. It's another classic instance of the insight fallacy: I know I should do it, but I never quite get around to it.

Get a leg up on your resolution by creating an environment that helps you. We are one of the few species on the planet capable of doing so. Rearrange your rewards, and create a contingency contract to cement the plan.

To help you modify your environment, here's another self-assessment.

CHECK YOURSELF: CONTROLLING YOUR ENVIRONMENT

Answer the following questions in terms of your behavior in the past week using a 5-point scale: 1 = Never, 2 = Seldom, 3 = Occasionally, 4 = Often, 5 = Repeatedly. Of course, be honest and realistic.

I kept things around my home or workplace that reminded me not to
give in to the problem.   _____
I left places where other people are encouraging the problem behavior. _____
I removed things from my home or workplace that reminded me of my
problem.   _____

A score of 3 or above on each item means that you are using as much environmental control as other people who've changed successfully. Congratulations, and keep it going! But if you score 2 or below on each item, you are mimicking those who don't succeed. Do not despair; ratchet up the power of your environment by employing the methods described in this step.

A Scientific Digression

Before pressing on, let me briefly digress so I can reveal more of the science taking place behind the scenes. I think you'll be impressed with how the three change catalysts of the Perspire step discussed so far fit together. Many of my students and clients tell me that they enjoy seeing how all the strategies work in concert (although they would not be the first to butter up their psychologist!).

You can also feel free to disregard this bit of geekish science. In fact, my wife and editor find their heads spinning when I get excited about this stuff. It works for me, but it may be a bit too much for most folks. Fair enough; do appreciate, though, that there is a lot of method (and science) behind my madness.

In earlier steps, you learned to become a behavioral detective in searching for the connections among the triggers of your problem, the behavior itself, and the consequences that follow and control the behavior. It's a well-defined sequence: triggers lead to your problem behavior, which then brings consequences. It's as simple as that. In my world, this is called a behavioral chain: one thing leads to another.

Now let me demonstrate how three particular catalysts fit together and naturally lead to solutions. Note the parallels between the behavior chain and the corresponding catalysts:

Behavior chain:	Triggers	→	Behavior	→	Consequences
Catalyst:	Controlling the Environment	→	Countering	→	Rewarding

As you will remember, *triggers* cue the environment for your problem. *Controlling the environment* reduces those triggers and temptations, as well as rearranges the environment to promote your goal. Should your problem occur anyway, *countering* replaces it with the healthier alternatives that cannot coexist with the problem itself. Finally, *rewarding* strengthens the healthy alternative and/or withdraws reinforcement from the problem behavior.

Each link of the behavior chain is covered; I love it! And you can love it, too, as you use all three strategies together. They complement one another perfectly because they address the entire chain. As one of my students quipped, "Just like the three amigos!"

HELPING RELATIONSHIPS AGAIN

Now that you have learned the first three strategies for the *roooar* of Perspire, your efforts should be aimed squarely at implementing each of them. Goethe got it exactly right when he wrote:

> *Knowing is not enough; we must apply.*
> *Willing is not enough; we must do.*

But wait, there's more, as they say in the infomercials. We also need to execute one more change catalyst—helping relationships—and avoid a three-headed demon before moving on to the next step.

Contrary to what you might assume by now, the research shows that strong helping relationships do *not* predict or favor who succeeds early in Perspire. You read that right: people on the road to change can survive for a few weeks without any social support even in the most hostile of environments. Their initial inspiration and action get them through by themselves or despite the sabotaging efforts of other people in their lives.

But once you're immersed in action for a few weeks, the quality and quantity of your helping relationships do count, and powerfully. To reiterate: helping relationships become critical at least 30 days into your effort.

Scores of research studies have demonstrated the impressive contributions of social support to your health and happiness. Ill health is more pronounced for those lacking social support, particularly for women. Simply stated, helping relationships improve our health and buffer us against the ravages of life.

The type of supportive relationship, as you'll recall, evolves from one step to another. In Plan, you can progress easily with a reassuring Socratic teacher in your court. But once you're in Perspire, you need to find an experienced coach if you don't have one on your team already. The change team you've already assembled will now be called upon for support, assistance, and an occasional challenge. It goes without saying that if you haven't seriously enlisted the help of others, now is the time to do so. Here I'll show you how to tailor your change team, make any necessary adjustments, and secure the services of an expert coach.

Listen and support. Any experienced psychotherapist will tell you that active listening and genuine support are the backbone of successful treatment. But your support team doesn't need to be composed of professionals; you can receive empathy and affirmation from all sorts of folks. Listening and being heard are extraordinarily powerful and tragically rare events in life. Cultivate and celebrate relationships that offer those.

Chat frequently. Keep in regular contact with your change team—several times a week, at a minimum, for a quick check-in and a healthy dose of support. Those recovering from hard-core addictions attend 90 self-help meetings in the first 90 days for a good reason; you, too, can check in daily for the duration of the Perspire step.

Express what you need. Your change team cannot read your mind. Do you want one of them to listen more, with fewer interruptions? Do you prefer more praise and acknowledgment? Or perhaps some concrete tips on how to navigate this roadblock? More help on a particular day? Tell them directly what you need. Be specific.

Keep it positive. What virtually everyone in Perspire needs is positivity. Ask your friends to stay positive toward your change, avoid doom-and-gloom predictions, and focus on your progress instead of the occasional slips. Firmly but graciously remind them that sarcasm, guilt, and embarrassment are not helpful forms of support!

Put me in, Coach. Assuming that you selected members of your team wisely, at least one of them will have experienced considerable success in his or her own change and will be able to offer more specific advice in terms of strategies. That person (or persons) effectively serves as your coach. Ask for tips or skills of the day. You don't need to endorse or implement every idea you receive, but you are collecting an assortment of skills. Experiment to find what works best for you.

Accept peer pressure. That term usually makes us think of the "bad influences" in school who led others into alcohol, drugs, and smokes. But peer pressure from online sites, faith communities, and work groups can also keep you on track and moving toward your goal. Monique, for instance, found that her religious community was unexpectedly helpful in following up on her progress.

Return the favor. When struggling with change, your efforts can preoccupy you and consume the majority of your thoughts—understandably so. But when dealing with friends, your efforts are probably not the central topic of their day. So ask your friends about their feelings, focus on their experiences, and balance the conversation.

Buddy up. One or more of your team may be undergoing a behavioral metamorphosis at the same time you are. But sometimes other friends and family will surprise you by announcing that they are joining you in changing their behavior. Positive health habits spread through networks of friends like a virus; researchers call the phenomenon "social contagion." We unconsciously mimic or emulate the behavior we see every day among friends and family. The buddy system works. Accept as many co-changers and training partners as your schedule can accommodate.

Race to the top. Friendly competition can spur people to greater heights. While working with other resolvers, create fun competitions. You'll reap many benefits: encouraging one another, tracking improvement, and yes, feeling guilty if you let the other person down.

Enlarge the team. Expand your notion of places where helping relationships can be found to include online support groups, work friends, neighbors, and others you did not identify in the Prep step. A fellow psychologist found it helpful to incorporate her family pet into her effort to walk more each day. She discovered that she couldn't ignore the dog's whining and urging to walk each morning, rain or shine.

Invite challenges. "Say what? You want me to invite a member of my change team to confront or criticize me?" Well, yes and no. Yes, you'll probably profit from the occasional loving correction, the caring challenge within a trusted relationship. Winning teams are candid and trusting. Decide on the rules of engagement so that you can hear the challenge and use it productively. But no, you don't need anyone to scream at or belittle you. You already do plenty of that to yourself.

Other dos and don'ts. When members of your team ask for direction, please let them know what is and what is not working for you. Dos include plenty of empathy, support, choices, availability, reassurance, optimism, and celebration. Common don'ts are lectures, impatience, mistrust, judgments, and despair. Please help your team members help you.

You can individualize your Tips for My Change Team on www.ChangeologyBook.com. Create a pithy, concise list that you can share with those supporting you.

CHECK YOURSELF: HELPING RELATIONSHIPS

Please report how frequently you engaged in the following behaviors in the past week using a 5-point scale: 1 = Never, 2 = Seldom, 3 = Occasionally, 4 = Often, 5 = Repeatedly. In the past week:

I received support and encouragement from other people for my
   behavior change.   _____
Someone listened when I needed to talk.   _____
There has been someone I could rely on when I needed help with my
   problem.   _____

People who make it through the Perspire step generally score at least 3 or 4 on each of these questions. Your score should remain high throughout the entire process of change. Remember that helping relationships become particularly crucial 30 days into your effort. If your scores are consistently below 3, you are at an elevated risk of failure. Please strengthen your social support before proceeding farther along the path.

THE THREE-HEADED DEMON

As a child in the 1960s, I was fascinated by the flick *Ghidorah, the Three-Headed Monster*, which featured a huge, ferocious beast spewing fire and wrecking havoc. It was part of the Godzilla series of films from Japan. A few years later, in junior high, I began reading about other mythological creatures blessed or cursed with three heads. One such demon was Cerberus, a three-headed hound that guarded the gates of the Underworld to prevent those who had crossed the river Styx from ever escaping. In a recent Harry Potter film, the young magician and friends must get past a vicious three-headed hound to obtain the Philosopher's Stone.

Three-headed demons occur not only in mythology and movies but also in one's quest to change. In the action step of Perspire, the demon's three heads are self-blaming, minimizing threat, and wishful thinking. *Self-blaming* is a perverse punishment that paralyzes motivation and momentum. You slide away from your goal a bit every time you resort to vicious internal name-calling—stupid!, incompetent!, loser!—and soon you're left with no motivation to continue with action. In the early days of Step 3, Andrew, for instance, started condemning himself for having overspent in the first place. Now that he was succeeding in controlling his spending for the first time in his life, he began beating himself up for his previous behavior.

Monique, on the other hand, temporarily *minimized the threat* of her alcohol use one Saturday evening during a friend's birthday party. Her "it wasn't that bad" moment sent her reeling backward into debating whether she should change, which led to a two-drink slip in her second week. Intentionally and unnecessarily subjecting yourself to temptation early on is self-defeating. I've heard of dieters stashing high-calorie goodies "in case company stops over," ex-smokers keeping a pack or two "just in case," drinkers keeping that one fine bottle of wine "for a special occasion." But like the proverbial apple in the Garden of Eden, temptation usually wins. In fact, Jim Prochaska, Carlo DiClemente, and I once discussed whether we had ever met someone who had played the "minimize-the-threat game" early in the Perspire step and won. None of us had ever met such a person.

Of course, eventually you'll need to confront your temptations, and you'll learn to do so gradually in the next couple of steps. But not in the first few days of Perspire. Keep a healthy distance from them for now, and don't underestimate the alluring power of your previous, ingrained behavior.

Monique also substituted *wishful thinking* for perspiration that one evening, before challenging the demonic thoughts in her head and resuming her action plan. She ignored the reality of her situation and believed for a moment—wished—that having two drinks wouldn't be a big deal. We all engage in wishful thinking, interpreting circumstances according to what we'd like to be the case rather than according to evidence or reality. You'll overspend during the holidays, wishfully thinking that your income will increase to cover your expenses. You'll ignore a problem colleague, wishfully thinking that the issue will resolve itself. You'll procrastinate on an important project, wishfully thinking that it'll get done on time easily.

Our research consistently finds that wishful thinking and self-blame lead to failure. These activities will defeat your efforts. The exercises and lessons revealed in this chapter will help you shun these self-defeating mental games and keep you on your path to success.

It turns out, of course, that the three-headed demon is not a monster threatening to destroy Tokyo; it's an internal monster, a self-inflicted demon. Beware and be watchful of your innate tendency toward self-blame. The following self-assessment will help you monitor the misuse of this self-defeating trio.

CHECK YOURSELF: AVOIDING THE THREE-HEADED DEMON

Answer the following questions about your thought processes in the past week using a 5-point scale: 1 = Never, 2 = Seldom, 3 = Occasionally, 4 = Often, 5 = Repeatedly.

I made light of the problem and refused to get too serious about it.   _____

I criticized, lectured, or blamed myself.   _____

I wished the problem would go away or somehow be over with.   _____

Unlike in the previous Check Yourselfs, higher scores on these items predict *failure*. Successful changeologists rated themselves a 2 on the first two items and a 3 on the last item (wishful thinking). By contrast, the unsuccessful gave themselves a 3 or 4 on the first two items and a whopping 4 or 5 on the wishful thinking item. If you are repeatedly wishing the problem away, you are probably not working at it enough.

Lower scores predict success here. Double-check your thinking as you shun the three-headed demon.

WHERE ARE YOU?

Let's bring the Perspire step to a close with a recap of where you have been, where you are, and where you are heading. We'll take a minute to look again at the road map, so to speak. You began in Psych, Step 1, for seven to fourteen days, followed by another week or two in Prep, Step 2. Now you are roaring down the highway in Perspire (Step 3), where you'll be for at least six weeks, perhaps more for those of you who are still struggling. Eventually you'll need to shift into Persevere (Step 4), where you'll handle your slips, and eventually into Persist (Step 5), where you will sustain the change forever.

How will you know when you graduate from action to early maintenance, from Perspire to Persist? Here are three guidelines to consider.

1. **You are devoting at least six weeks to Perspire.** I would love to tell you that you got the problem licked forever after a week or two, but we both realize that would be a book-selling fib. Your goal behavior will need to stabilize after the initial adrenaline rush of Psych and Plan. For most people and problems, that's six or more weeks before we can sensibly speak of moving into maintenance.

2. **You are walking the walk.** Your candid responses to the five Check Yourself exercises in this chapter should consistently reveal that you are using the catalysts associated with long-term success. Ensure that your Rewarding, Countering, Controlling Environment, and Helping Relationships scores are where they need to be. Check that your use of the three-headed demon responses falls below the threshold.

3. **You are feeling the confidence vibe.** This gut feeling is difficult to describe in precise terms, but you'll know it when you feel it. Think back to when you felt that you had largely mastered the skills of, say, riding a bike, driving an auto, or playing a sport. Not that you attained perfection, to be sure, but when you felt that quiet, realistic "I can do this."

In either case, whether you stay in Perspire or move to Persist, you'll profit from managing temptations and preventing slips back into your problem behavior. The next step is about learning to sustain the impressive action, that glorious *roooar,* of your hard work in Perspire. In the memorable words of Napoleon Hill, "Patience, persistence and perspiration make an unbeatable combination for success."

PERSEVERE: MANAGING SLIPS

Learn to say *no* and develop a plan for getting back on track after a slip. Avoid high-risk triggers, resist the urge, and keep a positive outlook. Slips need not become falls.

If you've ever watched world-class athletes compete in gymnastics or diving, you know that they try to "stick it"—to execute their performance without a slip, a wobble, or a fall. You know why we're so amazed by such an accomplishment? Because mortals can almost never do that! It's simply not human nature to complete tasks impeccably.

Once in a while, Olympians do manage to land a perfect score, but in the real world, virtually everyone falters in daily life. We all understand that when we first attempt to drive a car or ride a bike, we'll make mistakes. Behavior change is no different; it's a process of slipping, learning from the mistake, and trying again.

As you work to realize your goals and resolutions, expect to slip—probably multiple times. As Mark Twain once quipped, "To cease smoking is the easiest thing I ever did; I ought to know because I've done it a thousand times." Trying to change can be frustrating: you set a goal, you want to change, but sooner or later you err. If you understand and prepare for mistakes, however, they don't need to ruin your self-change effort.

Until fairly recently, neither behavioral researchers nor self-help authors addressed the inconvenient truth of relapse. They simply ignored the probability of relapse as though it didn't exist. It seems far more flattering to end a book or a research study on the success of achieving your goal for a week. Flattering, yes. Realistic, never. Prior to the 1990s, most self-help and treatment programs didn't even address how to respond to a single slip or a full relapse. The conventional wisdom of the time held that such a discussion might inadvertently encourage slips or create a self-fulfilling prophecy; merely talking about relapse would encourage it.

We are much wiser now and know the opposite to be true. Avoiding this important conversation about the blunders that will inevitably occur leaves people anxious and unprepared.

Fortunately, the pioneering research of Dr. G. Alan Marlatt of the University of Washington can help us minimize relapses. This step is all about persevering: understanding and overcoming the inevitable slips.

BLESSED AND CURSED WORDS

To persevere means to continue toward a goal in spite of discouragement or opposition. It speaks to the wondrous human capacity for determination, resilience, tenacity. For our purposes, to persevere is to continue toward your goal despite your urges to stop, cravings to regress, and slips on the road to success. To say that one is persevering is a true compliment, a blessed word.

In his book *The Emperor of All Maladies,* Dr. Siddhartha Mukherjee discusses the meaning of "relapse," a cursed word. "Relapse" comes from the Latin for "slipping backward" and "slipping again." Even though he writes about relapse with regard to cancer, his explanation is worthwhile: "[Relapse] signals not just a fall but another fall, a recurrent sin, a catastrophe that happens again. It carries a particularly chilling resonance in cancer—for it signals the reappearance of a disease that had once disappeared. When cancer recurs, it often does so in treatment-resistant or widely spread form. For many patients, it is relapse that presages the failure of all treatment. You may fear cancer, but what cancer patients fear is relapse."

The fear of relapse is not confined to the cancer patient. It goes hand in hand with virtually all of life's pursuits. You fear that you may fail, that you will fall backward, that you will embarrass yourself, that you cannot change. If ignored or minimized, the fear of relapse can contribute to your fall from grace. Your fear of falling can prevent you from even trying to change (as addressed in the Psych step). In your anxiety, you may even misinterpret a mere slip as a total fall.

Acknowledge your natural fear, understand its sources, and then march forward. You are persevering toward that blessed goal armed with your resilience and this chapter's skills.

A SLIP IS NOT A FALL

Practically everyone trying to realize a goal, on his own or with professional treatment, will experience at least one slip, or "lapse." A slip or lapse is a single event, a onetime reemergence of an unwanted behavior that doesn't need to lead to a fall or a relapse. So if your goal is to lose weight and you indulge in an especially delectable dessert after dinner one night, you've slipped but not fallen. With the help of a good plan for coping with slips, which I'll get to shortly, you can make a mistake without derailing your entire goal.

A fall or a relapse, by contrast, is a complete abandonment of the goal and a retreat into your old patterns of behavior. If that one dessert at that one dinner turns into a nightly habit, you've officially relapsed. You have let the slip become a fall; the lapse has graduated into a relapse.

Virtually every research study documents the high prevalence of lapses and relapses. In our studies, 58 to 71 percent of people slip at least once in the first 30 days of Perspire. The average number of slips is a breathtaking six! Slips are common—nearly universal—and understandable. As we say in psychology, "normalize it": consider it a normal part of living and learning.

Amazingly, your number of slips does not predict whether or not you will eventually reach your goal. Successful and unsuccessful New Year's resolvers, for example, don't differ in the number of their early slips. It's whether or not they permit a temporary slip to deteriorate into a permanent fall that determines who fails and who perseveres.

The good news is that you can transform slips into recommitments and resist the urge to give up altogether. We mortals accomplish this all of the time. In 1984, researchers at the University of Oregon telephoned, once a month, smokers trying to quit and found that many had sneaked a smoke once or twice but most hadn't reverted to smoking. In one of our New Year's resolutions studies, for another example, we followed hundreds of folks pursuing a mix of goals: budgeting their spending better, reducing their alcohol intake, being more patient, avoiding fast foods, improving their listening skills, learning to play the piano, and so on. By February, 11 percent of the resolvers had slipped and then fallen/relapsed, but far more—53 percent—had slipped but not fallen. Put another way, more than half had made mistakes without letting those mistakes lead to a total reversal of behavior change.

In the following pages, I'll teach you about the lapse process and how to persevere every small step of the way. The strategies entail:

♦ Avoiding high-risk triggers
♦ Practicing saying no
♦ Resisting the initial urge to slip
♦ Responding constructively if you do slip
♦ Preparing for the next time you slip

AVOIDING HIGH-RISK TRIGGERS

As you might expect, or just know from experience, a slip is typically preceded by a trigger, a high-risk situation that increases the chance that you'll return to your old ways. About 60 percent of self-changers report triggers surrounding their first slip. For instance, someone trying to lose weight might attack a pint of ice cream after a stressful day at work. Similarly, someone cutting back on alcohol shouldn't be spending his or her weeknights at the local watering hole, where drinking buddies and beer await.

Triggers can be practically anything that has historically been associated with the problem—from moods and behaviors to places, people, and physical cravings. Stress, negative moods, lack of control, positive emotions, and physical cravings lead the pack of the most common precipitants, as seen in the figure below. The figure shows the frequency of seven triggers of New Year resolvers' first slips at one month and three months.

Yes, even positive emotions can trigger slips! Emotions run wild, self-restraint takes a nap, and people celebrate in all of the wrong, unhealthy ways. With a little behavioral detective work, Andrew determined that his financial woes were commonly preceded by three events: cashing his paycheck ("and feeling that wad of money"), taking money out of an ATM ("not much good just sitting there"), and going out for a night on the town with friends. By completing the exercises and worksheets in this step, Andrew began to understand what precipitated his retreat into his old behaviors. Then he could anticipate and usually avoid the instigators that led him to squander his money.

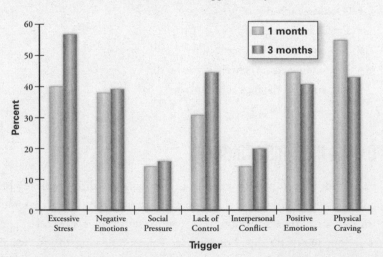

Most Common Triggers of Slips

Let's start by identifying your triggers. Ask yourself four of the classic *five W*s of newspaper writing: *where* (locations and circumstances), *what* (activities, feelings, thoughts), *when* (time of day or before or after a particular event), and *who* (people supporting or accompanying the old behaviors). For Andrew, the wheres were out with friends, the whats were happy and unplanned times, the whens were after receiving his paycheck and late at night, and the whos were a particular set of wealthy single friends who could afford a $200 Friday or Saturday bar tab.

Ask yourself these kinds of questions, observe your behavior, and become aware of your own high-risk situations. The results will inform an internal, red-alert emergency system that will go off when you are in these danger zones.

High-Risk Worksheet

 We can concretize this process by creating a worksheet to identify your high-risk situations, as shown below. Spend a few moments writing these down here or at www.Changeology Book.com. Record the situations that trigger your temptations; the entries below are some suggestions to get you started.

Beware: Danger Lurks Here

Where (in what locations and circumstances, easy access to the old behavior):

_____

_____

_____

_____

_____

Examples: Bar, bakery, smoke shop, shopping mall
Inactive, sedentary, or bored
After a fine dinner

What (activities, feelings, thoughts): _____

_____

_____

_____

_____

Examples: Feeling stressed or sad
Happy and celebrating
Struggling with cravings and temptations
Thinking "I can't do this," "It's beyond my control."

When (time of day or before or after a particular event): _____

_____

_____

_____

_____

Examples: Alone and feeling tired
After a long day and "needing to unwind"

Who (people supporting or accompanying the old behavior or triggering
stress): _____

_____

_____

_____

_____

Examples: Conflicts with other people
Social influences (friends who invite you to smoke, drink, spend, overeat, etc.)

After completing the worksheet, post it in a conspicuous place where
you can consult it regularly. Consider sharing it with your loved one and
perhaps your change team.

Reorient yourself to avoid these triggers. You can be creative here.
Andrew arranged for direct deposit instead of cashing his paycheck. To
avoid impulsive ATM withdrawals, he set a $50 daily limit on his cash
removals (with his bank's cooperation). To short-circuit other triggers, he
opted to minimize contact temporarily with his biggest-spending friends
and to plan specific fun activities that didn't cost a lot of money with
other (frugal) friends.

Minimize exposure to your chief triggers until you've built strong confidence that you can resist the temptations. Then, slowly, slowly make your way back to the people, places, and things that precipitated your old behavior. In the research, this is known as "cue exposure": gradually exposing the person to the trigger but having them perform the healthy, desired behavior.

For Monique, visiting a bar or going to a party with friends was *the* high-risk situation for her overdrinking and overeating. For several weeks, she smartly avoided parties and bars. Only after she had developed confidence in resisting temptations did she allow herself to revisit these seductive places. She made a short-term sacrifice for long-term health.

For many self-changers, the list of triggers will suffice. For others of you, however, the temptations come so frequently or powerfully that I recommend a continuous, daily log. Here, record each day the following specifics in three columns:

Triggers	Behaviors	Consequences
(where, what, when, who)	(coping strategy or slip)	(what happened and how you felt and what you thought afterward)

Whether you choose a general worksheet or a daily log, the purpose remains the same: to monitor your urges, identify warning signs, determine which of your coping responses work, and examine what transpired afterward. Your awareness and wisdom are increasing by the day, as you learn what triggers a fall and what coping responses prevent it.

PRACTICING SAYING NO

Probably the most difficult triggers come in twos or even as a group, whereby one trigger leads to another and then another. Say you argue with a friend, coworker, or family member. That's two triggers: a person and a feeling—stress and resentment. Or say you're at a friend's house for a party, and he or she encourages you to overeat and overdrink. That's a triple threat: a place (friend's house), a person (social pressure), and probably a feeling (a celebratory atmosphere). In such scenarios, it can be tough to say no.

That's why I encourage you to practice in advance for probable high-risk situations. Start by imagining a situation while in the comforts of home. Envision yourself in a scenario where temptations reign supreme. For instance, a woman in a troubled relationship imagines her partner making sarcastic or belittling remarks and feels the temptation to respond in kind. Or a smoker pictures himself outside on a stressful day with a friend who lights up; he can see the cigarette emerging from the pack, hear the flick of the lighter, smell the tobacco burning. The friend extends the pack and asks, "Want one?"

Begin in your imagination by saying no confidently and immediately. "No thanks, I don't want to bicker." "No, I'm quitting." Rehearse the scene in your head, and think of the best ways to react to the situation. Graduate to saying no out loud to yourself, and then practice with a member of your change team before saying it in a real situation. This way, when such triggers arise, as they inevitably do, you won't be panicked or feel unable to cope.

Pay attention to your feelings when you say no. Do you feel embarrassed? Not part of the crowd? Fearful that you'll lose a friend? Afraid that you'll come off brusque or offensive? Weak? Ungrateful? These feelings provide vital clues to your underlying psychological vulnerabilities. Identify and challenge the negative self-talk, and, if need be, revisit the previous step for additional work on strengthening your healthy opposites (countering) to the old behavior.

One day, Monique practiced declining drinks and smokes while standing in front of a mirror. The next day, she audiotaped herself saying no and refined her presentation. She felt at times that saying no might result in her not having much fun; she thought about that idea and concluded that it was an unfounded though natural fear. She also noticed that she hesitated when offered a drink, as though she were mulling it over and perhaps inviting encouragement. With practice, her response evolved into a firm and quick reply. She felt it, and she meant it.

After practicing inside your head, go to your support team for help. Ask them to practice with you by acting out a handful of problematic situations you're likely to encounter in the next two weeks. Virtually every goal has a corresponding skill set of saying no—drinks, food, a conflict—and all are variants of assertion training. Scores of research studies attest that practicing your firm but polite nos in advance of real-life triggers improves your perseverance.

That "No thanks" can be strengthened further by adding the *if-then* technique. Practice likely scenarios with "If this happens, I will do that." When Monique began to limit her alcohol intake, she anticipated that her friends would be pressing drinks on her. "If anyone offers me a drink," she decided, "I'll ask for a diet soda. If they ask me why I'm not drinking, I'll say that I am watching my weight and am driving tonight." Having a clear, ready response will enhance your confidence and make your "No thanks" even more convincing.

RESISTING THE INITIAL URGE

Despite your best efforts to identify and avoid triggers, at some point you'll undoubtedly confront the urge to regress into old ways. Smokers will crave a puff, overspenders will feel the need to buy, overeaters will plead for "just a bite," couch potatoes will find themselves reaching for the remote. It's the nature of change and growth.

But you can resist temptation. And so can I, usually. In fact, as I am writing this section, I'm encountering a high-risk temptation to my diet. Every time I walk to the secretary's office, I'm haunted by the sights and smells of post-Christmas goodies on the lobby table for everyone to sample. The fudge calls to me, "Just one won't hurt. Try one so you can tell Donna it was delicious." But I am resisting.

In the moment of intense temptation, you'll understandably protest, "You don't understand, John, it's just too strong! I can't stand it! I need it." And in that moment, it does indeed feel like "I'm gonna die if I don't give in to the urge."

How did I resist the siren song of temptation? How can you? Start by using the following 10 research-supported methods to resist the initial urge.

Ten Proven Ways to Resist the Urge

1. **Take a breather.** Take a few deep breaths, inhaling and exhaling slowly. Slow down your physical cravings and your runaway thinking. Relaxation will get you through a surprising number of potential slips.

2. **Knock it off.** Interrupt the thought process and challenge it vigorously. When you whine, "I neeeeeeed it!," dispute that nonsense. When you begin to believe a want is a must, forcibly tell yourself that you're not a five-year-old without free will or self-discipline. When my patients try to convince me that they are helpless, I ask simply, "Could you have resisted for a thousand dollars?" Ninety-nine percent of the time, they reply, "Of course." That proves they possess the skills to do so. Set your mind straight.

3. **Say "Yes, I can."** Remind yourself in no uncertain terms that you have resisted successfully many times before. Affirm your resilience.

4. **Walk it away.** Research shows that a brisk walk reduces cravings. For others, a slower, walking meditation works. Literally walk away your urges.

5. **Do the healthy opposite.** During periods of temptation and craving, employ the healthy alternatives that you discovered in the last step. Instead of shopping, go through your wardrobe for donations to others; instead of vegetating on the couch, get up and get active; instead of suffering in angry silence with your partner, initiate a calm, constructive conversation about your distress. Monique, for instance, decided not to visit a bar and wing joint to watch the Philadelphia Eagles game in favor of inviting friends over to her house, where she could control what drinks and eats were served. Be sure that your healthy opposites are ones that you genuinely enjoy; alternatives to triggers should never feel like punishments.

6. **Talk yourself down.** Ask your team to talk you down. They can speak with you for a few moments and support you.

7. **Distract yourself silly.** Find a distracting activity that fully engages both your hands and your mind. For me, it's getting on the computer and answering emails; for others, a good distraction might

be a puzzle, video game, or workout. Make a call, water the plants, scrub a floor, anything that will take up the couple of minutes that those cravings persist.

8. **Run away!** This is a sensible response should your urge become overwhelming. Leave the vicinity of the threat, and combine it with one or more of the aforementioned methods. When Andrew found himself in a high-risk situation with freewheeling friends, he would find a plausible reason to depart quickly—"I need to finish some paperwork" or "I need to return an urgent call." Then he would vigorously challenge his assumption that he "deserved" to engage in self-defeating behavior.

9. **Reward yourself.** As discussed in the previous steps, rewards works. When you're confronted with a craving, reinforce yourself for keeping on track. Strengthen your resolve by rewarding perseverance.

10. **Search your self.** Sooner or later, your urge to renew the old behavior will probably prompt the realization that you need to revisit your emotional reasons for the old behavior in the first place. You already accomplished much of this work in the Psych and Prep steps. Now return to those reasons for your old behavior—why you were consumed by the desire, what emotional gratification it was serving—and examine the underlying needs. Emotionally, what is not resolved is repeated. Remind yourself of the reason for your goal. Remember to use both sides (the two-headed push-pull) of the motivation: the push away from the disgusting behavior and the pull toward a brighter future. Such a process rarely stops a raging urge, but it powerfully reminds you of the psychological triggers in the past and the psychological payoffs in the future. That's the key, ultimately, to your emotional freedom.

As an aside, every psychologist is asked if hypnosis really reduces cravings. Yes, it frequently does so in a modest way. But the best hypnosis training is that which teaches you self-hypnosis. Neither is a panacea but a useful supplement to concerted self-change.

The research commends these 10 in-the-moment methods for

battling minor urges and ordinary temptations. They work well for mild and daily temptations, such as my resisting candy and cookies, but they typically don't work well for severe and intense cravings. In those cases, fighting the urges may actually feed them. This is when you need to do something called "urge surfing."

Surfing the Urge

In a famous series of experiments conducted at Yale University, participants were asked to suppress or fight a particular image, such as a white bear, in honor of the author Leo Tolstoy's challenging his brother not to think of a white bear. It turns out that trying to suppress an intense urge—for example, an image of a white bear—once it's implanted in your head, paradoxically feeds the urge. Trying to battle or not think of an intense urge magnifies it.

You can try this experiment yourself right now: Don't think of a pink elephant. Under no circumstances think of a pink elephant! How long did you last? Most people don't last a full minute without the image popping into their mind.

When to fight an urge and when to "surf" it, then, depends on its intensity. Created by Dr. Alan Marlatt, urge surfing is particularly useful for intense psychological or physiological cravings. The method derives from the Buddhist understanding of cravings as an inevitable part of life. Since some unpleasant urges will occur, we have to learn to accept the suffering they cause and develop a more mindful perspective. Then we can ride them out; we can let go without giving in.

Like any skill, urge surfing requires practice. First, practice by yourself when confronted with a minor urge. Then, after you become confident and comfortable with urge surfing, you can apply it to more intense cravings the moment they occur. For example, I began practicing with my small daily urges to eat sweets in my university department and private practice office. Friendly folks frequently bring in and share cookies, brownies, candy, and cakes. When I had become successful at avoiding those, I graduated to surfing the immense urge to eat breathtaking chocolate desserts at the end of a meal in a restaurant.

Here's how to develop the skills of urge surfing. Practice these steps for a few minutes, ideally in a comfortable, quiet place with no distractions, sitting down:

1. Imagine your urges as powerful ocean waves that arrive, crest, and then recede. They begin small, grow, then break up and dissipate.
2. Remember that urges, like big waves, pass by in a few moments.
3. Begin breathing slowly. Don't alter your breathing consciously; let the breath breathe itself.
4. Now visualize yourself surfing on an ocean wave. Don't fight the incoming wave; instead ride on top of it like a surfer.
5. Notice your thoughts. Without judging them, feeding them, or fighting them, gently bring your attention back to your breath.
6. Notice the craving as it affects your body. Focus on one particular area where you feel the urge, and notice what is occurring. Take note of its quality, position, and intensity. Notice how these change over time and with the in-breath and out-breath.
7. Be curious, like a behavioral detective, about what occurs and notice that the cravings pass in just a few moments—just like the rhythms of a wave.

The aim is to replace fighting or fearing the urge with relaxation and curiosity about it. We can become interested in the craving and watch it as if from outside ourselves—the cravings rise, crest, and subside like waves in the ocean. Fighting feeds the urge; nonjudgmentally watching it lets it subside and pass. Of course, such mindfulness requires practice, much as actual surfing does.

"For the life of me," Monique lamented, "I cannot resist sweets." And no wonder: for a lifetime she had given in to temptation and had never developed the skills to resist. What's more, she found that sweets led to a glass of wine and a smoke—a cascade of urges and responses that seemed to flow together seamlessly. Perseverance was certainly the most difficult step for Monique to master on her path to becoming a changeologist.

Monique started using the 10 proven ways to resist the urge, and they worked about 90 percent of the time ("the best I've ever done in my life"). She was understandably pleased. And she was amazed by the effectiveness of surfing the urge when she practiced in my office. She discovered her capacity to stand back, observe what was happening in a detached manner, and think about what she was doing rather than being on automatic pilot. She learned to watch the urge pass. Her cravings didn't need to dictate what she did.

Monique was particularly taken by the urge-surfing technique of seeing through the "PIG." The pig is a greedy, impulsive animal with a ravenous appetite; it stands for the "**P**roblem of **I**mmediate **G**ratification." The pig shows up, grunting "I'm starving. I'm craving. Feed me now." If you respond by giving the pig what it demands, it gets bigger and stronger. It begins to control you. When your pig says, "Give me, give me, give me now," talk to it. Relax, observe, become mindful. Remain in control.

I have found that identifying and surfing the PIG is a powerful method for many people, including psychotherapy patients and myself. Those of you who are having difficulty with the more abstract image of surfing the urge might prefer visualizing a loud, disgusting PIG demanding to be fed. See it rummaging; hear it grunting; smell its stench. That vivid image can help you experience the urge as something external and alien, something you can observe curiously rather than fight.

Surfing the urge didn't come easily or naturally to Monique at home; for most of us it's a new skill to be acquired. She practiced the exercise twice a day for a week. Until she mastered urge surfing and could resist temptation close to 99 percent of the time, she would rely on a slip plan, to which we now turn.

RESPONDING CONSTRUCTIVELY AFTER A SLIP

Your efforts to avoid high-risk triggers and to resist the initial urge have borne fruit: you are less likely to experience slips than during previous change attempts. Well done, friend!

But in spite of your valiant effort, you're human, you're not perfect (yet!), and you'll probably slip. What then? You'll respond constructively to the slip and prevent it from leading to a fall/relapse. In this section, I'll show you how to do so, beginning with a brief explanation of the chain of events that leads to relapse.

First, it helps to understand relapse as a process, a systematic chain of psychological events. A high-risk trigger arises, and at that point you have two choices. One choice would be to respond by using the techniques we just outlined; you could try one or more of the 10 ways to resist the urge, or you could surf the urge. You would feel more confident about your ability to maintain your goal or resolution, you would not slip, and you would be back on track. You would even feel stronger because you overcame the temptation.

The other choice leads to danger. After the high-risk trigger, you respond ineffectively and, as a result, feel weak, unconfident, embarrassed, guilty, incompetent. Monique, for example, began thinking, "Maybe I can't change these addictions. I don't have the willpower." A return to her old behavior began to look and feel more attractive. She temporarily expected positive outcomes from the old behavior. She rationalized that "a cigarette would be relaxing" and "a drink or two would hit the spot with a smoke." She ignored the negative consequences of "This cigarette will make me want to smoke more" and "Drinking brings a host of more problems."

Those two feelings—decreased self-efficacy and an attraction to old behaviors—conspire to instigate a slip. If you aren't prepared, that slip can provoke a torrent of nasty thoughts about your incompetence and your inability to keep on track. In the research, we call this the Abstinence Violation Effect (AVE), a psychological pattern that leads you to elevate a single slip into a disastrous fall.

Please don't feel intimidated by the research jargon; you already know the AVE by other terms. It's the saint-or-sinner complex, all-or-nothing thinking, the black-or-white view of life. If you subscribe to the AVE, you slip and immediately think, "Well, there's the proof of my inability to keep the goal. I might as well quit now and return to my old, comfortable behavior." Or, in a former patient's memorable observation, "If I slip and have a drink, I might as well go and get drunk." Of course, that's utter nonsense, but that's how many of us think after experiencing the disappointment of a slip.

How you respond to the slip—*not* the slip itself—determines which choice you make. If you lack an optimistic spirit and/or an effective plan for dealing with slips, more often than not you'll give your urges free rein and descend to the lower road. Once you understand how the relapse chain works, you're beautifully positioned to take the high road and blast that all-or-nothing thinking.

Here's how decades of scientific research and thousands of effective New Year's resolvers have prevented a slip from becoming a fall. The essence of these slip-busting strategies can be summed up as follows:

Slip Busters

Say it and believe it: A slip is not a fall. One swallow does not a summer make. Dispute the AVE. If you believe a slip will lead to a relapse, it probably will. If you believe a slip is a natural reminder to recommit, that's what you'll do. You control your mind, and your mind controls the outcome of a slip.

Go positive. Focus on what you have already accomplished, not the exception of a slip. You've succeeded 99 percent of the time since you committed to your goal. Are you really going to allow the 1 percent to determine how you proceed?

Think big picture. The path to relapse is filled with potholes of pessimism and despair. Instead of thinking "This slip is evidence I can't do it," look at the bigger picture: "To err is human, and I have faith and a plan not to repeat the slips." Yes, you've made a mistake, as we all do, but you haven't been defeated or even knocked down. Think of a slip literally: you did not fall, you caught yourself first.

Condemn the behavior, not the person. Avoid feeling guilty or depressed because of a single exception. Remember that you're human and it was the behavior that was temporarily derailed—not you.

Get back on the horse immediately. The old saying works. It's imperative to get back on the horse right away after you fall off. Return to your goal promptly, and focus on your next step.

Take one small step at a time. Twelve-step groups advise their members to take things a day at a time. Monique adopted "one thing/one day" as her personal motto because it encapsulated a proactive, realistic view of behavior change and reminded herself of her goal each day.

Unwrap the urge. To the extent that your strong urges to return to the problem express needs and feelings out of your immediate awareness, you can unwrap those urges to discover some underlying meanings. Take a few moments and reflect on your urges: What do they want? What feelings or images come to mind? Does a craving have a story or history to tell? In this way, you can understand the PIG and thereby transform it into a less insistent and harmful creature.

Learn from it. Studies show that if you view a slip as a learning experience and a natural part of behavior change, you're less likely to relapse. Respond to the slip as you would to other behavioral mistakes in life: use it as a learning experience; figure out what you did wrong and how to correct it next time. A Slip Card, presented in a few pages, is an excellent vehicle to do just that.

All these slip busters direct you to respond constructively to the slip. It's not a fall; it's not total success or total failure; it's an understandable and natural part of growth; it tells you that it's time to get back on track; it's a learning experience. You can persevere, think optimistically, and recommit immediately. In fact, slips can actually reinforce your resolve.

"Say what? A slip can actually strengthen me and my goal? What kind of psycho mumbo jumbo is that?" That's the typical response when I coach self-changers on this point.

In our studies, we found that 71 percent of New Year's resolvers felt that a slip had strengthened their commitment to their resolution. We probed further and asked, How so? The figure below summarizes their inspiring responses. Twenty-five percent of them said that a slip had rekindled their resolution, 13 percent said it had induced guilt, 10 percent said it had increased their awareness of their problem's severity, 10 percent said it had helped them refocus or refine their plan, and 10 percent said it had induced them to get back on track. And 6 percent confessed that the slip had intensified their drive to prove to themselves that they could do it.

All of these (and other) methods will collectively help you to recommit to your goal following a slip. In the words of President John Quincy Adams, "Patience and perseverance have a magical effect before which difficulties disappear and obstacles vanish." Such was the case with an impressive 71 percent of our research participants and with millions of successful changeologists.

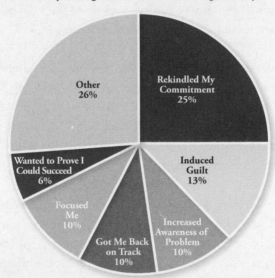

How a Slip Strengthened Resolvers' Change Attempts

- Other 26%
- Rekindled My Commitment 25%
- Wanted to Prove I Could Succeed 6%
- Induced Guilt 13%
- Focused Me 10%
- Got Me Back on Track 10%
- Increased Awareness of Problem 10%

PREPARING FOR THE NEXT TIME

All of the planning in the world won't necessarily prevent your first slip from happening. The good news is that a slip can be very informative, and even necessary, in helping you create a solid plan for future challenges. Once you've slipped, you'll want a plan that incorporates lessons learned and prepares you better. Otherwise, again you'll be like that skydiver sewing his parachute after he jumps. Let's adhere to the Boy Scout motto and be prepared.

Begin building your slip plan by identifying what you were thinking, what you were doing, what you were feeling, and whom you were with when you slipped. Not surprisingly, your answers will overlap with your high-risk triggers, identified earlier in this chapter.

Andrew first slipped when he thought that his money was sitting in his bank "not doing much." He was feeling lonely and decided to go clubbing with Ralph, "a trust fund baby with big appetites." Andrew also discovered that he was making tiny movemnts back to his old behavior. He made the decisions even though he knew they were leading to a probable downfall. For him, the triggers were lining up: thinking that his money was wasting away, his feelings of loneliness, and the invitation from Ralph to go out and socialize.

In your slip plan, you'll turn those triggers around and phrase them as the healthy opposites. Andrew learned to reverse his thought that saving is wasteful and remembered that saving protects his future; he stopped clubbing and found ways to advance his career by spending time elsewhere; when he felt lonely, he scheduled time for fun and friends; he avoided hanging with Ralph and socialized with financially prudent friends; and so on. What to think, what to do, what to feel, and who to do it with are the four categories that form the basis of your slip plan.

Here's Andrew's detailed slip plan for his overspending and conflicted relationships.

ANDREW'S SLIP PLAN

GETTING BACK ON TRACK AFTER I'VE SLIPPED

What to Think

Slips are just part of a process, an obstacle to overcome rather than a roadblock.

I know what to expect when a slip occurs—I have a plan.

I can meet my goal; it is not impossible or beyond my control.

I remember why I wanted to change, and I have not forgotten the negative effects of my problem.

A slip can rekindle my commitment.

Saving is strength for tomorrow, not a wasteful tonight.

Rather than wallowing in shame, I can immediately resume my plan and carry on.

What to Do

Avoid my triggers in the next week: Ralph, nightclubs, and expensive places.

Remind myself of the negative outcomes of the troubles.

Take a breather; get out of the situation immediately.

Engage in a healthy opposite—work for a while and distract myself.

I don't need to continue an argument; I can de-escalate just as I would at work.

Practice saying no more frequently before I'm in the situation.

What to Feel

Embarrassed by my slip but not about me.

Concerned that I slipped but not worried or depressed.

Determined to succeed despite obstacles.

Confident that I will succeed in the long run.

Cautious of triggers.

Glad that I recognized my mistake and that I am managing it.

Whom to Contact

Call Jack and maybe my parents.

Hang with my change team to combat loneliness.

Reach out for support immediately, don't wallow in self-pity for a day or two.

Now craft your own slip plan in terms of what to think, what to do, what to feel, and whom to contact. Yes, it will take a few moments, but the payback will prove huge. This road map shows you how to acquire effective strategies to prevent slips from becoming complete relapses.

_____'S SLIP PLAN

GETTING BACK ON TRACK AFTER I'VE SLIPPED

What to Think

What to Do

What to Feel

Whom to Contact

One of the best ways to prepare for future slips is to create a Slip Card, a pocket-sized cheat sheet designed to help you overcome slips the moment they occur. Your slip plan forms the basis for the shorter and punchier Slip Card, which you can carry with you. Record the dos and a couple of don'ts.

If you prefer, you can go online and create a Slip Card at www.ChangeologyBook.com.

Here, as an example, is Andrew's slip card.

ANDREW'S SLIP CARD

DO

Leave the situation immediately after slipping.

Reminder: a slip is *not* a fall. It can rekindle my commitment.

Remember that slips are part of the change process, an obstacle to overcome rather than a roadblock.

Feel embarrassed about the behavior, but not me as a person.

Know what to expect when a slip occurs—I have a plan.

Immediately start on a healthy alternative to overspending and conflict.

Call Jack and maybe my parents.

Reach out for support immediately.

DON'T

Overspend my way out of it.

Blame others for the relationship conflict.

Wallow in self-pity for a day or two.

Give up; one swallow does not make a summer.

Here's a blank slip card for you to complete. Make it shorter than Andrew's; a few dos and don'ts from your longer list. Carry it in your pocket, purse, or wallet through the next few weeks. Put it with your driver's license or your credit cards. Consider sharing it with your change team. You can also go online to personalize it, and print it out with your name on it.

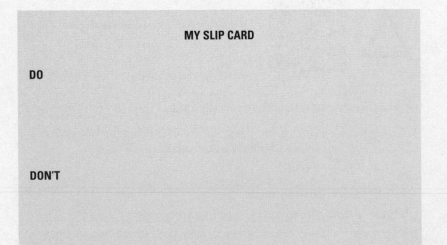

MY SLIP CARD

DO

DON'T

MOBILIZE YOUR CHANGE TEAM

During my clinical training, a favorite supervisor asked me how I would take an old refrigerator to the curb for disposal or recycling. I was surprised by the question but replied, "I would get a friend or a family member to help me move it." The supervisor responded, "That's right. A big project requires more than one person."

Achieving your goal, resolution, or transformation in 90 days is a big project. It requires more than one person. Now is the time to further mobilize the change team you created during the Prep step.

Getting social support for your self-change matters big time in the long run. Research consistently shows that the amount of help you receive from important people in your life predicts success a month into action. Not in the short run, mind you: it seems that we can muddle through on our own for a few weeks even in an unsupportive crowd. But in the long run, support becomes crucial.

Here you'll seek the support and guidance of others. They'll help you avoid high-risk triggers and practice saying no. They'll remind you to resist the initial urge to slip and offer constructive ways of responding if you do slip. For many resolvers, it helps to have members of the change team listed on the Slip Card, so you might want to think about adding them to that, too. Your team members are your consultants, your relapse prevention specialists.

As part of your training in Changeology, you have learned the skills of perseverance and the methods of relapse prevention. The essence of this step is keeping slips from turning into falls. We are working for the best but preparing for the worst.

Relapse is a process that can be thwarted at many points. You have learned how to: distinguish a slip from a fall, identify high-risk triggers, practice saying no to temptations, resist the initial urge to slip, respond positively if you do slip, and prepare for the next time. That next time you'll use your slip card and engage your change team.

Before moving on to the final step of Persist, let's conduct a self-assessment to ensure, in fact, that you are using these skills with sufficient frequency and effectiveness. Remember: it's not enough to simply *know* about these skills; it's essential that you actually *use* them.

CHECK YOURSELF: MANAGING SLIPS

Answer the following questions using a 5-point scale: 1 = Never, 2 = Seldom, 3 = Occasionally, 4 = Often, 5 = Repeatedly.

I am convinced that a slip does not constitute a fall.   _____

I am minimizing my exposure to triggers that may precipitate a slip.   _____

I am practicing saying no to requests to regress to my old behavior.   _____

I am skillfully resisting in-the-moment urges with the 10 proven methods. _____

Intense or prolonged cravings lead me to "surf the urge."   _____

I am maintaining a positive outlook, such as attending more to the
   numerous times I succeed than to the rare times I slip.   _____

If I slip, I condemn the behavior and situation, not myself as a person.   _____

I am learning from my previous slips which thoughts, behaviors,
   feelings, and relationships predispose me to slips.   _____

I am practicing the slip-busting methods as needed.   _____

I am on the lookout for any tiny steps backward that will lead me down
   the slippery path to relapse.   _____

I am carrying my Slip Card with me each day.   _____

I am reaching out to my change team for support as soon as I need it.   _____

I am aware of the negative consequences of my old behavior.   _____

If I do slip again, I feel prepared to respond constructively.   _____

Your ratings on these items should be at least a 4 (meaning "often") and preferably higher. In our studies, successful self-changers average close to 4. If so, you are skilled in Perseverance, and I congratulate you on your mastery of this step. Kindly proceed to the next chapter and the final step.

If you are not yet scoring 4s, please rework the respective skills in this step. Your occasional use of these methods places you at higher risk for not only slips but also eventual relapse.

We mere mortals cannot perfectly stick to our goals without slips or wobbles. None of us is a superhero; few of us are Olympic athletes. What we can achieve is another sort of stickiness: perseverance, persistence, resilience. As John D. Rockefeller observed, "I do not think there is any other quality so essential to success of any kind as the quality of perseverance. It overcomes almost everything, even nature." Perseverance certainly overcomes slips and is absolutely essential for *Changeology*.

STEP 5

PERSIST: MAINTAINING CHANGE

> **WEEK 12 AND BEYOND**
>
> **Keep using the strategies that maintain the new you. Have backup plans for those inevitable slips. Remind yourself that you can do this! Sustain self-change over the long haul.**

If you have been working the *Changeology* program, you're now a month or two into achieving lasting change. You deserve a hearty congratulations! You've steadily and successfully stepped from Psych to Prep to Perspire. You've learned how to use the right change catalysts at the right time and to avoid step mismatching. You've probably experienced temporary lapses but learned to Persevere. You are now entering the final step—Persist.

Even as you feel the pride of your success and bask in your accomplishments so far, residual anxiety remains. One of my patients perfectly encapsulated this mixed feeling when she remarked that Persistence felt like the opening line in Charles Dickens's *A Tale of Two Cities:* "It was the best of times, it was the worst of times." Best of times because she had realized her goal and was enjoying her new self; worst of times because she feared that success would not endure.

Almost every day I witness a failure in persistence, starting with a trail of slips. My research assistant informs me that she flosses her teeth for only three weeks after each dental visit and then gives up when the free sample of floss runs out. My golf partner concedes that his improved swing lasts about as long as the next round of golf because he fails to practice it as he once did. A patient admits that she returns to yelling at her spouse and "forgets" her new communication skills within a couple of weeks after their session with me. And my healthier eating and commitment to more exercise "magically" disappeared when I visited New York City to celebrate my son's birthday at a French restaurant.

None of these instances resulted from a dramatic relapse or a wrestling match with temptation. Instead, it was a slow, somber, almost incidental passing thanks to a few sequential, and sometimes seemingly minor, slips.

For all of the attention that we've paid to perseverance in the last step, many failures do not result from a sudden, volcanic eruption of a relapse; rather, it's frequently a gradual, almost imperceptible drift away. Failure announces its arrival with a soft whisper.

The previous step, Persevere, was about overcoming obstacles and lapses; this step, Persist, is about maintaining change over time. You need to master both in order to permanently establish your new behavior.

In the first part of the book, I outlined one of my research studies that demonstrated the power of moving from one step to the next. You nearly double the probability of your long-term success by graduating from one step to another. Congratulations again! Your efforts, as opposed to good intentions or boastful talk, exponentially improve the odds of succeeding months after starting.

That same study, however, also revealed an inconvenient truth. Success rates do gradually decline over time. That's why we take you through 90 days. The challenge is not just to get there but to stay there. All too often, people are on fire for four weeks but then turn to ashes for 48 weeks thereafter. And, as seen in the figure on page 23, most relapses occur within the first 90 days.

Persistence requires the mastery of a series of skills and a fundamental shift in thinking; lasting change is a marathon, not a 100-yard dash. And the challenge is to persist for not just 90 days but for a lifetime.

Otherwise we mimic the Greek mythological figure of Tantalus, the source of the English word "tantalize" and the proverbial description of goals beyond our reach. You may recall that Tantalus's punishment was to stand in a pool of water beneath a fruit tree with low branches. Whenever he reached for the fruit, the branches raised his intended meal from his grasp. Whenever he bent down to get a drink, the water receded before he could get any. His reach always exceeded his grasp.

This final step of Persist will help you avoid the curse of Tantalus. You'll learn how to:

+ Acquire proven methods for maintaining your new behavior
+ Boost your self-efficacy to continue your goal for a lifetime
+ Understand the spiral of change through the 5 steps
+ Distinguish between self-changes that end and those that require a lifetime of perseverance
+ Celebrate your success and end your journey through *Changeology* on a realistically positive note.

Throughout, several Check Yourself exercises will keep you on track, and, at the close of the book, I'll tell you about the joyful endings for Andrew, Monique, and me.

MAINTAINING NEW BEHAVIOR

When psychologists speak of *maintenance,* we refer to the consolidation and continuation of behavior change across time, usually after treatment ends. In this case, you'll be in maintenance following the completion of this book. Maintenance is more than preventing relapse. The word "persist" describes the intentional, active pursuit better than the laissez-faire, status quo "maintenance."

The core of this idea is embodied in the distinction between a *diet* and a *lifestyle.* The dreaded D word, diet, connotes limited, short-term deprivation. By contrast, lifestyle refers to a continual, long-term goal that enhances your life. When you think of persisting with your change, think of it as moving forward, as continually improving, as giving yourself an ongoing gift.

Monique understood this concept as she graduated from Perspire to

Persevere and then to Persist. She began the change process thinking that she needed to deprive herself of smokes, sweets, and drinks. She demonstrated her ability to live without them but did so reluctantly, begrudgingly, as though she were "missing her best friends." Monique battled her cravings and urges successfully but gradually learned that they were wolves in friends' clothing. The "friends," in actuality, were slowly poisoning her health, self-esteem, and relationships. She discarded the notion that she was depriving herself of her favorite things or penalizing herself in favor of giving herself good health. Short-term deprivation evolved into long-term self-care.

That's the cornerstone of persistence: it doesn't feel like dreary work anymore, it feels like healthy fun. Sure, even fun activities require some effort and sweat, but we perform them with an eager, vital attitude.

Here are scientific, time-tested methods that will prepare you for the long haul.

CONTINUING THE ACTION CATALYSTS

When you were perspiring (Step 3), you were constantly tracking your progress, calling on helping relationships, rewarding yourself, countering when necessary, and controlling your environment. You were, or should have been, working hard. That's the physical and psychological meaning of *perspire*.

The good news is that you will continue using these same strategies during persistence. They should be pleasant, almost automatic habits by now. The better news is that now you can tone down or moderate your use of them. You continue them all but will probably discover that you don't need to use them at the same rate and can reduce their frequency. In saying this, I always worry that some people will take it as license to breeze through Persist. That, as Andrew painfully discovered, would be a colossal error.

Andrew was riding the crest of success, having beaten back most of his demons. But he was feeling so improved and confident that he lost his way. He fell prey to overconfidence—"I got this beat!"—and the concomitant "My work is done." There was no volcanic relapse but a gentle regression in his behavior: he stopped calling his support team, he failed to reward himself for obtaining goals, he discontinued his budgeting, and he returned to the nightclubs and overspending. It all occurred gradually over three or four months.

Andrew experienced a dramatic reversal of gains, a poignant lesson for all of us on the failure to persist. The moral of his story: reducing your use of the change catalysts in the Persist step doesn't mean stopping them completely!

Do not despair about Andrew's plight, because we caught it in time. Andrew is now enjoying the healthy fun of long-term persistence, and he is much wiser and humbler as a result of the experience. We'll circle back and speak more of Andrew's temporary reversal in a few moments. But let's now review the formula for change that you've learned throughout this book and then turn to the action catalysts you will continue to use.

The Formula for Change, Redux

If change is a journey, the formula for change provides the map or GPS. It tells you when to turn, what to avoid, how fast you can go, and even where the rest stops are. Let's briefly return for another look at our map, originally introduced in Part I of this book.

90 days:	1 to 7–14	7–14 to 21	7–14 to 60	60 to 90	75+
Steps:	1. Psych	2. Prep	3. Perspire	4. Persevere	5. Persist
Tracking Progress					→
Committing					→
Raising Awareness		◉			
Arousing Emotions		◉			
Helping Relationships					→
Rewarding					→
Countering					→
Controlling Environment					→
Managing Slips					→

As you can see, you're mismatching if you're raising awareness of the problem and arousing negative emotions during this final step. The research convincingly tells us that using those strategies will send you reeling backward because you question the wisdom of your changes, begin blaming yourself, and engage in torturous rationalizations. It would be like a traveler who was two-thirds of her way to a destination suddenly questioning if she really wanted to travel in the first place!

On the other hand, the map tells us what to use from here on out. These are already firmly established in your repertoire, so we need only mention them again with the new wrinkles as they apply to persistence. "That which we persist in doing becomes easier," Emerson reminds us, "—not that the nature of the task has changed, but our ability to do has increased."

Tracking Your Progress

You have used this strategy throughout the 5 steps, probably to your great benefit, and you'll continue to use it with a few twists. Of course, tracking progress enables you to monitor your behavior closely and to detect any regression quickly. Andrew, by the way, conveniently "forgot" to track his progress for the first two months into Persist; that was the first and obvious tip that he was not persisting.

Here, you'll track your progress to determine: (1) which of the action catalysts are making a prime difference for you and (2) which environments (people, places, and things) prompt you to regress. At this point, not everyone is equally helped by all of the strategies. Tracking will enable you to decide which are absolutely critical to your maintenance and which can be tapered.

Likewise, closely observing your behavior will allow you to pinpoint the people, places, and things that precipitate regression. Yes, you did so in the last step when you identified your high-risk situations for a lapse. But here you'll do so again, focusing on more subtle regressions in your behavior than the explosive relapse.

Here's an example from my own life: Traveling and sampling the local cuisine pose the greatest threats to lapses in my fitness regimen and weight management. Under those circumstances, I'll temporarily reduce exercising and start eating comfort foods (especially club sandwiches, French fries, and local desserts). However, those circumstances prove *not* to be the triggers of subtle regressions. That dishonor falls to a frenetic workweek when I don't schedule the time to exercise regularly. My triggers for a sudden relapse are quite different than those for a gradual decay.

In Persist, you monitor your progress less frequently than in the earlier steps. Instead of weighing yourself several times a week, you might move to once a week. Instead of checking your budget every week, you may check it every two weeks.

Consider the ten thousand members in the National Weight Control Registry, all of whom have lost 30 pounds or more and maintained that loss for at least a year. The vast majority of members persist in tracking their food intake, counting calories or fat grams, and weighing themselves at least once a week. They engage in other behaviors, of course, but the point is that they have not stopped tracking their progress. They must not stop what is working for them!

Search for the people, places, and things that trigger any gradual slide in your goal behavior. Keep doing your behavioral detective work, and identify which strategies work best for you. Even in Persist, what is measured is improved.

Helping Relationships

Your change team was front and center during your perspiration days but is probably declining in prominence as you enter the final step. Monique, for example, was telephoning at least one friend daily during action; now, in maintenance, she is calling a friend two or three times a week to discuss her progress and secure support. That's understandable and effective, as long as she doesn't let her team and the support vanish altogether.

In the Prep step, we built your change team and evaluated its success by means of a Check Yourself. Let's repeat those same items, and this time please respond not as you are about to undertake the momentous change but as you are now persisting in that change.

Answer the following questions using a 5-point scale: 1 = Never, 2 = Seldom, 3 = Occasionally, 4 = Often, 5 = Repeatedly. In the past week:

I received support and encouragement from other people
   for my behavior change.   _____
Someone listened when I needed to talk.   _____
There has been someone I can rely on when I need help
   with my problem.   _____

   In Perspire, successful self-changers generally score a 4 or 5 on these questions. In Persist, your score can decline slightly, to 3 or 4. That's the magnitude, in concrete numbers, you can cut back on using these strategies. Going below that poses a real danger.

Continue to cultivate your change team to maintain your goals. You can choose people other than friends and family members for support; slowly add in neighbors, peers, coworkers, and perhaps online support groups. All of those people will become both cues to continue and potential sources of reinforcement.

Long-term social support acts like a buffer between us and the harsh realities of the world. Support never eliminates the ravages of life, but it does diminish them like a safe harbor during a storm. Heed the conclusions of dozens of longitudinal studies in psychology: maintain helping and loving relationships for 90 days and beyond.

So far, you've been *receiving* help from others, but in persistence, you'll also *offer* help to others. The twelfth and final step in 12-step groups involves helping others who are struggling with similar troubles. In Alcoholics Anonymous, for example, the step is: "Having had a spiritual awakening as the result of these steps, we tried to carry this message to alcoholics, and to practice these principles in all our affairs." Helping heals both those who receive it and those who give it.

Humans thrive on behaving altruistically and giving back. Volunteer for a cherished cause, or commit an hour or two a week to a charitable organization. You'll likely feel pride and gratitude, experience a sense of mastery, and expand your helping relationships even further. Again, Ralph Waldo Emerson put it beautifully: "It is one of the most beautiful compensations of life that no man can sincerely try to help another without helping himself."

Rewarding

One reason you can now rely less on helping relationships is that support and reinforcement increasingly come from within. Support from others fades (but never disappears) as your support for yourself blossoms. Naturally occurring self-rewards—positive self-statements and feelings of accomplishment—now predominate.

The magnitude of the rewards also fades. In the early going, rewards should be immediate and intense. In the long haul, rewards should be intermittent and meaningful.

It's been repeatedly proven that when we reward ourselves sporadically, we increase the chances that we continue toward our goal. Intermittent reinforcement leads to a high rate of response and intense resistance to stopping. It is, quite literally, "addictive." Gradually go from rewarding yourself continuously to rewarding yourself sporadically.

When she was young, my daughter once asked why I didn't get as excited anymore that she could ride a bike without training wheels by herself. I tried to explain that once a skill is mastered, we still celebrate but we do so internally and modestly. That's the rule for rewards during Persist. You begin to internalize, own, or literally become the change. Once it was outside of you as a distant goal; now it's part of you as your ongoing behavior. Occasional social support from others and intermittent self-affirmations keep it going strong.

Remember: studies show that long-term successful changeologists use more self-rewards and more positive self-statements. Keep on indefinitely with small contracts with yourself: attend to your health and goal before pursuing leisure activities.

Countering

The countering behavior, the healthy substitute for your problem, obviously helps you to maintain your goal. If you do the healthy opposite, the problem is solved. Voilà! As Buddhists say, "If we are facing in the right direction, all we have to do is keep on walking."

You may immediately inquire, "Dr. John, how long do I need to engage in that healthy substitute? How far do I need to keep on walking?" Those are fabulous questions, but they reflect the change-is-deprivation mind-set. A healthy substitute—relaxation, assertion, exercise, straight thinking, acceptance, and so on—ideally becomes part of your permanent lifestyle, as opposed to a temporary solution. And if it's healthy and working, why would you consider stopping?

For example, Monique continued eating mindfully, slowly, and always sitting. She countered her propensities to eat on the go, over the sink, and while watching television. Those self-taught behaviors became automatic, lifelong habits.

In his initial unsuccessful experience with Persist, Andrew abandoned his countering of spending with saving. His overconfident "I've licked this problem" caused him to stop the healthy substitute. He knows better now and is enjoying his second, successful experience with Persistence. Andrew learned what millions of self-changers have painfully learned: countering works only if it continues.

What happens, though, when you get bored and plateau with the countering? Well, you return to the strategies and add some variety and novelty into the mix. Spice it up by using interesting variations that are aligned with your preferences. Tired of the treadmill for exercise? Add walking outside, cycling, power walking, Pilates, or stretching. Switch the rewards—find new television shows or movies to watch, and then treat yourself to them when you complete the exercise. Getting complacent with the muscle relaxation? Alternate it with meditation, yoga, prayer, or singing.

If you ever get stuck looking for new techniques, I recommend three solutions: refer back to the earlier steps in this book; surf the Web for novel ideas; and ask successful changeologists. There's an inexhaustible supply of methods to activate catalysts while breaking plateaus and reversing complacency.

Controlling the Environment

In Perspire, you harnessed the power of the environment to promote your goal. You added people, places, and things into your life that supported change, while minimizing people, places, and things that triggered slips. Members of the National Weight Control Registry, for example, limit the number of times they eat out and avoid huge meals on holidays and special occasions. They understand the delicious lure of tempting environments.

In Persist, you continue to avoid the most alluring temptations while safely exposing yourself to some potential triggers. I covered this earlier, saying that in the addictions field, this is known as *cue exposure*: you slowly expose yourself to the cues or triggers that you avoided in the early days of your change. Such exposure allows you to practice coping responses in a wider range of high-risk circumstances. If you want to eat more healthfully in restaurants for the remainder of your life, it was a smart move to temporarily avoid those high-risk situations. But it's downright unrealistic to avoid them forever (particularly if someone is treating you to dinner!). So, in Persist, you'll both limit the times you dine out and safely practice in restaurants to exercise your new skills.

When I consistently began to decline sweets, pastries, and most desserts, I needed to carefully avoid not only the foods but also the whole set of sensory cues and surrounding contexts (sometimes known as the cue network or cue context). Sure, I enjoyed eating the food, but also I loved the aroma, the appearance, the dining with family and friends, the social reinforcement, and so on. A visit to a bakery or a walk through an outdoor food market could spell disaster after I began eating more healthily, so it was wise for me to avoid those environments for the short term. But in the long term, I deliberately reintroduced myself to those same situations, all without eating and without any reinforcement. Over time, I could look at and smell the desserts and I could admire the pastries without eating.

If you, like Andrew, want to return to taverns and nightclubs that used to cue overdrinking and spending, you'll safely and slowly confront the sight and smell of alcohol in a club for a brief amount of time. Then you'll use your arsenal of coping skills for dealing with the urges caused by such cues.

For all of Andrew's hiccups in maintaining his goals, he grasped this potent idea almost immediately. He constructed a plan and called it Safe Passage, using a boating metaphor of sailing between dangerous shores. After an entire month of avoiding the clubs, he began to allow himself one hour at a club per weekend with a maximum of two drinks. No buying drinks for others. No hiring limousines or heading out to expensive postclub restaurants. No telling friends that he would see them the next night. He gradually confronted the treacherous shoals, came away unscathed, and strengthened his coping abilities.

Safe passage for the rest of us entails avoiding high-risk triggers and cues during the early days of change and then gradually exposing ourselves to them and learning to cope with them constructively in the latter days of the journey. If you only avoid them, you fail to learn how to master them in the contexts in which they are likely to occur.

So, when asked whether it's more effective to avoid tempting situations or to learn to master them, you'll answer in the manner in which science directs us: "Yes, both. Avoid in the early going, and practice safe exposure and coping in the late going." In other words, use step matching: different things for different times.

BOOSTING YOUR SELF-EFFICACY PERMANENTLY

Earlier, we discussed and assessed your self-efficacy to change—how confident you were about achieving a particular goal. You may recall that that assessment was one of the best predictors of accomplishing your goal. In this step, we'll examine another type of self-efficacy: the realistic confidence to *maintain* that change over time.

Think of self-efficacy as a house, one that can be built by hard work and success or destroyed by the lack of same. Sixty days into your change, your confidence in your ability to continue grows. You build your own self-efficacy house. Success begets more success; success also begets more self-efficacy, which enables you to persist for 90 days and beyond.

To assess your self-efficacy, select the behavior for which you're in Persist. Remember that self-efficacy is behavior- and situation-specific, not a global evaluation of your self-esteem. Then make a list of a dozen situations, from the least difficult to the most difficult, in which you are tempted to give up. For each of those situations, evaluate how confident you are that you could persist with your goal/target behavior on a scale from 1 (not at all confident) to 10 (supremely confident).

Jonathon, my son and a contributor to this book, set a goal (target behavior) to drink a maximum of one diet soda per day. Phrased more positively, as every goal should be, his target is to drink healthier beverages. He unfortunately picked up the nasty habit of diet soda drinking from "a weak-willed paternal influence." As of this writing, he has restricted his daily intake of diet soda to one a day for two months and is fully immersed in maintenance. Here is his self-efficacy assessment for that goal.

JONATHON'S SELF-EFFICACY FOR CONSUMING HEALTHIER BEVERAGES

Situation or Feeling	Confidence Rating (1–10)
Going for a walk	10
Reading a book	8
Surfing the Internet	8
Feeling stressed	8
While working	7
Offered a diet soda by a friend	6
Eating out at a restaurant	6
Afternoon caffeine energy boost	5
Morning caffeine fix	4
At a movie theater	4
Pressured by his father to join him for a diet soda	3
The only other choice is disagreeable (e.g., tomato juice)	3

This exercise led Jonathon (and his father) to several realizations. First, he was quite successful in a variety of tempting situations. Second, he immediately identified his weak spots—the morning caffeine fix, the movie theater, and a resistant father who was not joining in the game plan. Third and relatedly, he can now focus on those risky triggers and develop alter-

 native plans. That's how he constructed his self-efficacy house.

Here's a blank Self-Efficacy exercise for you to complete. Do so for each behavior in Persist here or at www.ChangeologyBook

.com (where it will automatically compute your average self-efficacy rating). Do so by rating a range of situations (work, school, home) and feelings (sad, happy, relaxed). Do so separately for each goal.

MY SELF-EFFICACY FOR _____

Situation/Feeling	Confidence Rating (1–10)
_____	_____
_____	_____
_____	_____
_____	_____
_____	_____
_____	_____
_____	_____
_____	_____
_____	_____
_____	_____

Once you've completed the exercise, examine your ratings. Allow yourself, like Jonathon, to bask momentarily in your multiple successes. You have graduated to persistence by, well, persisting! Where are you the least confident? Is there a pattern?

Building Self-Efficacy

When I present public lectures or professional workshops on the science of change, by far the most frequent question is: How do I remain motivated and avoid sliding backward? It's asked at virtually every presentation and by practically everyone who consults me personally, usually in a tone that says, "Yes, big researcher and university professor, exactly how are you going to keep me going, since I've never done so in my entire life?!"

We tackled relapse prevention and I taught you perseverance skills in the last chapter, but persistence and self-efficacy factor here big time as well. So, at the risk of redundancy, let's take a few paragraphs to remind you of the strategies you can use to bolster your self-efficacy. Many of these methods repeat what has already been said, but repetition strengthens them.

- Success begets success; the most robust and genuine source of self-efficacy is success, while failure erodes it.
- Tip the balance in favor of the pros over the cons of changing. Complete another pros and cons exercise (online or in Step 1) and ensure that the pros are growing while the cons are shrinking.
- Think like the little train that could—I think I can, I think I can—in realistic terms. The train could not fly to the moon, but he could make it over the mountain. Stay positive but realistic.
- Keep rowing whether you feel motivated or not; of course, it's easier to remain motivated if there is a strong wind at your back pushing you forward. But "if there is no wind, row" as a Latin proverb wisely advises us.
- Focus on your high-priority goal, and don't dilute that commitment by undertaking too many new behaviors at once. Like a muscle, willpower can become fatigued and weakened. Sequence your lower-priority goals over time.
- Continue rewarding yourself; give yourself material incentives to maintain change.
- Congratulate yourself for small progress; take credit for your success in overcoming obstacles.
- Monitoring your behavior reminds you of that progress; tracking yourself keeps you on track.
- Calibrate the balance between self-support and social support; both boost self-efficacy.
- Observing a friend or peer succeed at a task strengthens your own confidence to do it; mimicry improves self-efficacy. Watch others grow and assist them.

- Seek encouragement from people, further reading, and the Internet; a few soothing words can significantly increase your confidence in a task.

- Keep and read a list of the harmful effects of your undesirable behaviors; you will remember how your life has improved.

- Maintain a list of the positive aspects of your behavior change; that will remind you of how far you've come.

- Negativity is the bane or opposite of self-efficacy; guard against negative statements about your goal, either to yourself or to others, and immediately replace them with positive statements.

- Think optimistically and realistically; focus on the 95 percent of the time that you are successful, not the few times you aren't.

- Periodically revisit a list of your top five values in life; think about how your change is linked to those values.

- Revisit the vivid pictures and self-affirmations of success created during the Psych step; practice and internalize them as a present actuality, not a future possibility.

- Remember the power of old environments to trigger old behaviors; safely and slowly approach those high-risk situations.

- Control your environment by avoiding pessimistic or scolding people; naysayers tend to decrease your self-efficacy and should be avoided.

- Practice the relapse prevention skills; it's not enough to know about them—put them into action.

- Doing the healthy opposite should become routine and almost automatic; it's impossible to simultaneously engage in both your goal and your old behavior.

- Interpret fear as fuel for change; successful changeologists feel fear, too, but they believe such feelings are normal and unrelated to their ability to maintain change.

- Invent your own "gumption reviver"; Sir Francis Galton once created that machine to wet his head periodically to keep him motivated during his long hours of study and research. What serves as your periodic reviver?

How many of these boosters should you utilize? Apply all that work for you, of course. And don't fret about the workload; these are methods that you have learned, practiced, and assessed throughout your voyage in the book.

Before moving on in this step, let's complete a brief Check Yourself on maintaining self-efficacy. This one is not nearly as situation-specific as the exercise you just completed, but it is as telling.

CHECK YOURSELF: MAINTAINING SELF-EFFICACY

Here are the two potent questions that will serve as your self-efficacy guideposts through Persistence:

How much realistic confidence do you have in your ability to maintain the changed behavior?
If you temporarily slip, how much realistic confidence do you have in your ability to get back on track?

Answer these questions "None," "A little," "Some," "Much," or "A great deal." The successful answer "Much" or "A great deal." The unsuccessful maintainers in our studies typically reply "Some" or "A little." On which side of the continental divide do you fall? If you are falling short here, please rework the respective steps earlier in the book. Don't sabotage all of your prior work to get there.

Remember, self-change does not require that you go it alone. Reach out to a support group, the Internet, or a professional for the added boost. Appendix B offers guidance on locating practitioners who will meet your needs and goals.

90 DAYS AND BEYOND: THE LONG HAUL

When interviewed by the media about New Year's resolutions, I speak of the difference between a 100-yard dash and a marathon. Change is not a mad dash; it's a marathon. Albert Einstein observed that "It's not that I'm so smart, it's just that I stay with problems longer."

No one would expect to master chess, tennis, or calculus after only a few lessons. But we harbor unrealistic expectations for personal growth, as though it should take only a single try or a few hours. Confront that nonsense!

One of the most vile, insidious prevarications of many self-help authors is the guarantee of spontaneous success. They promise superfast, 24-hour, magic-bullet results. That's a bogus claim and bogus self-help. Nowhere, no way has that ever been substantiated by scientific research. Any charlatan can recruit a few disciples to attest to an overnight miracle, but that's not science and it's not truthful.

To be sure, you may well experience dramatic success once you hit Perspire, but we both know that weeks (or months) of foundational work in Psych and Prep have paved the way for that success. Sustainable lifestyle changes take 90 days to come about.

As you know by now, matching particular catalysts to certain steps markedly reduces your workload, concretely shows you the way, and increases your effectiveness. This is a scientific breakthrough but not an instant guarantee or heavenly miracle. So let's square our shoulders and think realistically about change: it will take 90 days to reliably incorporate a new behavior.

The Spiral of Change

More than 30 years ago, when my colleagues and I began investigating how people changed their behavior on their own, we initially conceptualized people who move steadily and linearly through the steps:

This model accurately captured any single and successful attempt, but it's as rare as a dodo bird sighting. As you've learned, relapse is the rule rather than the exception. The vast majority of people will follow the above model three to six times before they reach the promised land of Persist for good. Linear progression is possible but a rare bird.

As a consequence, we needed to modify our original model to show that self-changers typically cycle through the steps several times. Our next scheme looked like this:

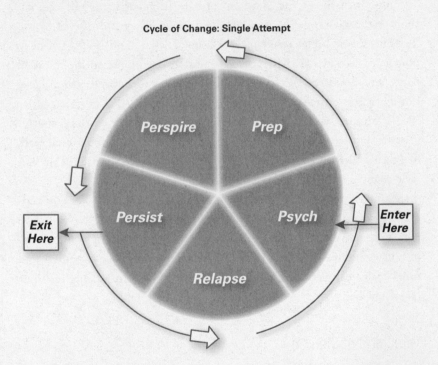

This wheel of change provides a more realistic look at how change actually occurs. People enter into Psych, progress to Prep, and then Perspire. If successful, they will Persist and then exit the cycle of change. In any single attempt, however, most will fail at persistence and then relapse, winding up back in Psych for another turn around.

Although the cycle of change proved far more realistic than the linear model, it was not yet quite complete. People were "going around in circles," as Billy Preston wailed in his old song. The cycle failed to recognize that we grow over time and progress with each subsequent change attempt.

Thus, the linear model gave way to the cyclical model that, in turn, gave way to the spiral of change. The spiral or helical pattern illustrates how most people actually move through the steps. A colleague once characterized it as the "double helix of behavior change," a complimentary allusion to the secret of DNA.

The spiral demonstrates that people do not revolve endlessly in circles, nor do they progress all the way back to where they began. Rather, self-changers recycle through the process, learn from their mistakes, and then marshal forward, wiser, for the next time. The route to behavior change is not a straight, linear line; it's a spiral path upward.

Spiral of Change: Multiple Attempts

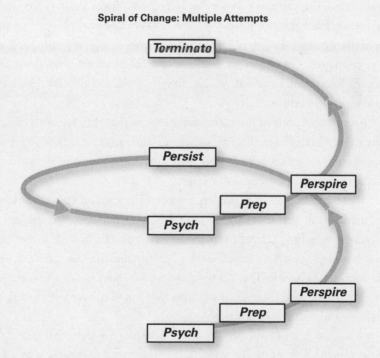

Living the spiral of change is a lot like walking the steps of the leaning tower of Pisa, as my long-term collaborator, Dr. Jim Prochaska, describes it: you walk upward for a while but then begin to travel sideways. It certainly can feel at times as though you're simply going around and around, but soon you discover you have, in fact, been progressing upward throughout. Keep that image and that realistic optimism with you.

DOES IT EVER END?

"Great is the art of beginning, but greater is the art of ending," according to Henry Wadsworth Longfellow. But does a spiral ever end? Do self-changers terminate the problem, reach their goals, and exit the path? Or are they forever persisting, always recovering but never recovered?

Researchers and practitioners have been arguing these questions for the past century and, to be honest, have become sadly polarized into two rival camps. On the one side are the Lifers, who insist that we are always recovering from most problems, always on the edge of slipping back into the darkness, and that success comes only with complete abstinence and hypervigilance. On the other side are the Terminators, who insist that most problems can be ended, we can fully recover, and that moderation is an achievable, realistic end.

An objective look at the controversy reveals that they are both correct. Like most dichotomies, this one generates more heat than light. In truth, some problems can be terminated. But other problems and personalities need to commit to a lifetime of Persist.

You can terminate the problem and exit the spiral if three conditions are met during Persist: (1) your temptation to regress or relapse across triggers is very low; (2) your self-efficacy to maintain is high across situations; and (3) you have established a healthy lifestyle that precludes the old problem behavior. That's 0 temptation, 100 percent confidence, and a solidly supportive lifestyle. If all three line up, you have triumphed, recovered, and terminated the problem.

What do I mean specifically by a healthier lifestyle that precludes the problem? The word "lifestyle" is as freely tossed around these days as Halloween candy on October 31, but my meaning comes from the compound word. Lifestyle literally refers to a permanent, affirmative style of life that stands in opposition to the negative behavior. It's not possible, for example, to live a sedentary lifestyle when exercise has been routinely and desirably incorporated into your daily activities for a year or so. The two simply cannot coexist. You have not only rooted out the old but have also built in the new, which is incompatible with the old.

A healthy lifestyle reflects the fact that you are becoming, growing into the kind of person you want to be. You continue to use the catalysts because they feel natural and positive and they are grounded in the conviction that maintaining change keeps your highly valued lifestyle intact. You think, "I can't imagine myself any other way." Your focus has changed from problems to growth.

Here are quick examples of terminated problems. I once made it a goal to floss my teeth each and every morning. Today I experience no temptation to relapse, have absolute confidence that I will do it, and have done it every morning, even when traveling, for the past 10 plus years. Monique's cigarette smoking also has been terminated. It took several months for the final cravings to pass, but they did, and she now encounters no temptations. Like many ex-smokers, it also took several months for her to develop 100 percent self-efficacy across high-risk triggers, but she did. She has been smoke-free for years, and when we last met, she said, "I can't believe it was even ever part of my life."

In correcting his partner-a-week debacle, Andrew also achieved termination. He worked the 5 steps hard and furiously. Despite his setbacks with the clubbing and drinking, he "got that one [relationships] right once and forever." Married now for several years, Andrew has 0 temptations, 100 percent confidence, and enjoys a meaningful, committed monogamous relationship that precludes his former problem.

Another recent example of termination absolutely floored me. After presenting to health care professionals at a hospital in another state, I was approached by two familiar faces that I vaguely recognized but couldn't quite place. The couple smiled and began talking, and then I instantly identified them as a couple I saw for marital therapy some 20 years earlier. They were health professionals who had relocated after only five or six therapy sessions, among the most contentious and grueling sessions of my early career as a clinical psychologist. In those sessions, they had been ferocious with each other, and when I had tried to intervene, they had turned their anger onto me. We all realized that I was seeing them then at their very worst: during a stressful relocation across the country, aggravated by the fact that they both came from dysfunctional families and had lousy communication and conflict resolution skills. Surely, I remember telling myself, if there were ever a couple that would wind up chronically distressed or divorced, it would be those two!

Yet, over a quick cup of coffee before I ran to catch my flight home, this couple told me that they had leveraged those few combative couple sessions and a weekend couples retreat into a lifetime of marital happiness by working together. I had to pinch myself to make sure that I was not dreaming; they had made it, they had exited a destructive relationship and created a new one—another reminder of the wonders and possibilities of change, even in the most unexpected of cases.

To be realistic, I should warn you that not everyone will achieve the ideal triad of 0 temptation, 100 percent self-efficacy, and a healthy lifestyle. For some personalities and problems, the temptations or cravings have been too strong for too long. Alcoholism and weight problems, for most people, fall into this category. Maintaining sobriety for life strikes most mental health professionals as a realistic position. Monique's temptations to drink and my cravings for junk food place us among those who will struggle for a lifetime.

Of course, that doesn't mean we will relapse. But it does mean that we'll need to continue to use the change catalysts to reduce the power of those triggers and beef up our self-efficacy. We'll persist with a new lifestyle that squelches the old problem. That lifestyle will preserve our hard-earned gains and will promote growth, but we have not—and honestly, may never—achieve 0 temptations and 100 percent self-efficacy. We're probably Lifers, and we're grateful to know it so we can avoid the pernicious yo-yoing of addictive behaviors.

Are you a Lifer or a Terminator for a particular goal? Answer these three questions:

1. Do you experience very low (close to 0) temptations across your prior triggers?

2. Is your self-efficacy to persist very high (close to 100 percent) across various situations?

3. Have you established a healthy lifestyle that precludes the old problem?

If you respond yes to all three, congratulations: you've exited the spiral of change for that goal. If you respond hesitantly or negatively to any one, please join Monique, Andrew, and the mass of humanity in long-term persistence.

Remember to adopt the middle ground in the debates on whether we can ever end or exit behavioral ailments. You'll definitely prove to be a Terminator on many counts; otherwise, we would all still be wearing diapers, crawling on our knees, and learning how to talk. We all exit the spiral of change on some goals and resolutions. At the same time—and in no way contradictory—we all are Lifers on other counts. That's a commonsense, research-supported position that simultaneously acknowledges our growth and respects our limits.

ANDREW, MONIQUE, AND ME

By this point in the book, you might be feeling as though Monique and Andrew are your personal friends. You've been through the 5 steps and a lot more together, and certainly you can relate to their multiple failures and some of their problems (self-esteem, eating, smoking, drinking, finances, relationships). The trajectories of their self-changes should also sound familiar: several initial failures before using step matching, years of despair, short-lived successes followed by painful relapses, a return to disillusionment and inaction, and finally success with the assistance of *Changeology*.

Before we depart, let me bring their respective stories to a close. With apologies to Sleeping Beauty and Prince Charming, their stories do sound like real-world fairy tales. Even the most grizzled of psychologists, hearing these tales of hope and triumph, would feel their eyes well up, as I certainly did during our final meetings.

Monique, you'll recall, typified so many people who struggle with addictions that temporarily bolster their abysmal self-esteem. She began our consults self-medicating with sweets, cigarettes, and alcohol—she was a "fat, nicotine, and booze hound," as she once put it. The Changeology system demystified the change process for her, and she learned to take on a maximum of two major goals at a time and then sequence the others. That's precisely what she did.

For years now, Monique has lived a life of confidence and security without tobacco or unhealthy weight. She exemplifies the Terminators with regard to self-esteem, weight, and tobacco. But even fairy tales occur in reality: Monique accepts that she is a Lifer with regard to alcohol use. She has not relapsed in many years, but she acknowledges a lifetime of recovery. Instead of calling herself a "fat, nicotine, and booze hound," Monique feels like a rich and svelte superstar. Not quite as rich as most true superstars, but wealthy in love and work. She telephones me every couple of years when she sees me appear on a national television show. She impresses me with every contact as among the happiest people I have ever been privileged to meet. I was a witness to her rebirth.

Andrew's changes proved to be a bumpier ride (I could have done without several of his thrills, to be honest). But ultimately, his success was equally satisfying. He fell prey to overconfidence and relapsed on two occasions, returning to excessive clubbing and overspending. However, he learned from those mistakes, got back on the horse, and eventually rode into the sunset. As I mentioned a few pages ago, Andrew has enjoyed the married and monogamous life for years now, sending me a holiday card with a photograph of his growing, charming family. Another rebirth I was privileged to midwife.

And me? Well, the progress on my own changes will bring us back to mundane reality—more like a television reality show than a fairy-tale movie. I'm grateful for more than my fair share of termination behaviors, such as flossing, exercising, and even undergoing that damn colonoscopy. But I struggle to persist on my weight control and overworking, and please, please don't even ask me about my daily consumption of caffeinated diet sodas.

IN CLOSING

As we take our leave, let's celebrate. Now and into the future, *Changeology* will increase your effectiveness and efficiency of losing weight, overcoming addictions, improving loving relationships, becoming less angry, and achieving scores of other life challenges and resolutions. All of those changes will result in your becoming freer, happier, and healthier. That's good reason to celebrate.

Such realistic optimism is not only deserving but also part of the change process. Don't let the naysayers and Puritans convince you otherwise. There is a tight link between celebrating your growth and perpetuating that growth. Whoop it up, feel rightfully proud, spread the cheer and encouragement. You can pay it forward to others and yourself.

Please learn to value your changes, even if they are less than or shorter than you originally desired. Critical thinking demands that we compare one outcome with another outcome. The alternative outcome for your simply wishing to change and not doing anything is zip (well, actually a 4 percent probability of success, as seen on page 22). Even temporary or incomplete change certainly beats nothing at all. That's the stance I ask— no, I implore—you to adopt as you look at your own spiral of change.

Monique, Andrew, and thousands of fellow travelers whom I have been privileged to study and coach for 30 years have transformed themselves, have been behaviorally reborn. They realized their goals, resolutions, and, yes, dreams. Self-change is no longer a temporary process but a permanent part of their healthy lifestyle. They, and now you, have become certified changeologists.

EPILOGUE

THE ADAPTATION OF CHANGEOLOGY

More than 100 million Americans resolve to change their behavior every January. That's more than one in three adults, but only a third of them succeed. What separates those who triumph from those who falter is the essence of this book.

The Changeology program, rooted in the 5 steps, has assisted tens of thousands of research participants to overcome dozens of behavioral ailments, from smoking and drinking to the patterns that lead to obesity, depression, unrelenting stress, and relationship distress, among others. Whether you aspire to start running marathons or to reduce your carbon footprint, *Changeology* affords you the structure and practical to-dos to make it happen within 90 days.

What else can *Changeology* do for you? Two of the questions I routinely get and I haven't yet addressed are the following: How can the system help one deal with forced, involuntary change? How can it improve society, perhaps even the world?

Those are fabulous questions, for there are just as many, if not more, people who are compelled to change something in their lives due to unexpected circumstances, such as job loss, death, divorce, or any event that shifts the status quo and demands that one adapts immediately. And we don't want to simply stop at the individual level of behavior change; we desire more systemic transformations in the health of the community as well.

This book has largely covered the changes we, as individuals, willfully make—the goals and ambitions we set out to achieve and the behaviors we attempt to modify. The good news is that all the lessons you've learned and the insights you've gained can help you with virtually any change—whether against your will or not. The strategies of Changeology can most definitely help you to manage involuntary change. The fact you've gotten this far in the book means you've likely changed at least one thing in your life for the better. This program can prove incredibly useful for dealing with all the demands that life throws at you.

If there's one overarching theme that this book intends to express, it's that *we can change.* We can adapt to life even when we're not 100 percent confident in that change from the get-go. Let's join our voices and yell it from the rooftops: self-change is possible, prevalent, and learnable! Even for involuntary and societal transformations not of our own making.

I wholeheartedly believe that the changes we seek at societal levels must start with each one of us. It may feel overwhelming and dubious to think that a single person can use the principles of *Changeology* to create massive change in an entire system, be it financial, economic, educational, or health. But for just a moment believe in the power of incremental change that amounts to massive transformation over time. Confucius said, "To put the world right in order, we must first put the nation in order; to put the nation in order, we must first put the family in order; to put the family in order, we must first cultivate our personal life; we must first set our hearts right."

Kristin Loberg, my collaborator and wordsmith on this project, encouraged me in this epilogue to "go big and bold, to demonstrate how the science of self-change can contribute to larger transformations in the world." She didn't need to prod me too much, as every clinical psychologist ultimately aims to repair the world, if only by one person every 50 minutes. I don't intend to go all 1960 hippie or 2013 New Agey on you. Of course there is a difference between one person stopping smoking and an entire species reversing global warming. Admittedly so, on one level. But on another level, the change process is quite similar.

My long-term colleague Dr. Jim Prochaska has immersed himself in societal transformation by matching the steps of change and their relevant catalysts for the past decade. He treats the entire state of Rhode Island as his laboratory for reducing obesity, smoking, depression, bullying, diabetes, skin cancer, and more. His wife, Dr. Jan Prochaska, has successfully applied the system to business organizations and social welfare organizations across the country. Another collaborator, Dr. Carlo DiClemente, has applied the steps to reduce alcohol abuse around the world via the Web. The British Humanist Association runs a Resolution Revolution each year to get more people volunteering and doing things to help others that is based on our research on New Year's resolvers. It can be, and has been, done.

Behavior change, however monumental and complex, is achievable by most anyone because of two fundamental facts that I've been instilling in you since the beginning of this book. For one, the catalysts that produce lasting, positive change are eminently teachable—and learnable. They are the heart and soul of *Changeology*. And two, we humans are incredibly resilient creatures. I've witnessed people who believed they were doomed to mediocrity transform their lives in a matter of weeks by implementing some of these catalysts, gaining a little confidence to keep going, and securing a modicum of human contact and support.

Throughout these pages, I've emphasized the value of making choices, learning skills, bolstering competence, and accepting responsibility for your behavior change. Please plant these ideas in your mind as you move forward and assume better control of your life and, in turn, your health and happiness. Every January 1, if you want to make just one realistic resolution for the New Year, make it to refresh your mind about the Changeology strategies and to reinforce where you are along the 5 steps for either behaviors you've started to modify or new ambitions on the horizon.

My ardent hope is that I have given you plenty of direction and skills to begin to make a tremendous difference in your life. I don't expect you to execute all of the ideas in this book or to transform your lifestyle overnight. Some of you may have read this entire book in one fell swoop, and now you're going back and actually applying the strategies over 90 days. Getting this far in the book means you've gained an awareness that puts you in a select group of people; that research-informed awareness will help you make the needed changes to live a more actively conscious life that will endure the test of time.

I know, in concrete terms, the value that feeling in control of your life and health brings because I see it day in and day out. I also see what ill-confidence, defeatism, and chronic failure breed in humans, no matter how privileged they are or how many people love them. Without the ability to change, life is much more difficult. But when you have the tools to adapt, many things are possible.

Whatever you hope to gain from reading this book, whether you think you're a bona fide changeologist or not, I hope that you at least embrace its call to personal action. As Paulo Coelho put it in his book *The Alchemist*, "There is only one way to learn. It's through action. Everything you need to know you have learned through your journey."

The person of action and the changeologist are one and the same. Be the change you wish to see in the world—and bring that self-change into the world.

ACKNOWLEDGMENTS

My life has been blessed in so many ways that I practically gush about my good fortune. I hail from a loving family that gave me both roots and wings. Three great brothers, to whom this book is dedicated. A superb education at Rutgers University, the University of Rhode Island, and Brown University Medical School. World-class mentors and collaborators on self-change in Drs. Jim Prochaska and Carlo DiClemente. Thousands of research participants teaching us how to change and what to avoid. Thousands of psychologists rating self-help resources and distinguishing the useful from the awful. A bevy of dedicated research assistants and splendid colleagues at the University of Scranton. Skilled psychologists and psychiatrists as office mates over the years. The best patients a clinical psychologist could have. A rewarding career combining teaching, research, and practice. A supportive wife, two wonderful children, and now a couple of rug-rat grandkids. I am eternally grateful to them all.

To top it off, I now have the pleasure and privilege of applying a lifetime of research to assist others in this book. A host of gifted professionals contributed to the effort.

Rich Benci started the adventure by encouraging me to update the stages of change in a new book bolstered by the interactive power of the Internet. He was instrumental in connecting me with ShareCare, Dr. Mehmet Oz, and Candice Fuhrman, who introduced me to my agent extraordinaire, Bonnie Solow. Bonnie expertly and patiently guided me through the book proposal, auction, launch, and foreign rights translations. Every author should have such an agent who pays attention to details and gives her creative energy and leadership every step of the way. Eric Watkins and Jack Reager of Blackout Design constructed a stellar Web page and enhanced our online presence. They are the humans behind the architecture of www.ChangeologyBook.com.

Trish Todd led the way brilliantly at Simon & Schuster. She polished the prose, streamlined the message, and improved our ability to connect with self-changers. I am forever grateful to her entire team: Molly Lindley, Kelly Welsh, Lynn Anderson, Jessica Abell, Jackie Seow, Richard Rhorer, and especially my publisher, Jonathan Karp.

My final, heartfelt acknowledgements go to my contributors, Kristin Loberg and Jonathon Norcross. What proud father wouldn't rave about his own son? But he has requested that I skip the mushy stuff and simply say, "Thank you, son. Well done." All the more reason to express deep gratitude to that writing marvel, Kristin Loberg. Her ability to translate my highfalutin science and impenetrable jargon into crisp, clear language is breathtaking. She tolerated my impatience and delays with therapeutic talents that would do any psychologist proud. It's been a pleasure, Kristin, and I am in your debt.

APPENDIX A

RECOMMENDED SELF-HELP RESOURCES

Self-help is concerted, self-initiated efforts to modify your behavior without professional treatment. However, it does not mean that you cannot, or should not, turn to useful books, films, websites, and support groups for additional assistance. You probably know that already; after all, you are at this moment reading a self-help book! But it's worth underscoring one point: self-help does not need to be a lonely or uncharted journey.

This year, in fact, more people will read a self-help book, attend a self-help group, and receive psychological advice from the Internet than will visit a mental health professional. We know from research that self-help is *the* major pathway to behavior change. More folks "do it" on their own than with the help of mental health professionals.

The rub lies in which self-help resource to trust and use. The self-help market has yielded an overwhelming, bewildering array of choices. Of the estimated 3,000 self-help books published annually, more than 95 percent are published without benefit of controlled scientific research on their effectiveness or safety as stand-alone self-help. Sifting through information on the Internet is like taking a two-year-old on a walk: the toddler picks up a few pretty pebbles but accumulates lots of garbage and dirt. Mental health professionals might know the difference between the good and the bad online, but rarely is the average person able to judge.

The self-help market resembles a Persian bazaar with proliferating choices but without clear answers: should you nurture others or nurture your inner child; seek success or simplicity; just say no or just do it; confront your fears or honor them? As the volume and accessibility of self-help soar, the question of quality becomes urgent.

Since 1998, colleagues and I have conducted research on the utility and quality of self-help resources for a myriad of behavioral disorders and life challenges. Our quest has been to guide mental health professionals in recommending useful self-help to their patients as well as consumers in selecting effective resources. Our research results were published in several editions of the *Authoritative Guide to Self-Help Resources in Mental Health,* which we recently updated and renamed *Self-Help That Works.* We appreciate the special permission of Oxford University Press in allowing us to share select results in this appendix.

On the following pages, I list the most highly rated self-help books and autobiographies for 20 of the most frequent goals of self-changers. The list is grounded in the results of our 12 national studies that secured expert consensus on effective self-help from nearly 5,000 clinical and counseling psychologists. Consensus, even expert consensus, promises no guarantees, but I prize these resources over individual judgments, arbitrary selection, or best-seller lists. (And, for the record, we receive no monetary compensation for recommending any particular resource. Our only incentive is helping people and professionals.)

Please use this appendix to guide your choice of self-help that fits you and to circumvent less effective remedies. Pick the categories that pertain to your goals, and then decide whether you would be most likely to benefit from a self-help book or an autobiography. (Those interested in the top-rated self-help films can find them at www.ChangeologyBook.com.) Or perhaps choose a personalized combination of several. Whatever the case, let thousands of professionals guide your selection and administration of self-help that will maximize your success.

Anger

Prisoners of Hate by Aaron T. Beck
The Anger Control Workbook by Matthew McKay and Peter Rogers
Letting Go of Anger by Ronald T. Potterby-Efron and Patricia S.
   Potterby-Efron
The Dance of Anger by Harriet Lerner
Angry All the Time by Ronald T. Potterby-Efron

Anxiety Disorders

The Anxiety and Phobia Workbook by Edmund J. Bourne
Mastery of Your Anxiety and Panic III by Michelle G. Craske and David
   H. Barlow

Mastering Your Fears and Phobias: Workbook by Martin M. Antony, Michelle G. Craske, and David H. Barlow

Overcoming Shyness and Social Phobia by Ronald M. Rapee

Worry by Edward M. Hallowell

The Earl Campbell Story by Earl Campbell (autobiography)

The Panic Attack Recovery Book by Shirley Swede and Seymour Sheppard Jaffe (autobiography)

A Mind of My Own by Chris Costner Sizemore (autobiography)

Assertiveness

Your Perfect Right by Robert E. Alberti and Michael Emmons

The Assertive Woman by Stanlee Phelps and Nancy Austin

The Assertiveness Workbook by Randy J. Paterson

Asserting Yourself by Sharon Anthony Bower and Gordon H. Bower

Stand Up, Speak Out, Talk Back! by Robert E. Alberti and Michael L. Emmons

Career Development

What Color Is Your Parachute? by Richard N. Bolles

Let Your Life Speak by Parker J. Palmer

Diversity and Women's Career Development by Helen S. Farmer and associates

Career Anchors by Edgar H. Schein

Life Choices by Richard S. Sharf

Communication and People Skills

You Just Don't Understand by Deborah Tannen

The Dance of Connection by Harriet Lerner

Boundaries by Henry Cloud and John Townsend

Shyness by Philip G. Zimbardo

How to Communicate by Matthew McKay, Martha Davis, and Patrick Fanning

Death and Grieving

How to Survive the Loss of a Love by Melba Colgrove, Harold H. Bloomfield, and Peter McWilliams

Life Lessons by Elisabeth Kübler-Ross and David Kessler

When Bad Things Happen to Good People by Harold S. Kushner

The Grief Recovery Handbook, Expanded Edition by John W. James and Russell Friedman

How to Go On Living When Someone You Love Dies by Therese A. Rando

Death Be Not Proud by John Gunther (autobiography)

A Grief Observed by C. S. Lewis (autobiography)

Letting Go by Morrie Schwartz (autobiography)

Depression

Feeling Good by David D. Burns

The Mindful Way Through Depression by Mark Williams, John Teasdale, Zindel Segal, and Jon Kabat-Zinn

Mind over Mood by Dennis Greenberger and Christine A. Padesky

The Feeling Good Handbook by David D. Burns

Control Your Depression by Peter M. Lewinsohn, Ricardo F. Muñoz, Mary Ann Youngren, and Antonette M. Zeiss

The Beast by Tracy Thompson (autobiography)

Darkness Visible by William Styron (autobiography)

The Noonday Demon by Andrew Solomon (autobiography)

Divorce

Crazy Time by Abigail Trafford

Dinosaurs Divorce by Marc Brown and Laurene Krasny Brown

The Boys and Girls Book About Divorce by Richard A. Gardner

Divorce by Rich Wemhoff

Helping Children Cope with Divorce by Edward Teyber

Eating Disorders

The Hunger Within by Marilyn Ann Migliore and Philip Ross

Overcoming Binge Eating by Christopher G. Fairburn

Dying to Be Thin by Ira M. Sacker and Marc A. Zimmer

Healing the Hungry Self by Deirdra Price

The Body Betrayed by Kathryn J. Zerbe

Feeding the Hungry Heart by Geneen Roth (autobiography)

Holy Hunger by Margaret Bullitt-Jonas (autobiography)
Am I Still Visible? by Sandra Harvey Heater (autobiography)

Families and Stepfamilies
The Shelter of Each Other by Mary Pipher
Mom's House, Dad's House by Isolina Ricci
Step-by Step-Parenting by James D. Eckler
Old Loyalties, New Ties by Emily B. Visher and John S. Visher
Love in the Blended Family by Angela Clubb

Love and Intimacy
Love Is Never Enough by Aaron T. Beck
In the Meantime by Iyanla VanZant
The Relationship Cure by John M. Gottman and Joan DeClaire
The Dance of Intimacy by Harriet Lerner
The Dance of Connection by Harriet Lerner

Marriage
Why Marriages Succeed or Fail . . . and How You Can Make Yours Last
     by John Gottman
We Love Each Other, But . . . by Ellen F. Wachtel
The Seven Principles for Making Marriage Work by John M. Gottman
     and Nan Silver
The 5 Love Languages by Gary Chapman
The Couple's Survival Workbook by David Olsen and Douglas Stephens

Obsessive-Compulsive Disorder
Obsessive-Compulsive Disorder for Dummies by Charles H. Elliott and
     Laura L. Smith
Brain Lock by Jeffrey M. Schwartz with Beverly Beyette
Stop Obsessing! by Edna B. Foa and Reid Wilson
Overcoming Obsessive-Compulsive Disorder by Gail Steketee
What to Do When Your Brain Gets Stuck by Dawn Huebner
Rewind, Replay, Repeat by Jeff Bell (autobiography)
Memoirs of an Amnesiac by Oscar Levant (autobiography)
The Boy Who Finally Stopped Washing by John B. (autobiography)

Parenting

Your Defiant Child by Russell A. Barkley and Christine M. Benton
Parenting the Strong-Willed Child by Rex Forehand and Nicholas
  Long
Parenting Young Children by Don Dinkmeyer, Sr., Gary D. McKay,
  James Dinkmeyer, Don Dinkmeyer, Jr., and Joyce L. McKay
The Blessing of a Skinned Knee by Wendy Mogel
How to Behave So Your Children Will, Too! by Sal Severe

Post-traumatic Stress Disorder

Trauma and Recovery by Judith Herman
Reclaiming Your Life After Rape by Barbara Olasov Rothbaum and
  Edna B. Foa
The PTSD Workbook by Mary Beth Williams and Soili Poijula
I Can't Get Over It by Aphrodite Matsakis
Survivor Guilt: A Self-Help Guide by Aphrodite Matsakis
I Am the Central Park Jogger by Trisha Meili (autobiography)
I Can Still Hear Their Cries, Even in My Sleep by E. Everett McFall
  (autobiography)
Soft Spots by Clint Van Winkle (autobiography)

Self-Management and Self-Enhancement

Get Out of Your Mind and into Your Life by Steven C. Hayes with
  Spencer Smith
The Last Lecture by Randy Pausch with Jeffrey Zaslow
Learned Optimism by Martin E. P. Seligman
Opening Up by James W. Pennebaker
The 7 Habits of Highly Effective People by Stephen R. Covey

Sexuality

Becoming Orgasmic by Julia Heiman and Joseph LoPiccolo
For Each Other: Sharing Sexual Intimacy by Lonnie Garfield
  Barbach
The New Male Sexuality by Bernie Zilbergeld
Sexual Awareness by Barry McCarthy and Emily McCarthy
The Family Book About Sexuality by Mary S. Calderone and Eric W.
  Johnson

Spiritual and Existential Concerns
Sacred Contracts by Caroline Myss
The American Paradox by David G. Myers
Finding Flow by Mihaly Csikszentmihalyi
Man's Search for Meaning by Viktor E. Frankl
When All You Ever Wanted Isn't Enough by Harold S. Kushner

Stress Management and Relaxation
The Relaxation and Stress Reduction Workbook by Martha Davis,
    Elizabeth Robbins Eshelman, and Matthew McKay
Wherever You Go, There You Are by Jon Kabat-Zinn
Staying on Top When Your World Turns Upside Down by Kathryn D.
    Cramer
Inner and Outer Peace Through Meditation by Rajinder Singh
The Stress and Relaxation Handbook by Jane Madders

Substance Abuse
Controlling Your Drinking by William R. Miller and Ricardo F. Muñoz
Sober for Good by Anne M. Fletcher
Responsible Drinking by Frederick Rotgers, Marc F. Kern, and Rudy
    Hoeltzel
The Addiction Workbook by Patrick Fanning and John T. O'Neill
Overcoming Your Alcohol or Drug Problem by Dennis C. Daley and
    G. Alan Marlatt
The Broken Cord by Michael Dorris (autobiography)
Note Found in a Bottle by Susan Cheever (autobiography)
A Drinking Life by Pete Hamill (autobiography)

Some self-help resources specifically apply the 5 steps to particular behavioral disorders. The stellar Pro-Change Behavior Systems (www.prochange.com) was developed by my collaborator Dr. Jim Prochaska and features low-cost online programs for exercise enhancement, stress management, weight regulation, healthy eating, depression prevention, smoking cessation, and medication adherence. I heartily recommend those online programs if you (or your organization) desire to keep working the *Changeology* steps.

APPENDIX B

SELECTING THE RIGHT PSYCHOTHERAPIST FOR YOU

Changeology has immersed you in the scientific study of behavior change and applied it to dozens of personal goals and self-improvements. As I have repeatedly emphasized, change occurs along a continuum, from doing it entirely on your own, on one end, to securing the assistance of a self-help book or group, to receiving professional treatment, on the other end. Please use as much self-help and treatment as necessary to realize your goals efficiently and effectively.

All change methods are complementary, not contradictory. Yes, a few rigid and insecure psychotherapists may still devalue self-change, and yes, a few anti-scientific self-help groups may still argue against psychotherapy and medication. But both the scientific research and clinical experience overwhelmingly support the natural synergy of self-change and treatment. They are friendly allies, not adversaries.

Thus, as a self-change researcher and clinical psychologist, I certainly recommend that some readers seek professional treatment during or after their efforts to change entirely on their own. Seeking professional help never constitutes a personal failure, although some readers will fail in their self-change or confront disorders that cannot be adequately resolved on one's own.

Why might you seek treatment in addition to using this book? Because you experience one or more of the Three Unables: unable to understand the material presented in this book; unable to apply its message to you or your situation; or unable to comply with the Changeology program. In these cases, please consider supplementing your self-change with professional help.

Some of you might initially experience the stigma that still exists against psychotherapy. Such antiquated bias results in the tragic underuse of psychological treatment and the needless suffering of millions. Only 30 percent of adults suffering from a mental disorder within the past year received professional help. Professional associations, such as the American Psychological Association (APA) and the American Psychiatric Association (APA), work hard to destigmatize mental health treatment, but its residue persists in some circles.

In this appendix, I offer research-driven guidance on selecting a psychotherapist tailored to your unique stage of change and treatment goal. The appendix is divided into four sections: introduction to the mental health professionals; generic advice on selecting a qualified professional; specific advice on finding a psychotherapist who fits your goal and stage; and finally, "test-driving" a psychotherapist for a few sessions to determine the optimal match. Much of this advice hails from a series of published studies that colleagues and I have conducted on how and where mental health professionals seek their own psychotherapists. After all, who better to offer guidance on selecting a psychotherapist than those who provide it and have received it themselves.

MENTAL HEALTH PROFESSIONALS

Here's a surprising fact: The term "psychotherapist" is not a legally protected or regulated term in most countries, certainly not in the United States. That means you can legally call yourself a psychotherapist or therapist, put it on a business card, and hang out a shingle. The lesson should be obvious: avoid anyone identifying and advertising as a psychotherapist. Instead, seek mental health services from someone licensed to practice by the particular state in which you reside.

Virtually all states license six mental health professionals: psychologists, psychiatrists, clinical social workers, counselors, psychiatric nurses, and marital/family therapists. Below are each profession's formal training, areas of expertise, and national organizations.

> **Psychologists** possess a doctoral degree in psychology (PhD, PsyD), generally receive the most training in psychotherapy, and spend one or two additional years as clinical interns. They alone provide psychological assessment and testing. In a few states, psychologists can also prescribe medication. Tip: Look for a psychologist who earned a doctorate in clinical or counseling psychology, not in a related field. Bonus tip: Search for a psychologist board-certified by the American Board of Professional Psychology (ABPP; www.abpp.org) or recognized

by the National Register of Health Service Providers in Psychology (www.nationalregister.org). The psychologist locators of the American Psychological Association (www.apa.org), the National Register (www .findapsychologist.org), and many state psychological associations can help you find a psychologist in your locale.

Psychiatrists possess a doctoral degree in medicine (MD, DO), and most have completed a formal residency in psychiatry. They prescribe medication and, compared with the other mental health professions, specialize in biological treatments. Tips: Look for a psychiatrist who is board certified in psychiatry and ascertain if he or she will only prescribe medication or will also offer psychotherapy (only a small percentage of psychiatrists now routinely conduct psychotherapy). The American Psychiatric Association (www.psych.org; 1-888-35-PSYCH) can offer assistance in finding a board-certified psychiatrist near you.

Clinical social workers possess a master's degree in social work or social sciences (MSW, MA) followed by supervised experience leading to state licensure and eligibility in the Academy of Certified Social Workers (ACSW). Clinical social workers offer psychotherapy and, compared with other mental health professions, specialize in community work. Tip: Look for a social worker who is extensively trained in clinical work and psychotherapy, not in social services or administration. Check out the National Association of Social Work (www.naswdc.org) and its National Social Worker Finder (www.helppro.com/nasw).

Counselors possess a master's degree (MA, MS) in counseling or an associated field and are licensed after several years of experience and completion of a national examination. Counselors offer services in many treatment settings. Tip: Look for one trained in individual, mental health, or clinical counseling, not career counseling (unless you are seeking direction regarding your career). The American Counseling Association (www.counseling.org) and its Counselor Find can generate names and details of licensed practitioners.

Psychiatric nurses are registered nurses (RN, BSN) who have earned a master's of science degree in nursing (MSN). Some go on to earn the

Nurse Practitioner (NP) designation and can then, in collaboration with a physician, prescribe medication. Some psychiatric nurses also offer psychotherapy. Tip: Look for a psychiatric nurse who specializes in psychotherapy, rather than administration or hospital care. A good resource is the American Psychiatric Nurses Association (www.apna.org).

Marriage and family therapists possess a master's degree in, naturally enough, marital and family therapy (MFT, MA) and tend to specialize in conducting couple and family work. A couple of jurisdictions call them by slightly different names: marriage and family therapists, child and family therapists, and so on. The American Association for Marriage and Family Therapy (www.aamft.org) as well as the state licensure boards can help you locate individual practitioners.

As you can see, there's a blizzard of mental health professionals out there. You can select among doctors (psychologists, psychiatrists) and master's-level professionals (social workers, counselors, psychiatric nurses, marriage and family therapists). Please insist upon someone licensed by the state and discount the plethora of unregulated certificates. Just the other day I received a letter from a "psychotherapist" who listed four sets of initials after her name, representing certificates earned after a couple of days of training. In other words, she was not licensed at all! Such certifications (certified grief counselor, certified trauma specialist, certified eating disorder specialist, ad nauseam) are largely designed, in my opinion, to impress and confuse you, the consumer. Cut through the torrent of misdirection and inquire about licensure. When in doubt about the licensure status of an individual practitioner, consult your state's website.

How, then, to select a mental health professional right for you? That's our next question and the next section.

SELECTING A QUALIFIED PROFESSIONAL

How do mental health professionals choose their own mental health professionals? Because members of these professions are care seekers as well as care providers, colleagues and I were curious to discover how licensed professionals selected someone for their own psychological treatment and why they choose them. We conducted our first study in the 1980s and then extended and replicated it in the late 2000s with more than 600 psychologists, counselors, and social workers.

Here are the experts' top reasons for selecting a psychotherapist in ranked order:

Competence
Warmth and caring
Clinical experience
Openness
Professional reputation
Active therapeutic style
Flexibility

In other words, the most trained change agents seek interpersonal qualities and professional competence in their own psychotherapists. Heed their example. Seek a close relationship—in which you will feel affirmed, appreciated, and respected by a fellow human being—with someone expert in his or her craft. Find a professional who is open, active, and flexible. Avoid passive "silent as a mirror" and dogmatic "my way or the highway" professionals.

Several selection criteria received ratings in the somewhat important range in our studies. That is, these factors sometimes mattered:

Theoretical orientation (psychodynamic, humanistic, cognitive,
    biological, etc.)
Success with similar patients
Being outside of my social/professional network
Specific profession or discipline
Cost per session

The specific profession or discipline will matter if you seek services provided by only that profession. Only psychologists, for example, perform psychological and neuropsychological testing; only psychiatrists, nurse practitioners, and, in a few states, psychologists prescribe psychotropic medications. But most members of the six professions can offer psychotherapy.

Cost per session and the professional being outside of your social network of friends will frequently come into play in your selection. As a rule, the doctoral-level practitioners charge more than the master's-level practitioners. Determine if your health insurance offers coverage for mental health care, and, when contacting professionals, ask directly about their billing and reimbursement rates. When seeking treatment themselves, mental health professionals wisely avoid seeing friends and close colleagues. The risk of complicating their lives and violating boundaries is just too high. Though you may initially feel more comfortable with someone you know from the neighborhood, church, or gym, avoid the temptation and get out of your fishbowl.

What do mental health professionals *not* value when searching for help themselves? Research productivity for starters; you are seeking an expert clinician, not an expert researcher. Nor do they highly value the professionals' demographics—gender, age, religious affiliation, or ethnic/racial background. They know what matters is the quality and qualifications of the person, not the color of his or her skin or a receding hairline.

That's not to say that these factors are inconsequential. To the contrary, recent studies demonstrate that patients expressing a strong preference for psychotherapists of a particular gender, ethnicity, religious persuasion, or sexual orientation should be matched with that desire. Being matched with your strong preference significantly reduces the chance of premature dropout and substantially increases the chance of a successful treatment. Note, that's a *strong* preference, as opposed to a take-it-or-leave-it inclination. So if you have strong desires for a particular type of psychotherapist, assertively try to secure that match.

FINDING A PSYCHOTHERAPIST WHO FITS YOU

Back in the day, when Model Ts roamed the earth and Freud ruled the consulting rooms, psychotherapists typically offered their identical treasured treatments to everyone who crossed their paths. It didn't matter if the treatment was psychoanalytic, humanistic, or behavioral; every patient, every disorder, and every goal received the same psychotherapy, depending upon the therapist's theory.

Today we frequently call that malpractice or professional negligence. Psychotherapy, as a clinical and ethical matter, is to be tailored or adapted to *your* needs, not to the practitioner's theory.

We have entered an era of evidence-based practice in which health care professionals personalize treatment to your specific problem and situation. Would you entrust your health to a physician who prescribed the identical treatment, say, antibiotics or neurosurgery, to every patient and illness? Or would you entrust your child to a child care professional who delivered the identical response, say, a smack on the bottom or a nondirective attitude, toward every misbehavior? Of course not! Nor should you tolerate any such nonsense from a psychotherapist.

You will seek a mental health professional who is prized not only for his or her competence, warmth, and openness but also for his or her flexibility and adaptability. Here are three routes through the psychotherapeutic maze to finding a practitioner who will meet your particular stage of change and needs.

The first tack is to locate a licensed professional whose theory matches your step. Psychoanalytic, psychodynamic, Adlerian, humanistic, existential, and motivational interviewing therapies are most frequently and effectively used for those in the Psych (contemplation) or Prep (preparation) steps. These approaches are particularly adept at identifying defenses, enhancing self-awareness, exploring choices, and increasing commitment. By contrast, cognitive, behavioral, rational-emotive, structural, solution-focused, systemic, and exposure treatments are most frequently and effectively suited for those in the Perspire (action) and Persevere (maintenance) steps. These approaches excel in developing healthy behaviors, employing reinforcement, harnessing the power of your environment, and preventing relapses. All psychotherapies have a place, but a step specific place, in the repertoires of mental health professionals.

The downside of this approach is that psychotherapists dedicated to one particular theory are likely to cover only half your steps. They can prepare you for the behavior change or, alternatively, can help you actually achieve it. Although half a loaf is better than none, we can probably do better.

The second route is to choose a professional who subscribes to an integrative or eclectic orientation. Not to worry about locating one; integrative is the most popular among psychotherapists. They realize that no single theory can accommodate all patients and problems; clinical reality has come to demand different strokes for different folks. Hence, an integrative therapist can guide you through the 5 steps and implement the change catalysts at the right time.

Even bolder—and to my way of thinking even better—is the third tack: select a licensed professional familiar with the stages of change. Not to fret here either: the vast majority of mental health and addiction professionals have been trained to some extent in the stages. Ask the potential practitioner if he or she is comfortable and skilled in leading you through the stages of change (precontemplation, contemplation, preparation, action, and maintenance).

You can minimize the probability of mental health professionals taking you in the wrong direction by insisting upon licensure, by matching your stage to their treatment approach, and finally, by avoiding those who practice discredited or ineffective therapies. The latter topic takes us into controversy, but my colleagues and I are working to develop an expert consensus on what treatments do not work better than placebo, chance, or the passage of time alone.

According to that expert consensus, here are discredited therapies to avoid:

Orgone energy accumulator   Future-lives therapy
Past-lives therapy   Color therapy
Rebirthing therapies   Thought Field Therapy
Primal scream therapy   Sexual reorientation therapy
Aromatherapy   Age-regression therapies
Erhard Seminar Training   Marathon encounter groups
Holding therapy   Neurolinguistic programming
Synanon-style boot camps   Angel therapy
Crystal healing
Treatments that attribute your distress to alien abduction or satanic ritual abuse

The chance of encountering one of these treatments from a licensed practitioner is, thankfully, quite small, but better safe than sorry.

TEST-DRIVING A PSYCHOTHERAPIST

Let's now implement this wealth of information and guidance on finding a psychotherapist that fits you. We conclude by walking the walk—actualizing these lessons and putting them into action.

♦ Collect a list of potential mental health professionals located in your area. Assertively ask for recommendations from health professionals, university psychology departments, current or past psychotherapists, community mental health centers, local hospitals, churches or synagogues, friends and family, and coworkers. Develop a final list of several frequently recommended professionals.

♦ Use the phone book and online find-a-therapist directories to locate professionals and their contact information, *but not to select a psychotherapist.* Such directories are marketing tools, not dispassionate indicators of quality. Would you entrust your best friend's or child's health to the best advertisers? Of course not. Not one online psychotherapist directory, to my knowledge, has independently or scientifically established the effectiveness of the folks paying to be listed there. So use it for informational purposes, not for making decisions about your health and happiness.

♦ Pinpoint where you get stuck in the change process. Your responses to the Check Yourself exercises sprinkled throughout *Changeology* can signify what particular assistance you seek from a mental health professional. Look back at your answers and reflect on your self-change collapses: perhaps you could not access your feelings or fears; perhaps you found the prospect of change too frightening; perhaps you could not assert yourself or control your environment; perhaps you could not resist temptation. Seek a psychotherapist seasoned and successful in those particular areas.

♦ Contact your health care insurance carrier to learn the particulars of your coverage (or lack thereof) for mental health services. Most of the treatment cost will probably be absorbed or reimbursed by your insurance carrier. And many psychotherapists, in both private practices and public clinics, will likely participate in the insurance plan. Specifically, ask: Does my insurance pay for mental health or addiction treatments? How many psychotherapy visits or sessions are covered per year? Is there an annual dollar limit for mental health coverage? Which services are covered—psychotherapy, medication, day hospital, inpatient hospital? What percentage of the treatment cost (or copay) do I pay? What is my deductible? Will I need a referral or authorization from my primary care physician? Can I select my own professional or do you provide a list from which I must select? If I seek psychotherapy outside the plan network, what amount will the insurance cover?

♦ If you learn that you do *not* have mental health benefits, you can probably still obtain some treatment with persistence and research. Here are common paths to securing psychotherapy without insurance coverage. First, pay directly out of pocket. Typical fees in private practices range between $50 and $200 per session, but fees in public clinics tend to run far less. Second, ask your employer (or a family member's employer) if it offers an Employee Assistance Program (EAP). These provide short-term counseling to help people identify and resolve personal problems and family struggles. Third, contact your state insurance, Medicare, and Medicaid offices to determine if you (or your family) are eligible for any government-funded insurance plans. Fourth, call or search on the Internet for local organizations that provide free or low-cost psychotherapy. These include community mental health centers, social service organizations, university psychology clinics, medical school psychiatry clinics, family service associations, and women's resource centers. Fifth, contact your local mental health agencies and ask about other possibilities. Please assert yourself; your health and happiness are at stake.

♦ If your health insurance does offer mental health benefits, call the two or three professionals on your finalist list and find out important information, such as scheduling, payment, policies, and fees. Don't expect extensive (and free) consultations by telephone, but responsible practice dictates that practitioners disclose the fundamentals of their costs and policies up front.

♦ Test-drive at least two psychotherapists, in the same way that you might research various automobiles, and then test-drive them. It's good to shop around for the professional who works best for you. Schedule an initial appointment with two psychotherapists. In my experience, effective practitioners are keen to match you with the best fit as well. Most therapists welcome proactive and well-informed customers.

♦ Ask informed questions at the first appointment: Is the therapist licensed? Has the license ever been revoked or suspended? Is he or she comfortable with and skilled in working with your particular problem? What kinds of treatments does the therapist use for your stage of change? Is the therapist familiar with the best available research to reach your goals? What is the cost of each session?

♦ Evaluate your experience after the first or second appointment, particularly in terms of the selection criteria presented in the previous sections of the appendix. A reliable gauge of whether a particular professional will prove helpful is whether you feel understood and helped in even the first meeting. Did you like what happened? Did you feel a relational connection? Did you trust and like him or her? Did he or she strike you as responsible and competent? Did he or she listen to and respect you? Did he or she ask the right questions? Did he or she set a treatment goal with you? Was he or she open to hearing your thoughts and eliciting your feedback?

♦ Comfort with the professional and the process is central to your success, but so, too, is movement toward your goal. Are you learning during sessions and experimenting with new behaviors between sessions? Does the therapy feel challenging but not overwhelming, as my London colleague Dr. Windy Dryden puts it? Are you on track to accomplish your treatment goals?

♦ Psychotherapy is at once a healing relationship and a treatment method. Find both the relationship and the method that fit you.

♦ If you do not feel comfortable with the person and/or feel that you are not making progress, consider switching practitioners. Keep in mind that your therapist works for *you,* not the other way around, and that you are purchasing a professional service.

♦ Invest yourself fully in the treatment. Bring the same high level of commitment and work that I have asked of you in using this book effectively. Become an active changeologist in both your self-help and in your psychotherapy.

Before you depart, kindly complete one last Check Yourself to ensure that you are mastering the requisite steps in locating and test-driving a mental health professional attuned to your needs and goals. You didn't honestly think that I would send you on your way without a final assessment of your skills, did you?

CHECK YOURSELF: SELECTING THE RIGHT PSYCHOTHERAPIST FOR YOU

Answer the following questions yes or no. Did you:

Challenge any lingering thoughts that getting professional help
   means failure?   _____

Embrace treatment as a natural compliment to your own
   self-change?   _____

Identify the education and qualifications of the major mental
   health professions?

Contact your health insurance carrier to learn the particulars of
  your coverage?   _____

Create a list of licensed mental health practitioners in your area? _____

Ask many friends and health care professionals for
  recommendations?   _____

Avoid reliance on online advertising directories?   _____

Research the therapists on your list to find out which one might
  work best for you?   _____

Call the finalists and find out important information (fees, policies,
  scheduling, etc.)?   _____

Make appointments with two of your finalists?   _____

Insist on seeing professionals licensed by your state?   _____

Express and pursue any strong preferences for a particular
  therapist characteristic?   _____

Pinpoint where you get stuck in the change process and let that
  inform your selection?   _____

Test-drive your therapist for a session or two?   _____

Ask specific questions during the initial visit to determine an
  optimal match with your needs?   _____

Select the practitioner for competence, warmth, caring,
  experience, and flexibility?   _____

Pick one that fits your treatment goal and your step of change?   _____

Avoid a psychotherapist who practices any of the discredited
  treatment methods?   _____

Ensure that you like, trust, and bond with the professional?   _____

Evaluate that therapist: is the treatment progressing toward
  your goals?   _____

Work hard and commit yourself to treatment; become a
  changeologist?   _____

NOTES

A few times while writing this book, I was encouraged to exclude scientific terminology and information that wasn't appropriate for the lay reader but that does reflect the real science. So I eventually surrendered to my editor and early readers, who convinced me to sneak those points into a notes section. Hence, let me share a few more ideas for those familiar with the research literature or hungry to know more details. I'll also point out specific references that are fully cited in the selected bibliography that follows.

Page 17: There is scant evidence in the research that an unmotivated person in precontemplation will make meaningful efforts to change on his own. I briefly mentioned the precontemplation stage for the sake of completeness and for those who are already familiar with the stages of change.

Page 19: To read more about Alfred Benjamin's take on ambivalence and the contemplation stage, I recommend his book *The Helping Interview* (1987).

Page 22: For those interested in the details of our meta-analysis of 39 published studies that demonstrate the power of moving from one step to another, please see the following article: Norcross, J. C., Krebs, P. M., & Prochaska, J. O. (2011). Stages of change. *Journal of Clinical Psychology, 67*, 143–154.

Page 22: The study performed on cardiac patients in a smoking cessation program can be found in Ockene, J., Ockene, I., & Kristellar, J. (1988). *The coronary artery smoking intervention study.* Worcester: National Heart Lung Blood Institute.

Page 25: To read the analysis of 87 self-help treatments showing the importance of honoring the stages and their inherent strategies, please see Krebs, P., Prochaska, J. O., & Rossi, J. S. (2011). Defining what works in tailoring: a meta-analysis of computer-tailored interventions for cancer-preventive behavior change. *Preventive Medicine, 51*, 214–221.

Page 25: The study of the 500 depressed patients is summarized in Levesque, D. A., Van Marter, D. F., Schneider, R. J., et al. (2011). Randomized trial of a computer-tailored intervention for patients with depression. *American Journal of Health Promotion, 26*(2), 77–79.

Page 27: Coupling behaviors that have something in common is known as "co-variation." That term comes from the fact that when we alter something about ourselves, we increase the likelihood that we alter other things about ourselves. To read more about the controlled studies carried out by colleagues at the University of Rhode Island, see Johnson, S., Prochaska, J., & Sherman, K. (2010, May). Co-variation: a promising approach to multiple behavior change interventions. Paper presented at the 31st annual meeting of the Society of Behavioral Medicine, Seattle, WA.

Page 27: To access the study done showing the relationship between smoking and drinking, see Lasser, K., Boyd, J. W., Woolhandler, S., et al. (2000). Smoking and mental illness: a population-based prevalence study. *Journal of the American Medical Association, 284*(20), 2606–2610.

Page 37: I fought hard to keep the word "catalyst" in the book despite my editor and collaborators' pleas to stick with "strategy." I then had to explain the difference between catalyst and technique, which forced me to go into how change catalysts occupy what I call a "midlevel of abstraction." So here we go.

There are literally hundreds of global theories of behavior change and psychotherapy, and we will probably never reach common ground on the theoretical level. There are also hundreds of specific techniques to modify behavior, and we will rarely agree on the specific, moment-to-moment methods to use. By contrast, the *catalysts of change* occupy a middle level of abstraction between global theories (such as psychoanalysis, behavior therapy, and humanistic) and specific techniques (such as dream analysis, progressive muscle relaxation, and reinforcement). The table below illustrates this intermediate level of abstraction. It has been adapted from my textbook with James O. Prochaska, *Systems of Psychotherapy* (2010).

It is at this intermediate level of analysis—catalysts of change—that meaningful points of convergence are found among the psychotherapies. It is also at this intermediate level that expert psychotherapists typically formulate their treatment plans—not in terms of global theories or specific techniques but as catalysts for their clients. Not too theoretical, not too technique-y; right in the middle is the sweet spot for behavior change.

LEVELS OF ABSTRACTION

Level	Abstraction	Examples
High	Theories	Psychoanalysis, cognitive, humanistic
Middle	Catalysts	Raising awareness, countering, tracking progress
Low	Techniques	Interpretation, two-chair technique, muscle relaxation

Page 40: To read more about the analysis of 47 studies proving the powerful connection between the steps and their respective catalysts, please see Rosen, C. S. (2000). Is the sequencing of change processes by stage consistent across health problems? A meta-analysis. *Health Psychology, 19*, 593–604.

Page 43: To read more about the research that contradicts the belief that "resolutions never succeed," please consult our scientific studies (listed in the Bibliography) conducted on New Year's resolvers.

Page 43: The quote from Oscar Wilde came from my copy of *The Picture of Dorian Gray*, originally published in 1909.

Page 45: In 2010, Sharon Begley of *Newsweek* wrote an entertaining piece called "My Alleles Made Me Do It," which summarized an original study done on blaming bad behavior on DNA by Suzanne O'Neill's group at Georgetown University. To read the original study, please see O'Neill, S., McBride, C. M., Alford, S. H., & Kaphingst, K. A. Preferences for genetic and behavioral health information: The impact of risk factors and disease attributions. *Annals of Behavioral Medicine, 40*, 127–137.

Page 47: The definition and cultivation of self-efficacy are summarized by the psychologist Albert Bandura in his 1982 article, Self-efficacy mechanism in human agency. *American Psychologist, 37*, 122–147.

Page 58: Tracking your progress is the same thing as what psychologists call "self-monitoring."

Page 62: Another way of saying "raising awareness" is "consciousness raising." Albert Einstein once said, "No problem can be solved from the same level of consciousness that created it." We need to elevate the dialogue, the awareness, the consciousness before modifying our behavior. We call this catalyst "consciousness raising" in our scholarly publications for exactly that reason.

Page 73: The symbolism of the two-headed llama owes its roots to the Janusian dialectic, which is brilliantly described in Albert Rothenberg's *The Creative Process of Psychotherapy* (Norton, 1988). Janus was a two-faced Roman deity, looking simultaneously forward and backward. In the Janusian tradition, motivation is optimally facilitated by being repelled by the problematic past and drawn toward the positive, problem-free future. The creative balance between past and future, negative and positive, dark and light is sometimes known as the Janusian dialectic.

Page 76: The practical process of weighing the pros and cons is what psychologists call a "decisional balance."

Page 85: To read more about the "fascinating line of research" that shows how extensive planning can backfire among perfectionists, please see the following references: (1) Powers, T. A., Koestner, R., & Topciu, R. A. (2005). Implementation intentions, perfectionism, and goal progress: Perhaps the road to hell is paved with good intentions. *Personality and Social Psychology Bulletin, 31,* 902–912. (2) Wittenberg, K. J., & Norcross, J. C. (2001). Practitioner perfectionism: Relationship to ambiguity tolerance and work satisfaction. *Journal of Clinical Psychology, 57,* 1543–1550.

Page 90: Patterns exist in all that we do, and that is especially true when it comes to behavior patterns that follow a specific sequence of events. Certain times of the day, certain situations, certain feelings, and certain rewards can predictably lead to the same behavior. Psychologists label this "temporal contiguity," meaning that one behavior causally leads to another across time in a behavioral chain.

Page 98: For an engaging and scholarly review of the power of going public, I encourage you to check out Robert B. Cialdini's 2008 book *Influence: Science and Practice* (5th ed).

Page 100: The research on writing behavior has been ably reviewed by Robert Boice in his book *Advice for New Faculty Members* (2000).

Page 100: The notion of thinking in terms of baby steps was immortalized by Bill Murray's character in the film *What About Bob?* In that movie, Murray's anxious character remained calm and motivated by reminding himself to take "baby steps, just baby steps." I use this example in my speaking engagements because it hits home for many people.

Page 101: A look at Robert Cialdini's (2008) book *Influence: Science and Practice* will get you started in understanding the evidence that commitment is most effective in improving your self-image and realizing future goals when it's active, public, and effortful.

Page 113: For a scholarly review on the downside of rumination, see Nolen-Hoeksema, S., Wisco, B. E., & Lyubomirsky, S. (2008). Rethinking rumination. *Perspectives on Psychological Science, 3,* 400–424.

Page 123: David Levy has written extensively on the skills of critical thinking. To read more and understand the "insight fallacy," check out his book *Tools of Critical Thinking: Metathoughts for Psychology,* 2nd ed.

Page 124: To read more about the 32 research studies on the effectiveness of various types of self-talk, see the following article: Hatzigeorgiadis, A., Zourbanos, N., Galanis, E., & Theodorakis, Y. (2011). Self-talk and sports performance: A meta-analysis. *Perspectives on Psychological Science, 6*(4), 348–356.

Page 138: Another way of saying "control your environment" is "stimulus control," which is what researchers call this catalyst.

Page 153: For more on the late Dr. Alan Marlatt's seminal work on minimizing relapses, please see Marlatt, G. A., & Donovan, D. M. (Eds.). (2007). *Relapse prevention: maintenance strategies in the treatment of addictive behaviors* (2nd ed). New York: Guilford.

Page 164: In research circles, *surfing the urge* is frequently known as "mindfulness-based relapse prevention." For more detail on this, see *Relapse prevention: maintenance strategies in the treatment of addictive behaviors.*

Page 184: For more information about the National Weight Control Registry, please go to www.nwcr.ws.

Page 186: In behavioral research, the process of backing away from external sources of rewards as you begin to cultivate self-rewards is known as "fading reinforcement." We gradually decrease the frequency of rewards from others and substitute rewards from ourselves.

Page 203: Our unrealistic expectations for personal growth was eloquently described by Sigmund Freud in 1933: "No reader of an account of astronomy will feel disappointed and contemptuous of science if he is shown the frontiers at which our knowledge of the universe melts into haziness. Only in psychology is it otherwise. There, mankind's constitutional unfitness for scientific research comes fully into the open. What people seem to demand of psychology is not progress in knowledge, but satisfactions of some other sort; every unsolved problem, every admitted uncertainty is made into a reproach against it."

Page 219: The "Three Unables" were detailed in my first book, *Changing for Good,* with Drs. Prochaska and DiClemente (1994).

Page 220: The fact that only 30 percent of adults suffering from a mental disorder receive professional help has been confirmed by numerous studies. To see some of this research, please consult the following two classic references: (1) Corrigan, P. (2004). How stigma interferes with mental health care. *American Psychologist, 59,* 614–625. (2) Kessler, R., McGonagle, K. A., Zhao, S., et al. (1994). Lifetime and 12-month prevalence of DSM-III-R psychiatric disorders in the United States. *Archives of General Psychiatry, 51,* 8–19.

Page 225: To understand how researchers established the "expert consensus" on discredited therapies, please refer to the following three sources: (1) Norcross, J. C., Koocher, G. P., Fala, N. C., & Wexler, H. K. (2010). What doesn't work? Expert consensus on discredited treatments in the addictions. *Journal of Addiction Medicine, 4*(3), 174–180. (2) Lilienfeld, S. O., Lynn, S. J., & Lohr, J. M. (Eds.). (2003). *Science and pseudoscience in clinical psychology.* New York: Guilford. (3) Norcross, J. C., Koocher, G. P., & Garofalo, A. (2006). Discredited psychological treatments and tests: A Delphi poll. *Professional Psychology: Research & Practice, 37,* 515–522.

SELECTED BIBLIOGRAPHY

At the time this book went to press, I could have amassed hundreds, if not thousands, of studies attesting to the effectiveness of step matching and the change catalysts described herein. As I stated at the beginning, the 5-step process that encompasses *Changeology* reflects decades of scientific research in both laboratory and clinical settings that continue to this day. A book that showcased every single published study on the stages of change would run thousands of pages, for it's impossible to list all the studies that have emerged in the last 30 years.

What follows, then, is an annotated bibliography that highlights some of the more prominent studies published, including the ones featured in this book. To access more research and an updated list of references, visit my website at www.ChangeologyBook.com and check out the National Institutes of Health's online publication library at www.pubmed.com.

Bandura, A. (1982). Self-efficacy mechanism in human agency. *American Psychologist, 37,* 122–147.

Baumeister, R. F., & Tierney, J. (2011). *Willpower: rediscovering the greatest human strength.* New York: Penguin.

Beck, A. T., Rush, A. J., Shaw, B. F., & Emery, G. (1979). *Cognitive therapy of depression.* New York: Guilford.

Begley, S. (2010, June 14). My alleles made me do it: the folly of blaming bad behavior on wonky DNA. www.thedailybeast.com/newsweek/blogs/ the-human-condition/2010/06/13/my-alleles-made-me-do-it-bad-behavior -blamed-on-wonky-dna.html.

Benjamin, A. (1987). *The helping interview.* Boston: Houghton Mifflin.

Bike, D. H., Norcross, J. C., & Schatz, D. M. (2009). Processes and outcomes of psychotherapists' personal therapy: replication and extension 20 years later. *Psychotherapy, 46,* 19–31.

Boice, R. (2000). *Advice for new faculty members.* Boston: Allyn & Bacon.

Borland, R. (1990). Slip-ups and relapse in attempts to quit smoking. *Addictive Behaviors, 15,* 235–245.

Brogan, M. M., Prochaska, J. O., & Prochaska, J. M. (1999). Predicting termination and continuation status in psychotherapy using the transtheoretical model. *Psychotherapy, 36,* 105–113.

Brownell, K. D., Marlatt, G. A., Lichtenstein, E., & Wilson, G. T. (1986). Understanding and preventing relapse. *American Psychologist, 41,* 765–782.

Burns, D. (1999). *Feeling good: the new mood therapy.* New York: Avon.

Carroll, K. M. (1996). Relapse prevention as a psychosocial treatment: a review of controlled clinical trials. *Experimental and Clinical Psychopharmacology, 4,* 765–782.

Chouinard, M. C., & Robichaud-Ekstrand, S. (2007). Predictive value of the transtheoretical model to smoking cessation in hospitalized patients with cardiovascular disease. *European Journal of Cardiovascular Prevention and Rehabilitation, 14*(1), 51–58.

Cialdini, R. B. (2008). *Influence: science and practice* (5th ed). New York: Prentice Hall.

Coelho, P. (1993). *The alchemist.* New York: HarperCollins.

Colino, S. (2001, January). The decision that changed my life. *Ladies' Home Journal,* 84–86.

Corrigan, P. (2004). How stigma interferes with mental health care. *American Psychologist, 59,* 614–625.

Cuijpers, P. (1997). Bibliotherapy in unipolar depression: a meta-analysis. *Journal of Behavior Therapy and Experimental Psychiatry, 28,* 139–147.

Curry, S. G., & Marlatt, G. A. (1985). Unaided quitters' strategies for coping with temptations to smoke. In S. Shiffman & T. A. Wills (Eds.), *Coping and substance use* (pp. 243–265). New York: Academic Press.

DiClemente, C. C. (2003). *Addiction and change: how addictions develop and addicted people recover.* New York: Guilford.

DiClemente, C. C., Prochaska, J. O., Fairhurst, S. K., et al. (1991). The process of smoking cessation: an analysis of precontemplation, contemplation and preparation stages of change. *Journal of Consulting and Clinical Psychology, 59,* 295–304.

Eisenberg, D. M., Davis, R. B., Ettner, S. L., et al. (1998). Trends in alternative medicine use in the United States, 1990–1997. *Journal of the American Medical Association, 280,* 1589–1575.

Epcot Poll. (1985). *Resolutions not kept long by most Americans.* Lake Buena Vista, Fla.: Walt Disney World.

Geller, J. D., Norcross, J. C., & Orlinsky, D. E. (Eds.). (2005). *The psychotherapist's own psychotherapy: patient and clinician perspectives.* New York: Oxford University Press.

Gibbs, N. (2004, July 5). Made your July 1 resolutions? *Time,* 98–99.

Gollwitzer, P. M. (1999). Implementation intentions: strong effects of simple plans. *American Psychologist, 54,* 493–503.

Goodwin, D. K. (2006). *Team of rivals: the political genius of Abraham Lincoln.* New York: Simon & Schuster.

Greenwald, J. (1998, November). Herbal healing. *Time,* 61–68.

Gritz, E. R., Carr, C. R., & Marcus, A. C. (1988). Unaided smoking cessation: Great American Smokeout and New Year's Day quitters. *Journal of Psychosocial Oncology, 6,* 217–234.

Hall, K. L., & Rossi, J. S. (2008). Meta-analytic examination of the strong and weak principles across 48 health behaviors. *Preventive Medicine, 46*(3), 266–274.

Hatzigeorgiadis, A., Zourbanos, N., Galanis, E., & Theodorakis, Y. (2011). Self-talk and sports performance: a meta-analysis. *Perspectives on Psychological Science, 6*(4), 348–356.

Isenhart, C. E. (1997). Pretreatment readiness for change in male alcohol dependent subjects: predictors of one-year follow-up status. *Journal of Studies on Alcohol, 58*(4), 351–357.

James, W. (1890). *Principles of Psychology.* http://psychclassics.yorku.ca/James/Principles/index.htm.

Johnson, S., Prochaska, J., & Sherman, K. (2010, May). Co-variation: A promising approach to multiple behavior change interventions. Paper presented at the 31st Annual Meeting of the Society of Behavioral Medicine, Seattle, WA.

Kazdin, A. E. (2008). *Behavior modification in applied settings* (6th ed). Long Grove, IL: Waveland Press.

Kessler, R., McGonagle, K. A., Zhao, S., et al. (1994). Lifetime and 12-month prevalence of DSM-III-R psychiatric disorders in the United States. *Archives of General Psychiatry, 51,* 8–19.

Klingemann, H., & Carter-Sobell, L. (Eds.). (2007). *Promoting self-change from addictive behaviors.* New York: Springer.

Kobayashi, M., Mrykalo, M. S., & Norcross, J. C. (1997, April). Slips and falls: a naturalistic study of lapses and relapses in self-initiated behavior change. Poster presented at the 68th Annual Meeting of the Eastern Psychological Association, Washington, D.C.

Koocher, G. P., Norcross, J. C., & Greene, B. A. (Eds.). (2013). *Psychologists' desk reference* (3rd ed). New York: Oxford University Press.

Krebs, P., Prochaska, J. O., & Rossi, J. S. (2011). Defining what works in tailoring: a meta-analysis of computer-tailored interventions for cancer-preventive behavior change. *Preventive Medicine, 67,* 143–154.

Lasser, K., Boyd, J. W., Woolhandler, S., et al. (2000). Smoking and mental illness: a population-based prevalence study. *Journal of the American Medical Association, 284*(20), 2606–2610.

Levesque, D. A., Van Marter, D. F., Schneider, R. J., et al. (2011). Randomized trial of a computer-tailored intervention for patients with depression. *American Journal of Health Promotion, 26*(2), 77–79.

Levy, D. A. (2009). *Tools of critical thinking: metathoughts for psychology* (2nd ed). Long Grove, IL: Waveland Press.

Lilienfeld, S. O. (1998). Pseudoscience in contemporary clinical psychology: what it is and what we can do about it. *The Clinical Psychologist, 51*(4), 3–9.

Lilienfeld, S. O., Lynn, S. J., & Lohr, J. M. (Eds.). (2003). *Science and pseudoscience in clinical psychology.* New York: Guilford.

Marlatt, G. A., & Donovan, D. M. (Eds.). (2007). *Relapse prevention: maintenance strategies in the treatment of addictive behaviors* (2nd ed). New York: Guilford.

Marlatt, G. A., & Kaplan, B. E. (1972). Self-initiated attempts to change behavior: a study of New Year's resolutions. *Psychological Reports, 30,* 123–131.

McConnaughy, E. A., DiClemente, C. C., Prochaska, J. O., & Velicer, W. F. (1989). Stages of change in psychotherapy: a follow-up report. *Psychotherapy, 26,* 494–503.

McConnaughy, E. A., Prochaska, J. O., & Velicer, W. F. (1983). Stages of change in psychotherapy: measurement and sample profiles. *Psychotherapy, 20,* 368–375.

Miller, E., & Marlatt, A. (1997). *How to keep up with those New Year's Resolutions: researchers find commitment is the secret of success.* University of Washington study.

Miller, W. R., & Rollnick, S. (2002). (Eds.). *Motivational interviewing: preparing people for change* (2nd ed). New York: Guilford.

Miller, W. R., & Tonigan, J. S. (1996). Assessing drinkers' motivation for change: the Stages of Change Readiness and Treatment Eagerness Scale (SOCRATES). *Psychology of Addictive Behaviors, 10*(2), 81–89.

Miller, W. R., Wilbourne, P. L., & Hettema, J. E. (2003). What works? A summary of alcohol treatment outcome research. In R. K. Hester & W. R. Miller (Eds.), *Handbook of alcoholism treatment approaches: effective alternatives* (3rd ed., pp. 13–63). Boston: Allyn & Bacon.

Mukherjee, Siddhartha. (2010). *The emperor of all maladies.* New York: Scribner.

Nolen-Hoeksema, S., Wisco, B. E., & Lyubomirsky, S. (2008). Rethinking rumination. *Perspectives on Psychological Science, 3,* 400–424.

Norcross, J. C. (2000). Here comes the self-help revolution in mental health. *Psychotherapy, 37,* 370–377.

Norcross, J. C. (2005). The psychotherapist's own psychotherapy: educating and developing psychologists. *American Psychologist, 60,* 840–850.

Norcross, J. C. (2006). Integrating self-help into psychotherapy: 16 practical suggestions. *Professional Psychology: Research & Practice, 37,* 683–693.

Norcross, J. C. (Ed.). (2011). *Psychotherapy relationships that work* (2nd ed). New York: Oxford University Press.

Norcross, J. C., & Beutler, L. E. (2011). Integrative psychotherapies. In R. J. Corsini & D. Wedding (Eds.), *Current psychotherapies* (9th ed). Belmont, CA: Brooks/Cole Cengage.

Norcross, J. C., Beutler, L. E., & Levant, R. F. (Eds.). (2006). *Evidence-based practices in mental health: debate and dialogue on the fundamental questions.* Washington, DC: American Psychological Association.

Norcross, J. C., Bike, D. H., & Evans, K. L. (2009). The therapist's therapist: a replication and extension 20 years later. *Psychotherapy, 46,* 32–41.

Norcross, J. C., Campbell, L. F., Grohol, J. M., et al. (2013). *Self-help that works* (4th ed). New York: Oxford University Press.

Norcross, J. C., & Goldfried, M. R. (Eds.). (2005). *Handbook of psychotherapy integration* (2nd ed). New York: Oxford University Press.

Norcross, J. C., & Guy, J. D. (2005). The prevalence and parameters of personal therapy in the United States. In J. D. Geller, J. C. Norcross, & D. E. Orlinsky (Eds.), *The psychotherapist's own psychotherapy.* New York: Oxford University Press.

Norcross, J. C., & Guy, J. D. (2007). *Leaving it at the office: a guide to psychotherapist self-care.* New York: Guilford.

Norcross, J. C., Hedges, M., & Castle, P. H. (2002). Psychologists conducting psychotherapy in 2001: a study of the Division 29 membership. *Psychotherapy, 39,* 97–102.

Norcross, J. C., Hogan, T. P., & Koocher, G. P. (2008). *Clinician's guide to evidence-based practices: mental health and the addictions.* New York: Oxford University Press.

Norcross, J. C., & Karpiak, C. P. (2012). Clinical psychologists in the 2010s: fifty years of the APA Division of Clinical Psychology. *Clinical Psychology: Science and Practice, 19*(1), 1–12.

Norcross, J. C., Koocher, G. P., Fala, N. C., & Wexler, H. K. (2010). What doesn't work? Expert consensus on discredited treatments in the addictions. *Journal of Addiction Medicine, 4*(3), 174–180.

Norcross, J. C., Koocher, G. P., & Garofalo, A. (2006). Discredited psychological treatments and tests: a Delphi poll. *Professional Psychology: Research & Practice, 37,* 515–522.

Norcross, J. C., Krebs, P. M., & Prochaska, J. O. (2011). Stages of change. *Journal of Clinical Psychology, 67,* 143–154.

Norcross, J. C., Mrykalo, M. S., & Blagys, M. D. (2002). *Auld lang syne:* Success predictors, change processes, and self-reported outcomes of New Year's resolvers and nonresolvers. *Journal of Clinical Psychology, 58,* 397–405.

Norcross, J. C., & Prochaska, J. O. (1984). Where do behavior (and other) therapists take their troubles? II. *The Behavior Therapist, 7,* 26–27.

Norcross, J. C., Ratzin, A. C., & Payne, D. (1989). Ringing in the New Year: the change processes and reported outcomes of resolutions. *Addictive Behaviors, 14,* 205–212.

Norcross, J. C., Santrock, J. W., Campbell, L. F., et al. (2003). *Authoritative guide to self-help resources in mental health* (3rd ed). New York: Guilford.

Norcross, J. C., & Sayette, M. A. (2012). *Insider's guide to graduate programs in clinical and counseling psychology* (2012/13 edition). New York: Guilford.

Norcross, J. C., Strausser, D. J., & Faltus, F. J. (1988). The therapist's therapist. *American Journal of Psychotherapy, 42,* 53–66.

Norcross, J. C., VandenBos, G. R., & Freedheim, D. K. (Eds.). (2011). *History of psychotherapy: continuity and change* (2nd ed). Washington, DC: American Psychological Association.

Norcross, J. C., & Vangarelli, D. J. (1989). The resolution solution: longitudinal examination of New Year's change attempts. *Journal of Substance Abuse, 1,* 127–134.

Norcross, J. C., & Wampold, B. E. (2011). What works for whom: adapting psychotherapy to the person. *Journal of Clinical Psychology, 67,* 127–132.

Ockene, J., Kristellar, J., Ockene, I., & Goldberg, R. (1992). Smoking cessation and severity of illness. *Health Psychology, 11,* 119–126.

Ockene, J., Ockene, I., & Kristellar, J. (1988). *The coronary artery smoking intervention study.* Worcester: National Heart Lung Blood Institute.

O'Neill, S., McBride, C. M., Alford, S. H., & Kaphingst, K. A. (2010). Preferences for genetic and behavioral health information: the impact of risk factors and disease attributions. *Annals of Behavioral Medicine, 40,* 127–37.

Ouimette, P. C., Finney, J. W., & Moos, R. H. (1997). Twelve-step and cognitive-behavioral treatment for substance abuse: a comparison of treatment effectiveness. *Journal of Consulting & Clinical Psychology, 65,* 230–240.

Pantalon, M. V., Lubetkin, B. S., & Fishman, S. T. (1995). Use and effectiveness of self-help books in the practice of cognitive and behavioral therapy. *Cognitive and Behavioral Practice, 2,* 213–222.

Powers, T. A., Koestner, R., & Topciu, R. A. (2005). Implementation intentions, perfectionism, and goal progress: perhaps the road to Hell is paved with good intentions. *Personality and Social Psychology Bulletin, 31,* 902–912.

Prochaska, J. O. (2004). Population treatment for addictions. *Current Directions in Psychological Science, 13,* 242–246.

Prochaska, J. O., & DiClemente, C. C. (1985). Common processes of self-change in smoking, weight control, and psychological distress. In S. Shiffman & T. Wills (Eds.), *Coping and substance abuse: a conceptual framework* (pp. 345–363). New York: Academic Press.

Prochaska, J. O., DiClemente, C. C., & Norcross, J. C. (1992). In search of how people change: applications to addictive behaviors. *American Psychologist, 47,* 1102–1114.

Prochaska, J. O., DiClemente, C. C., Velicer, W. F., et al. (1985). Predicting change in smoking status for self-changers. *Addictive Behaviors, 10,* 395–406.

Prochaska, J. O., & Norcross, J. C. (2010). *Systems of psychotherapy: a transtheoretical analysis* (7th ed). Pacific Grove, CA: Brooks/Cole Cengage.

Prochaska, J. O., Norcross, J. C., & DiClemente, C. C. (1995). *Changing for good.* New York: Avon.

Prochaska, J. O., Norcross, J. C., & DiClemente, C. C. (2005). Stages of change: prescriptive guidelines. In G. P. Koocher, J. C. Norcross, & S. S. Hill (Eds.), *Psychologists' desk reference* (2nd ed). New York: Oxford University Press.

Prochaska, J. O., Norcross, J. C., Fowler, J., et al. (1992). Attendance and outcome in a worksite weight control program: processes and stages of change as process and predictor variables. *Addictive Behaviors, 17,* 35–45.

Prochaska, J. O., Velicer, W. F., Fava, J. L., et al. (2001). Counselor and stimulus control enhancements of a stage-matched expert system intervention for smokers in a managed care setting. *Preventive Medicine, 32,* 23–32.

Prochaska, J. O., Velicer, W. F., Rossi, J. S., et al. (1994). Stages of change and decisional balance for twelve problem behaviors. *Health Psychology, 13,* 39–46.

Project MATCH Research Group. (1997). Matching alcoholism treatments to client heterogeneity: Project MATCH posttreatment drinking outcomes. *Journal of Studies on Alcohol, 58,* 7–29.

Rosen, C. S. (2000). Is the sequencing of change processes by stage consistent across health problems? A meta-analysis. *Health Psychology, 19,* 593–604.

Rosen, G. M. (1993). Self-help or hype? Comments on psychology's failure to advance self-care. *Professional Psychology: Research and Practice, 24,* 340–345.

Schwarzer, R., & Leppin, A. (1989). Social support and health: a meta-analysis. *Psychology & Health, 31,* 1–15.

Scogin, F., Bynum, J., & Calhoun, S. (1990). Efficacy of self-administered treatment programs: meta-analytic review. *Professional Psychology: Research and Practice, 21,* 42–47.

Seligman, M. E. P. (2007). *What you can change and what you can't.* New York: Vintage.

Shiffman, S., Paty, J. A., Gnys, M., et al. (1996). First lapses to smoking: within-subjects analysis of real-time reports. *Journal of Consulting and Clinical Psychology, 64,* 366–379.

Skow, J. (1999, April 26). Lost in cyberspace. *Time,* 61.

Valasquez, M. M., Maurer, G., Crouch, C., & DiClemente, C. C. (2001). *Group treatment for substance abuse: a stages-of-change therapy manual.* New York: Guilford.

Velicer, W. F., Fava, J. L., Prochaska, J. O., et al. (1995). Distribution of smokers by stage in three representative samples. *Preventive Medicine, 24*(4), 401–411.

Watzlawick, P. (1983). *The situation is hopeless but not serious.* New York: Norton.

Wierzbicki, M., & Pekarik, G. (1993). A meta-analysis of psychotherapy dropout. *Professional Psychology: Research and Practice, 29,* 190–195.

Wiggers, L. C. W., Oort, F. J., Dijkstra, A., et al. (2005). Cognitive changes in cardiovascular patients following a tailored behavioral smoking cessation intervention. *Preventive Medicine, 40*(6), 812–821.

Wilde, O. (1909). *The picture of Dorian Gray.* New York: Pearson.

Witkiewitz, K. (2012). Preventing relapse. In G. P. Koocher, J. C. Norcross, & B. A. Green (Eds.), *Psychologists' desk reference* (3rd ed). New York: Oxford University Press.

Wittenberg, K. J., & Norcross, J. C. (2001). Practitioner perfectionism: relationship to ambiguity tolerance and work satisfaction. *Journal of Clinical Psychology, 57,* 1543–1550.

INDEX

Abstinence Violation Effect (AVE), 167, 168

acceptance, as countering method, 125–26, 134–36

action
description/characteristics of, 19–20
Perspire as taking, 111–51
as stage of change, 19–20
timeline for, 36–37
See also Action plan; change catalysts; *specific action*

action catalysts. *See* change catalysts

Action Plan, 83–84, 85, 102–7

"AEIOU and always Y" guide, 63

airplane jump analogy, 83, 107–8

Alcoholics Anonymous, 84, 185

Andrew (patient)
Action Plan of, 102, 105
awareness of, 64–65
change catalysts and, 181–82
change team/support for, 95, 180
commitment of, 100, 101–2
confidence of, 181, 187, 202
countering by, 133–34, 187
ending of problem for, 199
environment and, 141, 188–89
as example of 5 step process, 54, 201, 202, 203
fears of, 74
goals of, 56, 86–87
imagery and, 133–34
as learning from mistakes, 202
long-term consequences and, 71
mantra/motto of, 79

optimism and, 72
patterns of, 112
Persevere and, 156, 157, 158, 163, 171–72, 173–74
Persist and, 181–82, 183, 187, 188–89
Perspire and, 111–12, 122, 133–34, 141, 148
Prep and, 86–87, 95, 100, 101–2, 105
as preparing for future slips, 171
problems of, 54
Psych and, 54, 56, 58, 64–65, 71, 74
reevaluation of yourself and, 67
relapses/slips of, 171–72, 173–74, 202
rewards and punishments for, 119, 122, 180
slip plan/card of, 171–72, 173–74
three-headed demon and, 148
tracking progress of, 58, 183
triggers for, 112, 156, 157, 158, 163, 171

assertion, as countering method, 125, 126, 131

athletes, 124, 152

Auden, W. H., 16

avoidance
of pain, 134
of triggers, 152, 155–59, 189
See also exposure

awareness
adaptation of Changeology and, 206
arousing emotions and, 68, 75
as change catalyst, 37, 53, 62–67, 82
Check Yourself and, 65, 66, 109
and difference between preparation and taking action, 112–14

awareness (*cont.*)
  of high-risk triggers, 159
  maintaining change and, 182
  methods for raising, 63–66
  pros and cons exercise and, 76
  Psych goals and, 53
  questions to ask about, 64
  reevaluation of yourself and, 66–67
  responding constructively to slips and,
      169
  step matching and, 39
  tracking, 62
  tracking progress and, 88

Baumeister, Roy, 98
Beck, Aaron, 127
Beck, Judith, 108
Beckett, Samuel, 104
behavioral chain, 89, 143–44
"behaviorial detectives," 88–90, 100, 139,
      143
Benjamin, Alfred, 19
Bergman, Ingmar, 71
blame, 84, 148, 149, 174, 183
blogging, 60
bribery, 122
British Humanist Association, 206
buddy system, 146
business organizations, Changeology applied
      to, 205–6

Caldwell, Nancy A., 60
catastrophic thinking, 128–29
cell phone apps, tracking progress and, 61
change
  ambivalence about, 15–16
  as ending, 180, 198–201
  formula for, 39–40, 182–83
  incremental, 205
  integrated approach to, 10, 38–39
  involuntary, 205
  keys for succeeding at, 35–50
  linear model of, 195–97
  measuring your stage of, 29–31
  myths about, 42–47
  need for, 9, 10–11, 18, 26
  as never ending, 198–201
  of other people, 26
  over- and underestimating ability to, 135
  paradox of, 15–16, 69–70
  as possible, prevalent, and learnable, 205

  prioritizing, 28
  process of, 1–2, 3, 6–7, 17
  readiness for, 17–18, 28
  resistance to, 15–16, 69–70
  self-assessment for, 31
  spiral of, 180, 195–201
  stages of, 3, 17–20, 29–31
  strategies for, 24–25
  structure of, 16–20, 35, 38
  temporary/incomplete, 203
  timeline for, 36–37
  types of, 16–17
  what you want to, 26
  See also specific topic
change catalysts
  adaptation of Changeology and, 206
  behavioral chain and, 143–44
  commitment and, 97
  examples of, 37
  helping relationships and, 144
  keys for success and, 35, 37–39
  long haul and, 195, 199, 200
  sources of methods for activation of, 187
  spiral of change and, 199
  step matching and, 39–42
  as teachable and learnable, 206
  techniques for, 37–38
  timeline for change and, 37–38
  See also specific catalyst
change team
  Action Plan and, 106
  activities/function of, 94–95, 144–48,
      175
  adjustments in, 145–48
  and articulation of what is needed, 94
  assembling/mobilizing the, 83, 92–96,
      109, 175, 185
  Check Yourself and, 96, 109
  commitment and, 98
  contingency contracts and, 117–18, 137
  countering and, 131
  cyber-, 92
  dos and don'ts with, 147
  formal invitation to, 93–94
  importance of, 175
  maintaining change and, 184, 185
  number of people on, 92, 146
  Perspire goals and, 111
  pessimism and, 93
  Prep goals and, 83
  saying no to triggers and, 160–61, 162

self-efficacy and, 96
sharing worksheet for high-risk triggers
    with, 158
slips and, 94, 145, 172, 174, 175
starting date and, 104
tracking progress and, 94
trust and, 95
type of support and, 92
your relationship with, 95, 145
Changeology
    as action, 207
    adaptation of, 204–7
    as advocate of integration of multiple
        sources of healing, 10
    benefits of, 203, 204–7
    business applications of, 205–6
    differences between other self-help
        programs and, 2, 4–6
    importance of, 10–11
    Integrated approach to, 38–39
    as program of success, 204
    for social change, 204–7
    website for, 6
    See also specific topic
ChangeologyBook.com
    Action Plan and, 102, 106, 107
    Determine My Behavioral Chain and, 89
    movies concerning fear of change on, 71
    and Norcross as member of change team,
        95
    pros and cons sheets on, 78
    self-efficacy exercise and, 190–91
    Slip Cards and, 173
    as source for online support, 6
    Tips for My Change Team and, 147
    tracking progress and, 61
    weekly reminders from, 140
    worksheet for high-risk triggers and,
        157
Changing for Good (Norcross, Prochaska, and
    DiClemente), 5, 17–18
Check Yourself
    for Action Plan, 107
    arousing emotions and, 75, 109
    assessment of step and, 29–31
    for awareness, 65, 66, 109
    benchmarks for, 84, 109–10
    change team and, 96, 109
    commitment and, 81, 101, 109
    for controlling your environment, 142,
        151

countering and, 137, 151
effective use of 5 step process and, 7, 8
5 steps of change and, 29–31
function of, 7, 8, 29–31
goals and, 87, 88, 109
and going from Perspire to Persist, 151
importance of, 82, 108
for keys to self-change, 49–50
maintaining change and, 180, 184–85
reevaluation of yourself and, 67, 68
rewards and, 123, 151
selection of psychotherapists and, 229–30
for self-efficacy, 48, 194
for slips, 175–76
for support/helping relationships, 147–48,
    151, 184–85
for three-headed demon, 150, 151
tracking progress and, 91, 109
checklist, for contingency contract, 118–19
chronic contemplation, 104
Coelho, Paulo, 207
cognitive therapy, 126, 127, 128, 131
commitment
    as change catalyst, 37–38, 53, 78–82, 97
    change team and, 98
    Check Yourself and, 81, 101, 109
    definition of, 78
    desire differentiated from, 97
    getting back on track after slips and, 172
    goals and, 37–38, 99, 102
    going public and, 98–99
    internalizing your model or mentor and,
        80
    maintaining change and, 182
    motivation and, 99–100, 102
    myths and, 44
    Prep goals and, 83
    priorities and, 98, 99
    Psych goals and, 53
    responding constructively to slips and,
        169–70
    Roosevelt's comments about, 80
    and slips as recommitments, 155
    stages of change and, 19
    support groups and, 81
    to timeline for change, 36–37
    willpower and, 78–79, 98
competition, 146
compliments, self-, 119
confidence, 7, 48, 151, 172, 198, 206.
    See also self-efficacy

consequences
  building self-efficacy and, 193
  doubling of, 121
  long-term versus short-term, 71, 89
  of not changing behavior, 69–70
  Psych goals and, 53
  punishment as, 119–23
  rewards as, 114–23
  tracking progress and, 88–91
  of triggers, 143, 159
contemplation stage
  description/characteristics of, 18–19
  5 steps of change and, 20
  timeline for, 36–37
  See also Psych
contingency contracts, 117–19, 122, 137, 142
control
  acceptance and, 134, 135
  adaptation of Changeology and, 206–7
  of environment, 138–42, 187–89
  goals and, 55–56
  identification of need for change and, 26
Corby, Rebecca A., 186
countering
  acceptance and, 125–26, 134–36
  behavior chain and, 143–44
  building self-efficacy and, 193
  as change catalyst, 112, 124–38
  change team and, 131
  characteristics of, 123–24
  Check Yourself and, 137, 151
  complaints about, 136–37
  exposure and, 130–32
  healthy thoughts as, 125, 126–29, 131
  identification of healthy alternatives and,
    100–101
  imagery and, 132–34
  maintaining change and, 180, 182,
    186–87, 193
  methods for, 124–38
  Perspire goals and, 111
  preparing for next slip and, 172
  rewards and, 130, 131, 136–37
  See also specific method
cravings, 164–66
"cue exposure," 159, 188
cue network/context, 188

Daily Burn (website), 61
daily logs. See journaling
denial of need for change, 9, 18, 29

Deutsch, Morton, 98–99
DiClemente, Carlo C., 2, 5, 17–18, 149,
    206
distractions, 162–63
diversions, 125, 126
dreaded chores, 119
Drucker, Peter, 58, 97

Einstein, Albert, 63, 195
Ellis, Albert, 127
Emerson, Ralph Waldo, 78, 105, 114, 183,
    185
Emma (patient), 32–34
emotions
  arousing, 53, 68–75, 76, 109
  awareness and, 68
  as change catalyst, 53, 68–75, 82
  Check Yourself and, 75, 109
  and difference between preparation and
    taking action, 112–14
  maintaining change and, 182
  Psych goals and, 53
  resisting the urge and, 163
  saying no and, 160
  step matching and, 39, 40
  as triggers, 156
environment
  behavior chain and, 143–44
  building self-efficacy and, 193
  as change catalyst, 112, 138–42
  Check Yourself for, 142, 151
  control of, 138–42, 151, 187–89
  maintaining change and, 180, 182, 183,
    187–89, 193
  Perspire goals and, 111
  slips and, 188
  step matching and, 39–40
  triggers and, 188–89
exercise, as countering method, 125, 126,
    162
exposure, as countering method, 125,
    130–32

failure(s)
  adaptation of Changeology and, 207
  blame for, 84
  commitment and, 97
  countering and, 128
  fear of, 46–47, 153–54
  learning from mistakes and, 105
  myths about, 45–47

in persistence, 178–79
to prepare, 82
reasons for, 105
relapse as presage of, 153
See also prior efforts
fairness, countering and, 127–28
falls. *See* relapse/lapse; slips
fear(s)
  arousing emotions and, 69
  balancing desire for change and, 73–75
  building self-efficacy and, 193
  of change, 15–16, 53, 69, 70, 71, 72–75,
    77, 83
  commitment and, 78
  confronting, 137
  countering and, 130–32
  denial and dismissal of, 69
  of dogs, 130
  of failure, 46–47, 153–54
  feeling the, 70, 72–75
  as fuel for change, 193
  pros and cons of change and, 77
  of relapse, 153–54, 178
  selection of change team and, 94
feedback, raising awareness and, 64
feelings. *See* emotions; *specific feeling*
50 new beginnings, 103
5 stages of change
  effectiveness of, 25
  identification of, 1–2
  timeline for, 36–37
5 steps of change
  Check Yourself and, 29–31
  duration of each step in, 21
  ineffective use of, 8–10
  overview about, 21–28
  process of change and, 17
  as sounds, 111
  and spiral of change and, 180
  structure of change and, 35
  successfulness of, 3–4
  timeline for, 35, 36–37
  See also Changeology; Persevere; Persist;
    Perspire; Prep; Psych
Freud, Sigmund, 5, 62, 69–70
future, embracing a positive, 72

genetics, 42, 44–45
Gerard, Harold, 98–99
Ghidorah, the Three-Headed Monster (movie),
  148

"go long," 71–72
goals
  assessment of steps and, 29–31
  Check Yourself and, 87, 88, 109
  commitment and, 37–38, 99, 102
  defining/identifying, 54–57, 82, 83,
    85–88
  5 steps of change and, 8, 9, 20
  identification of need for change and, 26
  limiting, 54
  long-term versus short-term, 86–87
  measurement of, 55, 85, 86
  multiple, 8, 27–28, 30–31
  myths about, 42, 43–44
  planning for change and, 84
  positive versus negative, 56
  Prep goals and your, 83
  prioritizing of, 28, 98, 99, 192
  private declaration of, 98
  process of change and, 1–2, 6–7
  publicizing, 79, 83, 98–99, 102
  realistic, 55
  remembering, 99
  setting, 109
  SMART, 85–86, 87
  stages of change and, 19
  sub-, 57, 85, 87
  tantalizing, 179–80
  tracking progress and, 58–62, 88–91
  types of change and, 16
  as under your control, 55–56
  writing down the, 106
  See also specific patient
good-bye letters, 74–75
Google Calendar, 60
Grandma's rule, 116–17
guilt, 73

habits
  arousing emotions and, 69
  bad, 3, 16, 26
  eradication of, 5
  need for change and, 26
  reevaluation of yourself and, 67
  types of change and, 16
Hamill, Peter, 65
happiness, countering and, 129
health insurance, 119, 227, 228
health maintenance organization (example),
  25
healthy alternatives/opposites. *See* countering

healthy thoughts, as countering method, 125, 126–29, 131
helping relationships. *See* change team; other people; support
Hill, Napoleon, 151
hypnosis, self-, 163

if-then technique, 161
imagery, 72, 74, 125, 132–34, 160, 165, 166
individual, limitations of self-help programs and the, 4, 5–6
insight fallacy, 123, 142
inspiration
    mentors and, 80
    See also mantras/motto; motivation
Internet
    tracking progress and, 60, 61
    See also websites; *specific website*

journaling, 60, 73, 89, 159

Keynes, John Maynard, 42
Knapp, Caroline, 65
Kübler-Ross, Elisabeth, 1

life satisfaction, 17, 26
lifestyle
    long haul and, 195, 200, 201
    meaning of term, 180, 198–99
    as persisting change, 180
    self-change as part of healthy, 203
    spiral of change and, 198–99
listening, importance of, 145
Loberg, Kristin, 205
love, countering and, 129

maintenance
    behavioral detective work and, 91
    description/characteristics of, 20
    meaning of, 180
    proven methods for, 180–81
    stages of change and, 20
    step matching and, 40, 42
    timeline for, 36–37
    tracking progress and, 91
    See also Persevere; Persist
mantras/motto, 79, 105
Marden, Orison Swett, 139
Marlatt, G. Alan, 153, 164
May, Rollo, 80

measurement
    of stage of change, 29–31
    See also tracking progress
medications, 9
meditation, 135, 136
mental health professionals
    Check Yourself about, 229–30
    effective use of Changeology and, 9–10
    raising awareness and, 65
    selection of qualified, 222–30
    types of, 220–22
    See also psychotherapists
mentors, 80
mindfulness, 135, 136, 165, 166
"minimize-the-threat game," 148–49
mirror work, 75
mistakes, learning from, 105
Monique (patient)
    change team/support for, 93, 184
    commitment of, 97
    confidence of, 54, 159, 202
    countering of, 126, 135–36, 187
    ending of problem for, 199, 200
    environment of, 140–41
    as example of 5 step process, 54, 201, 202, 203
    fears of, 70
    goals of, 56, 79, 86, 202
    helping relationships and, 146
    and learning from mistakes, 105
    maintaining new behavior and, 180–81
    mantra/motto of, 79
    optimism of, 72, 74
    Persevere and, 159, 160, 161, 162, 165–66, 167, 169
    Persist and, 180–81, 184, 187
    Perspire and, 112, 121–22, 126, 135–36, 140–41, 146, 148–49
    planning of, 84, 102
    Prep and, 84, 86, 89, 93, 97, 101, 102
    prior efforts/failures of, 84, 97
    problems of, 54, 202
    pros and cons of, 76–77
    Psych and, 54, 56, 58, 61, 64, 65, 67, 70, 72, 74, 76–77, 79
    raising awareness and, 64, 65
    reevaluation of yourself and, 67
    resisting the urge and, 161, 162, 165–66
    rewards/punishments for, 121–22
    as saying no, 160, 161
    slips/relapses of, 167, 169, 202

step matching and, 54
three-headed demon and, 148–49
tracking progress and, 58, 61, 89
triggers for, 140–41, 159, 160, 161, 162
urge surfing and, 165–66
motivation
blame and, 148
building self-efficacy and, 191–94
commitment and, 97, 99–100, 102
countering and, 137
importance of planning and, 108
overestimating value of, 53
self-talk for, 124
movies
making your own, 132, 133–34
raising awareness and, 65
Mukherjee, Siddhartha, 153
myths, destructive, 36, 42–47

negativity, countering and, 125–29
"neurotic paradox," 69–70, 71, 117
new beginnings, 103
New Year's resolutions, 3, 22–23, 43, 48, 154–55, 156, 169–70, 194–95, 204, 206
Niebuhr, Reinhold, 135
ninety day program
beyond the, 194–98
commitment to, 5–6, 7
effective use of 5 step process and, 7, 8
importance to change process of, 5–6, 7
ineffectiveness of 5 step process and, 9
no, saying, 152, 155, 159–61, 172, 175
Norcross, John C.
as change team member, 95
colonoscopy problem of, 29, 70, 202
ending of problem for, 199
as example of 5 step process, 201, 202
excessive worry of, 125–26
flossing problem of, 29, 179–80, 199, 202
professional background of, 2–3
weight/exercise problem for, 29, 104, 183–84, 202
Norcross, Jonathan, 58–59, 130, 189–90

online support group, 92
optimism/pessimism, 72, 93, 145, 152, 168, 169, 192, 193, 203

other people
building self-efficacy and, 192
change of, 26
defining goals and, 55
importance of, 34
offering help to, 146, 185, 192
pain of, 71
pros and cons exercise and, 76
overgeneralizing, 47, 127

pain
avoidance of, 134
feeling, 70
of other people, 71
patterns, 90–91, 127
peers, as helping relationships, 146
perfectionism, 85, 110, 126, 127, 152
Persevere (Step 4), 152–77
blessed and cursed words and, 153–54
change team and, 158, 160–61, 162, 172, 174, 175
commitment and, 155, 169–70, 172
and definition of persevere, 153
goal for, 31, 152
high-risk worksheet and, 157–58
importance of, 24, 177
need for lifetime of, 180
positive outlooks and, 152, 168
preparing for next slip and, 170–74, 175
resisting initial urge and, 161–66
responding constructively after a slip and, 152, 155, 166–70, 175
saying "no" and, 152, 155, 159–61, 172, 175
slips/falls and, 150, 152–77
step matching and, 39–40
structure for self-change and, 21–23, 35
timeline for, 36–37
tracking progress and, 150
triggers and, 152, 155–66, 167, 171, 172, 175
urge surfing and, 164–66, 167
See also specific topic
Persist (Step 5), 178–203
backup plans for slips and, 178
beyond the 90 days and, 194–98
celebration of success and, 180
change catalysts and, 181–89, 195, 199, 200
change team/support and, 180, 184–85, 192, 198

Persist (Step 5) (*cont.*)
    countering and, 180, 186–87
    end of problem and, 180, 198–201
    environment and, 180, 183, 187–89, 193
    failure during, 178–79
    formula for change and, 182–83
    goals for, 31, 178
    going from Perspire to, 150–51
    importance of, 24
    long haul and, 180, 194–98
    as maintaining change, 150, 178–203
    rewards and, 180, 186, 192
    self-efficacy and, 180, 189–94, 198, 200,
        201
    slips/relapse and, 178–79, 183, 184
    spiral of change and, 180, 195–201
    step matching and, 182, 189
    structure for self-change and, 21–23, 35
    success and, 178, 179
    timeline for, 36–37
    tracking progress and, 150, 180, 183–84
    triggers and, 183, 184, 188–89, 193, 198
    See also specific topic
Perspire (Step 3), 111–51
    awareness and, 112–14
    building new behaviors and, 111
    change catalysts and, 112, 137, 143–44
    change team and, 111, 117–18, 137,
        144–45
    contingency contracts and, 117–19, 122,
        137, 142
    countering/counter conditioning and,
        111, 112, 123–38, 143–44
    emotions and, 68–69, 112–14
    environment and, 111, 112, 138–42,
        143–44, 187–88
    goals for, 31, 111
    and going from Perspire to Persist, 150–51
    helping relationships and, 111, 112,
        144–48
    importance/purpose of, 24, 113–14
    and meaning of word perspire, 180
    moving forward and, 112–14
    punishing yourself and, 119–23
    recap for, 150–51
    relapses/lapses during, 154
    rewards and, 111, 112, 114–23, 136–37,
        142, 143–44
    self-efficacy and, 124
    sound of, 111
    spiral of change and, 196

step matching and, 39–40, 112, 114
    structure for self-change and, 21–23, 35
    as taking action, 111–51
    three-headed demon and, 148–50
    timeline/duration for, 36–37, 112, 150,
        151
    tracking progress and, 150
    triggers and, 139, 140–41, 143
    and what not to do, 112–14
    See also specific topic
pessimism. *See* optimism/pessimism
photographs, tracking progress and, 61–62
PIG (Problem of Immediate Gratification),
    166, 169
plan/planning
    5 steps of change and, 20
    flexible, 84
    for getting back on track after slips, 152,
        155, 166–70, 175
    and how long for need to plan, 107–8
    importance of, 84
    for next slips, 170–74, 175, 178
    perfectionism and, 85
    and revision of plans, 84
    See also Action Plan; Prep
positive outlook. *See* optimism/pessimism
precontemplation, 18, 111
Prep (Step 2), 83–110
    Action Plan and, 83–84, 85, 102–7
    change catalysts and, 97
    change team/support and, 83, 92–96, 98
    commitment and, 83, 97–102
    consequences and, 88–91
    countering and, 100–101
    description/characteristics of, 19
    effective use of 5 step process and, 7
    failure to prepare and, 82
    fifty new beginnings and, 103
    getting ready for, 107–10
    goals and, 83, 84, 85–88, 98–99, 102
    goals for, 31, 83–84
    importance of, 24, 108
    planning for change and, 83–110
    pros and cons and, 77
    self-assessments and, 108–10, 163
    self-efficacy and, 96
    spiral of change and, 196
    as stage for change, 19
    step matching and, 39–40
    structure for self-change and, 19, 21–23,
        35

timeline/duration for, 36–37, 150
tracking progress and, 83, 86, 88–91, 150
triggers and, 88–91
virtuous cycle and, 99–100
See also specific topic
Preston, Billy, 196
primal scream therapy, 69
prior efforts, 45–47, 49. *See also* failure(s)
priorities, 82, 98, 99, 192
Prochaska, James O., 2, 3, 5, 17–18, 25, 62, 149, 197, 205
Prochaska, Jan, 205–6
pros and cons exercise, 76–78, 79, 192
Psych (Step 1), 53–82
    awareness and, 53, 62–66, 75, 76, 82, 88
    building self-efficacy and, 193
    change catalysts and, 53, 77, 82
    Check Yourself and, 109
    commitment and, 53, 78–82, 97
    doubt and, 80
    effective use of 5 step process and, 7
    emotions and, 53, 68–75, 76, 82
    envisioning a positive future and, 72
    failure to prepare and, 82
    fear of change and, 53, 70, 71, 72–75
    as getting ready for change, 53–82
    goals and, 31, 32, 54–57, 62, 79, 82, 98
    goals for, 53
    identification of emotional reasons for old behavior and, 163
    importance of, 24, 82
    mentors and, 80
    priorities and, 82
    pros and cons and, 76–78, 79
    reevaluating yourself and, 66–68
    rushing through, 82
    spiral of change and, 196
    step matching and, 39–40
    structure for self-change and, 21–23, 35
    support groups and, 81
    timeline/duration for, 36–37, 62, 150
    tracking progress and, 53, 58–62, 82, 88, 150
    See also specific topic
psychotherapists
    Check Yourself about, 229–30
    selection of right, 10, 194, 219–30
    studies of change in, 3
    See also mental health professionals
punishment, 119–23, 148
push-pull llama, 69, 73–75, 79, 94, 163

reactivity, 62, 90
reevaluating yourself, 66–68. *See also* Check Yourself
relapse/lapse
    building self-efficacy and, 193
    commitment to 90 day program and, 7
    definition of, 167
    drift into, 179
    effective use of 5 step process and, 7
    fear of, 153–54, 178
    long haul and, 195–96, 200
    meaning of, 153
    Persevere as dealing with, 152–77
    Persist and, 179, 183, 184, 191–94, 195–96, 200
    as presage of failure, 153
    prevalence of, 154
    responding constructively after a slip and, 167, 175
    slips differentiated from, 154, 175
    spiral of change and, 195–96
    stages of change and, 20
    step matching and, 41–42
    See also slips
relationships
    identification of need for change and, 26
    as type of change, 17
    See also Andrew; change team; helping relationships; support
relaxation methods, 125, 126, 131, 162, 165, 166, 172
research. *See* science/research; *specific scientist or institution*
resisting the urge, 161–66
resources. *See* self-help resources/books
responsibility, hyper-, 128
rewards
    behavior chain and, 143–44
    as bribery, 122
    building self-efficacy and, 192
    as change catalyst, 37, 38, 112, 114–23
    Check Yourself and, 123, 151
    as consequences, 114–23
    contingency contracts and, 117–19
    controlling the environment and, 142
    countering and, 130, 131, 136–37
    cycle of, 89
    definition of, 114–15
    delayed versus immediate, 116, 117
    effectiveness of, 120
    intermittent/sporadic, 186

rewards (*cont.*)
    maintaining change and, 180, 182, 186, 192
    Perspire goals and, 111
    punishment combined with, 121
    resisting the urge and, 163
    step matching and, 39–40
    techniques for, 115–19
    tracking progress and, 58, 89, 90
    types of, 115
rule of two, 27–28

sabotage, self-, 125
science/research
    as basis for behavioral change, 11, 15–34
    change catalysts and, 37
    failure of self-help programs and, 4–5
    importance of, 34
    integrated approach to changeology and, 38–39
"selective abstraction," 128
self
    criticism of, 85
    image of, 19, 73, 102, 119, 132
    sabotage of, 125
    searching your, 163
    talking to your, 73, 75, 124
self-assessments
    Prep and, 108–10, 163
    See also Check Yourself
self-change
    Check Yourself for keys to, 49–50
    history of studies of, 2–4
    See also specific topic
self-efficacy
    assessing, 189–91
    building, 191–94
    change team and, 96
    Check Yourself for, 48
    definition of, 47
    importance of, 49
    keys to success and, 47–50
    long haul and, 200, 201
    maintaining change and, 180, 189–94, 198, 200, 201
    motivational self-talk and, 124
    self-esteem differentiated from, 47–48
    slips and, 167
    spiral of change and, 198
self-esteem, self-efficacy differentiated from, 47–48

self-evaluation. *See* Check Yourself
self-help, definition of, 211
self-help programs, limitations of, 4–5
self-help resources/books, 2, 3, 4–6, 8–10, 65, 71, 129, 193, 211–17
Seligman, Martin, 134
Serenity Prayer (Niebuhr), 135
"shaping," 116
slip busters, 168–69
Slip Cards, 169, 173–74, 175
slips
    change team and, 94, 145, 175
    Check Yourself for, 175–76
    constructive responses to, 166–70, 175
    definition of, 154
    environment and, 188
    going from Perspire to Persist and, 151
    learning from, 169
    maintaining change and, 178–80, 182, 188
    "normalizing" of, 154
    Persevere and, 150, 152–77
    plans for getting back on track after, 152, 155, 166–70, 175
    plans for next, 170–74, 178
    and preventing slips from becoming falls, 168–70
    as recommitments, 155
    relapse/lapse differentiated from, 154, 175
    resisting initial urge for, 155, 161–66, 175
    saying no and, 152, 155, 159–61, 172, 175
    slip busting strategies and, 168–70
    step matching and, 41–42
    See also triggers
small steps
    rewards for, 116, 121
    taking, 100, 101
SMART (Specific, Measurable, Attainable, Relevant, Time-specific) goals, 85–86, 87, 118
social change, Changeology for, 204–7
SparkPeople (website), 61
spiral of change, 180, 195–201
stages of change
    assessment/measurement of, 29–31
    description of, 18–20
    process of change and, 17
    readiness for change and, 17–18
    studies about, 3
    See also specific stage

start date, 102–3, 104
step matching, 24–25, 33, 39–42, 47, 112, 114, 182, 189
stories, telling yourself, 73
strategies
    failure of self-help programs and, 4, 5
    See also specific topic or strategy
success
    building self-efficacy and, 192
    celebration of, 180
    Changeology program as, 204
    fear of endurance of, 178
    5 steps of change and, 22–23
    Hill's words about, 151
    keys to, 35–50
    long haul and, 195
    maintaining change and, 178, 179, 180, 189, 192, 195
    at onset, 104
    success as begetting more, 189, 192
support
    building self-efficacy and, 192, 193, 194
    as change catalyst, 37, 112, 144–48
    Check Yourself for, 147–48, 151, 184–85
    commitment and, 81
    effective use of 5 step process and, 8, 9
    importance of, 144
    long-term, 185
    maintaining change and, 180, 182, 184–85, 192, 193, 194, 198
    myths about change and, 47
    online, 6, 92
    Perspire goals and, 111
    planning for future slips and, 174
    Prep goals and, 83
    quality and quantity of, 144
    spiral of change and, 198
    step matching and, 40
    tracking progress and, 60
    See also change team; rewards
Suzuki, Shinichi, 138

talking to yourself, 73, 75, 124
Tantalus (mythological figure), 179–80
"teacher's fallacy," 68
termination of problems, 198–201
three-headed demon, 144, 148–50, 151
time-outs, 121
timeline for change, 35, 36–38

To Dos, function of, 7
tracking progress
    benefits of, 58, 60, 62
    as change catalyst, 37, 53, 58–62, 82, 88–91
    change team and, 94
    Check Yourself and, 91, 109
    consequences and, 88–91
    establishing baseline behavior and, 58
    goals and, 86
    importance of, 59–60
    maintaining change and, 91, 180, 182, 183–84
    measurement and, 90
    methods and tools for, 50, 60–62
    patterns and, 90–91
    Prep goals and, 83
    Psych goals and, 53
    purpose of, 58
    rewards and, 58, 89, 90
    spontaneous improvement and, 62
    triggers and, 88–91, 94, 183–84
triggers
    avoiding, 152, 155–59, 189
    awareness of, 159
    building self-efficacy and, 193
    change team as help with, 175
    consequences of, 143, 159
    controlling the environment and, 139, 140–41, 188–89
    examples of, 156
    getting back on track after slips and, 172
    identification of, 156–57, 175
    long haul and, 200
    methods/strategies to resist, 161–64
    planning for future slips and, 171, 172
    questions about, 156–57
    and resisting the initial urge, 161–66, j259 167
    saying no to, 152, 155, 159–61, 175
    spiral of change and, 198
    strategies for dealing with, 158–59
    tracking progress and, 88–91, 94, 183–84
    W questions about, 156–58
    worksheet to identify high-risk, 157–58, 159
twelve-step groups, 169, 185
two-headed llama. *See* push-pull llama

University of Miami, and sounds for steps of change, 111

University of Oregon, slips of smokers study at, 155

University of Rhode Island, change studies at, 27

"urge surfing," 164–66, 167

values, your, 66, 76, 193

virtuous cycle, 99–100

visualization. *See* imagery

website(s), 6, 8, 60. *See also specific website*

weed analogy, 100

willpower

    Action Plan and, 102, 105

    building self-efficacy and, 192

    commitment and, 78–79, 98

myths about, 42, 44, 45

Persist and, 192

Prep and, 98, 102, 105

Winehouse, Amy, 71

wishful thinking, 149, 203

worksheet, for high-risk triggers, 157–58, 159

worrying (countering example), 125–26

Ws (where, what, when, who), four, 156–58

Yale University, urge surfing study at, 164

Zach (patient), 41, 42

Zelma (patient), 40–41, 42

Zoe (patient), 41–42

ABOUT THE AUTHOR

John C. Norcross, PhD, ABPP, is an internationally recognized expert on behavior change, psychotherapy, and New Year's resolutions. He is Distinguished Professor of Psychology at the University of Scranton, Adjunct Professor of Psychiatry at SUNY Upstate Medical University, and a board-certified clinical psychologist in part-time practice.

Dr. Norcross has authored more than 300 scholarly publications and 20 professional books. His research on self-change and New Year's resolutions has been featured in hundreds of media outlets, and he has appeared on dozens of national news shows, such as *Today, Good Morning America,* CNN, *CBS News Sunday Morning, The Early Show, Anderson Cooper 360,* MSNBC, and the PBS special *This Emotional Life.*

Dr. Norcross is past president of the American Psychological Association's Division of Clinical Psychology, the APA Division of Psychotherapy, and the International Society of Clinical Psychology. His national awards reflect his simultaneous distinction in research, practice, and teaching. Among those awards are the Pennsylvania Professor of the Year from the Carnegie Foundation, the Distinguished Career Contributions to Education and Training from the American Psychological Association, and election to the National Academies of Practice.

The father of two grown children, Dr. Norcross lives in northeast Pennsylvania with his wife.

ABOUT THE COLLABORATORS

Kristin Loberg is a professional writer with multiple *New York Times* and *Wall Street Journal* bestsellers to her credit, including Phil Town's *Rule #1* and *Payback Time,* Brenda Watson's *The Fiber35 Diet,* and Dr. David B. Agus's *The End of Illness.* A graduate of Cornell University, she lives in her hometown of Los Angeles.

Jonathon Norcross graduated from St. Joseph's University, where he studied English and film. He lives in New York City, where he works in the film and television industry.